MW00529421

TRADIVOX
VOLUME III

TRADIVOX

CATHOLIC CATECHISM INDEX

VOLUME III

Richard Challoner

Edited by
Aaron Seng

SOPHIA INSTITUTE PRESS
MANCHESTER, NEW HAMPSHIRE

This book is an original derivative work comprising newly typeset and
reformatted editions of the following Catholic catechisms, once issued with
ecclesiastical approval and now found in the public domain:

Challoner, Richard. *An Abridgment of Christian Doctrine*. English Secret Press, 1759.
Challoner, Richard. *The Catholick Christian Instructed*. London, 1737.
Challoner, Richard. *The Grounds of the Catholick Doctrine*. English Secret Press, 1752.

Scripture references follow the Douay-Rheims Bible,
per the imprint of John Murphy Company (Baltimore, 1899).

Printed in the United States of America. All rights reserved.

Cover and interior design by Perceptions Design Studio.
Unless otherwise noted, all illustrations are in the public domain.

Sophia Institute Press
Box 5284, Manchester, NH 03108
1-800-888-9344

www.SophiaInstitute.com

Sophia Institute Press® is a registered trademark of Sophia Institute.

ISBN 978-1-64413-354-5
LCCN 2020952306

The Manner of Execution at Tyburn.

Dedicated with love and deepest respect
to all the English Martyrs and Confessors.
Orate pro nobis.

CONTENTS

CONTENTS

ACKNOWLEDGEMENTS

THE publication of this series is due primarily to the generosity of countless volunteers and donors from several countries. Special thanks are owed to Mr. and Mrs. Phil Seng, Mr. and Mrs. Michael Over, Mr. and Mrs. Jim McElwee, as well the visionary priests and faithful of St. Stanislaus Bishop and Martyr parish in South Bend, Indiana, and St. Patrick's Oratory in Green Bay, Wisconsin. May God richly reward their commitment to handing on the Catholic faith.

FOREWORD

The Catholic faith remains always the same throughout the centuries and millennia until the coming of our Lord at the end of the time, likewise "Jesus Christ is the same yesterday, today and forever" (Heb 13:8). The Catholic faith is "the faith, which was once delivered unto the saints" (Jude 1:3). The Magisterium of the Church teaches us solemnly the same truth in the following words of the First Vatican Council: "The doctrine of the faith which God has revealed, is put forward not as some philosophical discovery capable of being perfected by human intelligence, but as a divine deposit committed to the spouse of Christ to be faithfully protected and infallibly promulgated. Hence, too, that meaning of the sacred dogmas is ever to be maintained, which has once been declared by holy mother Church, and there must never be any abandonment of this sense under the pretext or in the name of a more profound understanding. May understanding, knowledge and wisdom increase as ages and centuries roll along, and greatly and vigorously flourish, in each and all, in the individual and the whole Church: but this only in its own proper kind, that is to say, in the same doctrine, the same sense, and the same understanding (cf. *Vincentius Lerinensis, Commonitorium*, 28)."[1]

An authentically Catholic catechism has the function of learning and teaching the unchanging Catholic faith throughout all generations. The Roman Pontiffs indeed, taught: "There is nothing more effective than catechetical instruction to spread the glory of God

---

[1] Vatican I, Dogmatic Constitution *Dei Filius de fide catholica*, Ch. 4

and to secure the salvation of souls."[2] Saint Pius X said, that "the great loss of souls is due to ignorance of divine things."[3] Therefore, the traditional catechisms have enduring value in our own day and age, which is marked by an enormous doctrinal confusion, which reigns in the life of the Church in the past six decades, and which reaches its peak in our days.

I welcome and bless the great project of the "Tradivox" in cataloguing and preserving the hundreds of long-lost Catholic catechisms issued with episcopal approval over the last millennium. This project will convincingly show the essentially unchanging nature of the apostolic doctrine across time and space, and so I invite the faithful of the entire world to support this historic effort, as we seek to restore the perennial catechism of the Church. The project of a catechism restoration on behalf of "Tradivox" will surely be of great benefit not only to many confused and disoriented Catholic faithful, but also to all people who are sincerely seeking the ultimate and authentic truth about God and man, which one can find only in the Catholic and apostolic faith, and which is the only religion and faith willed by God and to which God calls all men.

+Athanasius Schneider, O.R.C.,
Titular Bishop of Celerina
Auxiliary Bishop of the Archdiocese of Saint Mary in Astana

[2] Pope Benedict XIV, Apostolic Constitution *Etsi minime*, n. 13
[3] Cf. Pope St. Pius X, Encyclical *Acerbo nimis*, n. 27

PREFACE

S OME are surprised to find that when a given Catholic is asked to "look something up in the catechism," he may well respond: "Which one?" The history of the Catholic Church across the last millennium is in fact filled with the publication of numerous catechisms, issued in every major language on earth; and for centuries, these concise "guidebooks" to Catholic doctrine have served countless men and women seeking a clear and concise presentation of that faith forever entrusted by Jesus Christ to his one, holy, Catholic, and apostolic Church.

Taken together, the many catechisms issued with episcopal approval can offer a kind of "window" on to the universal ordinary magisterium—a glimpse of those truths which have been held and taught in the Church *everywhere, always, and by all.* For, as St. Paul reminds us, the tenets of this Faith do not change from age to age: "Jesus Christ yesterday and today and the same for ever. Be not led away with various and strange doctrines" (Heb 13:8-9).

The catechisms included in our *Tradivox Catholic Catechism Index* are selected for their orthodoxy and historical significance, in the interest of demonstrating to contemporary readers the remarkable continuity of Catholic doctrine across time and space. Long regarded as reliable summaries of Church teaching on matters of faith and morals, we are proud to reproduce these works of centuries past, composed and endorsed by countless priests, bishops, and popes devoted to "giving voice to tradition."

IN THIS VOLUME

The three texts that together comprise Volume III are the work of
the eminent Bishop Richard Challoner, whose prodigious work as
a Catholic professor, priest, bishop, and vicar apostolic has placed
him in the estimation of many historians as the leading figure of
English Catholicism in the 1700s: a period described as the most
discouraging and apparently hopeless for Catholics in that country.
Like a new Athanasius, Bishop Challoner would arise in those days
to devote all of his considerable apostolic energies to growing and
strengthening the Church against nearly impossible odds. While
space does not permit a full account of his life and work, several
important details must be shared here, in order to better highlight
the humble beginnings and inspiring career of this great champion
of Catholic tradition in England.

Born the only son of a Presbyterian vintner in Sussex, Richard
Challoner did not become a Catholic until his early teen years, following the death of his father. Widowed suddenly in her twenties,
Mrs. Challoner was left with very little means to raise her only son,
and worked as a housekeeper. She soon found employment with
the Gage family, one of a dwindling number of Catholic house-
holds in Firle amid mounting anti-Catholic legislation. Why exactly
the Gages opened their home to the struggling Challoners at this
time remains unclear, since the old Catholic families typically employed only Catholic servants, giving them and their families access
to those private chapels which for centuries were among the only
places of regular Catholic worship in the country. Like so many
decisions that make up what one presumes to call an "ordinary
life," in God's providence, this little change of family associations
would go on to shape the lives (and perhaps save the souls) of untold
thousands, both in England and beyond.

Employment with the Gages placed Mrs. Challoner and her son
in the circles of the prominent Stafford-Holman family of Wark-
worth Castle, to whom Mrs. Challoner transferred her employment.

The matron of this deeply pious family was the Lady Anastasia, daughter of the Viscount William Stafford, who had been martyred some ten years before Richard was born. Chaplain to this devout family was the widely known author, Fr. John Gother, who both instructed and received the young Challoner into the Church during his time in residence there. Observing a sincere reverence and intellectual aptitude in the young man, Fr. Gother secured entry for Richard at Douay College in 1705, which was now in its second century of training English missionary priests. Although sailing for the famous college would mean twelve years of separation from his dear mother, a longing to serve Jesus Christ and his persecuted Church had by this time planted itself in the heart of Richard Challoner, and he resolved to make the journey. He spent the next twenty-five years with the college: first as a student, then as professor and priest, and finally as vice-president. In 1708 he vowed to return to the English mission whenever required, and a signed copy of this oath remains in the Westminster archives. It merits quotation:

> I, Richard Challoner, an Alumnus of the English College at Douay, considering the divine benefits which I have received, particularly that which has led me from my country now afflicted with heresy, and which has made me a member of His Catholic Church . . . promise and swear before Almighty God that I am ready and will ever be ready, so far as His most holy Grace shall help me, to receive Holy Orders in due time and to return to England in order to gain the souls of others as often and where it shall seem good to the Superior of this College so to command.

His return to England to "gain souls" would not come until 1730, following his priestly ordination (1716) and first publication: a little book of meditations entitled *Think Well On't* (1728). Challoner's depth of personal prayer, focused studiousness, and educator's gift for driving home the spiritual import of Catholic doctrine with good cheer and quiet fervor made him an ideal candidate for the mission.

He was sent back to London, which would remain the center of his missionary operations for the rest of his life. The penal laws were still in full force against priests in those days, and like so many of his fellow Catholics, Challoner was forced to live as an outlaw, frequently moving from place to place, and working under assumed names to elude informants. Everyone knew of the handsome incentives for turning in Catholics to government officers, and some had even begun to make their living at "priest-hunting," as the capture of clergy could at times fetch £100 or more (around $23,000 by today's standards). Undaunted, Challoner undertook his priestly ministry in constant danger, and was soon so beloved among those who refused submission to the state-imposed Anglican religion that his name became a kind of badge of allegiance among these so-called "recusants." Disguised as a layman under several aliases, Challoner spent years tending to his flock and celebrating secret Masses in private homes, hotels, pubs, and other discreet locations. With the heart of a true pastor, he could be found in the prisons and poorest parts of town, bringing the sacraments and as much encouragement, counsel, and catechesis as time would allow.

His spare hours were spent in such vigorous writing that even an author in normal circumstances would have been proud to match his output. With the aid of the underground Catholic press in England and several international connections, Challoner published a wide range of tracts, books, translations of classical texts, and even multi-volume works on Catholic doctrine, morals, apologetics, prayer, hagiography, and liturgy. His book of daily *Meditations* and his frequently republished *Garden of the Soul* became instant classics, molding the devotional life of English Catholics for generations, and his compendious *Memoirs of Missionary Priests* remains the greatest reference work on the English martyrs. His most widely known literary achievement, however, is certainly his update to the English translation of the Bible: a version eventually synonymous with the "Douay-Rheims Bible," which for Catholics remained the most widely used and frequently referenced English version of Scripture until the 20th century.

Little wonder, then, that Challoner was consecrated as coadjutor bishop while yet in his forties, and installed as vicar apostolic of the London District in 1758; a position placing him in governance not only of thousands of souls in lower England, but also of the growing Catholic population in the Thirteen Colonies on the far side of the Atlantic—a jurisdiction that he would be the last English bishop to exercise. As a bishop, his energies seemed boundless: navigating complex legal hurdles intended for Catholic suppression, establishing several schools, inaugurating clergy conferences, and helping to launch a major charitable organization for the relief of the poor, whom he always loved. He would serve nearly forty years in the episcopate, and his upright character and remarkable achievements became so well known that admirers could be found even among his enemies. The Anglican pastor later tasked with officiating at Challoner's civic burial would record him as "a very pious and good man, of great learning and extensive abilities."

Even so, the aged bishop would barely escape the fiercely anti-Catholic Gordon Riots of 1780, the most destructive rioting in the city's history. The so-called "King Mob" spent several days and nights looting and burning chapels, businesses, private homes, and foreign embassies suspected of any Catholic ties: a chilling precursor to the horrors of the French Revolution that were soon to come. Never completely recovering from the ordeal, Bishop Richard Challoner would die of an apparent stroke just months later, passing quietly in a friend's home on January 12, 1781. A few years earlier, he had assured his close friend, Bishop George Hay of Scotland: "You will see, there will be a new people," prophesying (as Hay believed) the Catholic revival in England that he would not live to see. Having formed a pact with Challoner to celebrate three Masses a week for the repose of the soul of whichever of the two friends died first, Bishop Hay would honor their arrangement for nearly a quarter century after Challoner's death, until age and infirmity finally rendered him physically unable to offer Mass any longer.

THIS VOLUME RECOVERS three of Challoner's catechisms from editions published in the author's lifetime. The first is *An Abridgment of Christian Doctrine*, a twice-distilled synopsis of an earlier text by the same name (the famous "Douay Catechism" of Fr. Turberville, included in Volume II of our *Index*), which was penned almost a century earlier at the alma mater of both authors. Recovered here is the 1759 edition of Challoner's *Abridgment*, apparently the very first printing of this simple, question-answer booklet for the instruction of young Catholics. The work was found to be so immediately useful that it ran in several editions throughout the country, later becoming the prototype for the most recognizable English Catholic catechism of all: the so-called "Penny Catechism." The *Abridgment's* final chapter contains an act of the love of neighbor that is rendered all the more moving by its having been recited by Catholics on not a few English scaffolds of the day:

> O my God, thou hast commanded me to love every neighbor as myself, for thy sake. O give me grace to fulfill this commandment. I desire to love every neighbor, whether friend or enemy, in thee and for thee. I renounce every thought, word, or deed that is contrary to this love. I forgive all that have any way offended me, and I beg thy mercy, grace, and salvation for all the world.

THE SECOND TEXT included in this volume is the first edition of *The Catholick Christian Instructed in the Sacraments, Sacrifice and Ceremonies of the Church* (1737). This is a much longer, heavily annotated, and rather unique work for its time, and one that proved critical for strengthening mystagogical catechesis among Catholics throughout what is now the United Kingdom. Having by this time suffered generations of separation from their liturgical heritage due to government prohibitions of Catholic worship, the English faithful were in sore need of a religious instruction that was shaped by and ordered toward ritual worship and the sacramental life—something that other catechisms often abbreviated or omitted altogether.

The Catholick Christian Instructed met this need for Catholics, while also offering non-Catholics of that time an "insider's look" at many Catholic rites and prayers that, having been celebrated throughout England since the sixth century, were suddenly being punished as criminal acts. Its many citations of protestant scholars made the work particularly effective in this regard.

The book also generated the most heated persecution for its author, perhaps lending credence to the old Catholic truism: "It's the Mass that matters." In the lengthy Preface of the original (omitted in this volume), Challoner engaged the claims of an Anglican contemporary who had published an attack on the "paganism of Popery." His book-length rejoinder, with its thorough explanation and defense of the beauty, symbolism, and sanctity of the Roman Rite, quickly gained so wide a readership that the affronted Anglican divine set the law in motion against him in retribution. Pressure for Challoner's discovery and arrest became so extreme that he was obliged to leave the country for several months, before returning to London to continue his work. *The Catholick Christian Instructed* remains a valuable explanation of the faith by means of sacred signs and symbols, and a lasting witness to the Church's love for those divine mysteries enacted upon her altars. Contemporary readers unfamiliar with the traditional Roman Rite will find a deep richness and clarity in the ceremonies expounded in these instructions, now nearly three hundred years old—and Catholics who worship according to the *usus antiquior* today will be struck by the familiarity of what Challoner describes.

THIRD IN THIS VOLUME is Challoner's *The Grounds of the Catholick Doctrine*, first published in 1732. Intended for the poorly educated faithful or non-Catholic inquirers, this text offers another simple, question-answer catechism based on the *Professio Fidei Tridentina*, one of the four major Creeds of the Catholic Church. First promulgated during the Council of Trent by Pope Pius IV, this Creed spotlights many doctrines often challenged by protestants, serving well as a framework for Challoner's small catechism in sectarian England. Like his *Abridgment*, Challoner's *Grounds* was inexpensively printed and bound, and it is unclear whether any original editions survived the centuries as a result. However, several subsequent editions were printed during the author's lifetime, and we are proud to reclaim the seventh (English Secret Press, 1752) in the pages below. Nearly a century and a half after its first appearance, Challoner's *Grounds* was endorsed by the Catholic bishops of England and published again, without any noteworthy alterations (see Washbourne's edition of 1868), thus demonstrating the work's doctrinal accuracy and abiding catechetical value.

EDITORIAL NOTE

Our *Catholic Catechism Index* series generally retains only the doctrinal content of those catechisms it seeks to reproduce, as well as that front matter most essential to establishing the credibility of each work as an authentic expression of the Church's common doctrine, e.g., any episcopal endorsement, *nihil obstat*, or *imprimatur*. However, it should be noted that especially prior to the eighteenth century, a number of catechisms were so immediately and universally received as reliably orthodox texts (often simply by the reputation of the author or publisher), that they received no such "official" approval; or if they did, it was often years later and in subsequent editions. We therefore include both the original printing date in our Table of Contents, and further edition information in the Preface above.

Our primary goal has been to bring these historical texts back into publication in readable English copy. Due to the wide range of time periods, cultures, and unique author styles represented in this series, we have made a number of editorial adjustments to allow for a less fatiguing read, more rapid cross-reference throughout the series, and greater research potential for the future. While not affecting the original content, these adjustments have included adopting a cleaner typesetting and simpler standard for capitalization and

Woodcut depicting an early method used in the production of Catholic catechisms, circa 1568.

annotation, as well as remedying certain anachronisms in spelling or grammar.

At the same time, in deepest respect for the venerable age and subject matter of these works, we have been at pains to adhere as closely as possible to the original text: retaining archaisms such as "doth" and "hallowed," and avoiding any alterations that might affect the doctrinal content or authorial voice. We have painstakingly restored original artwork wherever possible, and where the rare explanatory note has been deemed necessary, it is not made in the text itself, but only in a marginal note. In some cases, our editorial refusal to "modernize" the content of these classical works may require a higher degree of attention from today's reader, who we trust will be richly rewarded by the effort.

We pray that our work continues to yield highly readable, faithful reproductions of these time-honored monuments to Catholic religious instruction: catechisms once penned, promulgated, and praised by bishops across the globe. May these texts that once served to guide and shape the faith and lives of millions now do so again; and may the scholars and saints once involved in their first publication now intercede for all who take them up anew. *Tolle lege!*

Sincerely in Christ,
Aaron Seng

TRADIVOX
VOLUME III

AN

ABRIDGMENT

OF

Chriſtian Doctrine:

Reviſed and enlarged

by R. C.

And publiſhed for the uſe of the L---n
diſtrict.

Printed in the Year M DCC LIX

Original Title Page
(*English Secret Press, 1759*)

An Abridgment
of
Christian Doctrine

Revised and enlarged
by R. C.
And published for the use of the L– – –n
district.

Printed in the Year 1759

Chapter 1

1. Who made you?
God.

2. Why did he make you?
That I might know him, love him, and serve him in this world,
and be happy with him forever in the next.

3. To whose likeness did he make you?
To his own image and likeness.

4. Is this likeness in your body, or in your soul?
In the soul.

5. In what is your soul like to God?
Because my soul is a spirit, endowed with understanding and
free-will; and is immortal, that is to say, it can never die.

6. In what else?
That as in God there are three Persons and one God; so in man
there is one soul and three powers.

7. Which are the three powers?
Will, memory, and understanding.

8. Which must we take most care of: our body, or our soul?
Of our soul.

9. Why so?

"What will it avail a man to gain the whole world, and lose his own soul?"[1]

10. What must we do to save our soul?

We must worship God by faith, hope, and charity. That is, we must believe in him, hope in him, and love him with all our hearts.

11. What is faith?

It is to believe, without doubting, all that God teaches; because he is the very truth, and cannot deceive, nor be deceived.

12. And how shall we know what the things are which God teaches?

From the testimony of the Catholic Church of God, which he has established by innumerable miracles, and illustrated by the lives and deaths of innumerable saints.

Chapter 2

The Apostles' Creed

13. What are the chief things which God teaches?

They are contained in the Apostles' Creed.

14. Say the Apostles' Creed.

I believe in God, the Father Almighty, Creator of heaven and earth; and in Jesus Christ, his only Son our Lord; who was conceived by the Holy Ghost, born of the Virgin Mary;

---

[1] Mt 16:26

suffered under Pontius Pilate, was crucified, dead and buried; he descended into hell; the third day he rose again from the dead; he ascended into heaven, sits at the right hand of God the Father Almighty; from thence he shall come to judge the living and the dead. I believe in the Holy Ghost, the holy Catholic Church, the communion of saints; the forgiveness of sins; the resurrection of the body; and life everlasting. Amen.

The First Article of the Creed

15. Which is the first article of the Apostles' Creed?
I believe in God, the Father Almighty, Creator of heaven and earth.

16. What is God?
He is Maker and Lord of heaven and earth.

17. Why is he called almighty?
Because he can do all things, whatever he pleases, and nothing is hard or impossible to him.

18. Why is he called Creator of heaven and earth?
Because he made heaven and earth and all things, out of nothing, by his only Word.

19. Had God any beginning?
No. He always was, and always will be.

20. Where is God?
God is everywhere.

21. Does God know and see all things?
Yes, he does know and see all things.

22. Has God any body?

No, God has no body; he is a pure spirit.

23. Is there then but one God?

Yes, in God there are three Persons.

24. Which are they?

God the Father, God the Son, and God the Holy Ghost.

25. Are they not three gods?

No. The Father, the Son, and the Holy Ghost, are all but one and the same God.

The Second Article

26. Which is the second article of the Creed?

And in Jesus Christ, his only Son, our Lord.

27. What do you believe of Jesus Christ?

I believe he is the Son of God, the second Person of the Blessed Trinity, true God, and true man.

28. Why is he true God?

Because he is the true and only Son of God the Father, born of him before all ages, and perfectly equal to him.

29. Why is he true man?

Because he is the true son of the Blessed Virgin Mary, and has a body and soul like us.

30. Was he always both God and man?

He was always God, equal to his Father from all eternity; but he was not always man, but only from the time that he came down from heaven for our redemption.

31. Why was he made man?
To save us from sin and hell.

32. Was Jesus Christ the Father, or the Holy Ghost?
No, he was neither God the Father, nor God the Holy Ghost, but only God the Son.

The Third Article

33. Which is the third article of the Creed?
Who was conceived by the Holy Ghost, born of the Virgin Mary.

34. How was Christ made man?
He was conceived and made man by the power of the Holy Ghost, in the womb of the Virgin Mary, without having any man for his father.

35. Where was our Savior born?
In a stable at Bethlehem.

36. Upon what day was our Savior born?
Upon Christmas-day.

The Fourth Article

37. Which is the fourth article of the Creed?
Suffered under Pontius Pilate, was crucified, dead, and buried.

38. What did Christ suffer?
A bloody sweat, whipping at the pillar, crowning with thorns, and the carriage of his cross.

39. What else?
He was nailed to a cross, and died upon it between two thieves.

40. Why did he suffer?
For our sins.

41. Upon what day did he suffer?
On Good Friday.

42. Where did he suffer?
On Mount Calvary.

43. Why do Catholics make the sign of the cross?
To put us in mind of the Blessed Trinity, and that the second Person became man, and died on a cross.

44. What puts us in mind of the Blessed Trinity, when we make the sign of the cross?
These words: In the name of the Father, and of the Son, and of the Holy Ghost.

45. What puts us in mind that Christ became man, and suffered on a cross?
The very making or signing ourselves with the sign of the cross.

The Fifth Article

46. Which is the fifth article of the Creed?
He descended into hell, the third day he rose again from the dead.

47. Whither did the soul of our Savior go after his death?
His soul went down into that part of hell called limbo.

48. What do you mean by limbo?
I mean a place of rest, where the souls of the saints were.

49. Did none go up to heaven before our Savior?
No. They expected him to carry them up thither.

50. What means, *the third day he rose again from the dead?*
It means, that after he was dead and buried for part of three days, he raised himself to life again the third day.

51. On what day did Christ rise again from the dead?
On Easter-day.

The Sixth Article

52. Which is the sixth article of the Creed?
He ascended into heaven, sits at the right hand of God the Father Almighty.

53. When did our Savior go up to heaven?
Forty days after he rose again.

54. Why is he said to sit at the right hand of God the Father? Has God the Father any hands?

No. But the meaning of the words is, that Christ as God is equal to his Father, and as man is in the highest place of heaven.

55. On what day did our Savior go up to heaven?

On Ascension-day.

The Seventh Article

56. Which is the seventh article of the Creed?

From thence he shall come to judge the living and the dead.

57. Will Christ ever come again?

Yes, he will come down from heaven at the last day, to judge all men.

58. What are the things he will judge?

All our thoughts, words, and works.

59. What will he say to the wicked?

Go ye cursed into everlasting fire.[2]

60. What will he say to the just?

"Come, you blessed of my Father, receive ye the kingdom which is prepared for you."[3]

61. Shall not every man be judged at his death, as well as at the last day?

Yes, he shall.

[2] Cf. Mt 25:41
[3] Mt 25:34

The Eighth Article

62. Which is the eighth article of the Creed?
I believe in the Holy Ghost.

63. Who is the Holy Ghost?
He is the third Person of the Blessed Trinity.

64. From whom doth he proceed?
From the Father and the Son.

65. Is he equal to them?
Yes, he is the same Lord and God as they are.

66. When did the Holy Ghost come down on the apostles in fiery tongues?
On Whit-Sunday.

67. Why did he come upon them?
To enable them to preach the gospel and to plant the Church.

The Ninth Article

68. Which is the ninth article of the Creed?
The holy Catholic Church, the communion of saints.

69. What is the Catholic Church?
All the faithful under one head.

70. Who is that head?
Christ Jesus our Lord.

71. Has the Church any visible head on earth?

Yes, the bishop of Rome, who is the successor of St. Peter, and commonly called the pope.

72. Has the Church of Christ any marks by which you may know it?

Yes, it has these four marks: it is one, it is holy, it is Catholic, and apostolical.

73. How is the Church *one*?

Because all its members agree in one faith, are all in one communion, and are all under one head.

74. How is the Church *holy*?

By teaching a holy doctrine, by inviting all to a holy life, and by the eminent holiness of so many thousands of her children.

75. How is the Church *Catholic* or *universal*?

Because she subsists in all ages; teaches all nations; and maintains all truths.

76. How is the Church *apostolical*?

Because she comes down by a perpetual succession from the apostles of Christ; and has her doctrine, her orders, and her mission from them.

77. Can the Church err in what she teaches?

No, she cannot err in matters of faith.

78. Why so?

Because Christ has promised that hell's gates shall not prevail against his Church; and that the Holy Ghost shall teach her all truth; and that he himself will abide with her forever.[4]

[4] Cf. Mt 16:18; Jn 14:26, 16:13; Mt 28:20

79. What is meant by the communion of saints?
That in the Church of God there is a communion of all holy persons in all holy things.

80. And have we any communion with the saints in heaven?
Yes, we communicate with them, as our fellow-members under the same head, Christ Jesus; and we are helped by their prayers.

81. And are the souls in purgatory helped by our prayers?
Yes, they are.

82. What do you mean by purgatory?
A middle state of souls, suffering for a time, on account of their sins.

83. In what cases do souls go to purgatory?
When they die in lesser sins, which we call venial; or when they have not satisfied the justice of God for former transgressions.

84. How do you prove there is a purgatory?
Because the scripture often teaches that God will render to every man according to his works; and that nothing undefiled can enter heaven; and that some Christians shall be saved, yet so as by fire.[5]

The Tenth Article

85. Which is the tenth article of the Creed?
The forgiveness of sins.

---

[5] Cf. Rom 2:6; Apoc 21:27; 1 Cor 3:15

86. What is meant by this article?
That there is in the Church of God, a forgiveness of sins, for such as properly apply for it.

87. To whom has Christ given power to forgive sins?
To the apostles and their successors, the bishops and priests of the Church.

88. By what sacraments are sins forgiven?
By baptism and penance.

89. What is sin?
An offence of God; or any thought, word, or deed against the law of God.

90. What is original sin?
It is the sin in which we were born.

91. How came we to be born in sin?
By Adam's sin, when he ate the forbidden fruit.

92. What is actual sin?
All the sin we commit ourselves.

93. What is mortal sin?
That which kills the soul, and deserves hell.

94. How does mortal sin kill the soul?
By destroying the life of the soul, which is the grace of God.

95. What is venial sin?
That which does not kill the soul, yet displeases God.

The Eleventh Article

96. Which is the eleventh article of the Creed?
The resurrection of the body.

97. What means, *the resurrection of the body*?
That we shall all rise again with the same bodies at the day of judgment.

The Twelfth Article

98. Which is the twelfth article of the Creed?
Life everlasting.

99. What means, *life everlasting*?
That the good shall live forever happy in heaven.

100. What is the happiness of heaven?
To see, love, and enjoy God for evermore.

101. And shall not the wicked also live forever?
They shall be punished forever in the flames of hell.

Chapter 3

The Lord's Prayer

102. Will faith alone save us?
No, it will not without good works.

103. Can we do any good towards our salvation, of ourselves?
No, we cannot, without the help of God's grace.

104. How may we obtain God's grace?
By prayer.

105. What is prayer?
It is the raising up of our minds to God.

106. What think you of those, who at their prayer think not of God, nor of what they say?
If these distractions are willful, such prayers instead of pleasing God, offend him.

107. Which is the best of all prayers?
The Lord's Prayer.

108. Who made the Lord's Prayer?
Christ our Lord.

109. Say the Lord's Prayer.
Our Father who art in heaven; hallowed be thy name; thy kingdom come; thy will be done on earth, as it is in heaven. Give us this day our daily bread; and forgive us our trespasses, as we forgive them that trespass against us; and lead us not into temptation, but deliver us from evil. Amen.

110. Who is it that is here called our Father?
God who made us all, and who, by his grace is the Father of all good Christians.

111. Why do you say *Our Father* and not *My Father*?
Because we are not to pray for ourselves alone, but for all others.

**112. What do we pray for when we say *hallowed be thy name?*

That God may be honored and served by all his creatures.

113. What means, *thy kingdom come?*

We pray that God may come, and be king in all hearts by his grace; and bring us all hereafter to his heavenly kingdom.

114. What means, *thy will be done on earth, as it is in heaven?*

That God would enable us by his grace, to do his will in all things, as the blessed do in heaven.

115. What means, *give us this day our daily bread?*

We beg by these words all necessaries for soul and body.

116. What means, *forgive us our trespasses, as we forgive them that trespass against us?*

We beg that God will forgive us our sins, as we forgive others their injuries.

117. What means, *lead us not into temptation?*

That God would give us grace not to yield to temptation.

118. What means, *deliver us from evil?*

We beg that God will free us from all evil of soul and body.

119. May we desire the saints and angels to pray for us?

Yes, we may.

120. How do you prove that the saints and angels can hear us?

"There shall be joy before the angels of God over one sinner that repents."[6]

---

[6] Lk 15:10

121. What is the prayer to our Blessed Lady which the Church teaches us?
The Hail Mary.

The Hail Mary

122. Say the Hail Mary.
Hail Mary, full of grace, our Lord is with thee. Blessed art thou amongst women; and blessed is the fruit of thy womb, Jesus. Holy Mary, Mother of God, pray for us sinners, now, and in the hour of our death. Amen.

123. How many parts are there in the Hail Mary?
Three parts.

124. Who made the two first parts?
The angel Gabriel, and St. Elizabeth, inspired by the Holy Ghost.

125. Who made the third part?
The Church of God, against those who denied the Virgin Mary to be the Mother of God.

126. Why say you the Hail Mary so often?
To put us in mind of the Son of God being made man for us.

127. For what other reason?
To honor the Blessed Virgin Mother of God, and to beg her prayers for us.

Chapter 4

The Ten Commandments

128. How many commandments are there?
Ten.

129. Who gave the ten commandments?
God himself in the old law; and Christ confirmed them in the new.

130. Which is the first commandment?
I am the Lord thy God, who brought thee out of the land of Egypt, and out of the house of bondage. Thou shalt not have strange gods before me. Thou shalt not make to thyself any graven thing; nor the likeness of anything that is in heaven above, or in the earth beneath, or in the waters under the earth. Thou shalt not adore them, nor serve them.

131. What are we commanded by this?
To believe, hope, love, and serve one true and living God, and no more.

132. What is forbidden by this commandment?
To worship false gods, or idols; or to give anything else whatsoever the honor which belongs to God.

133. What else is forbidden by this commandment?
All false religions; all dealing with the devil; and enquiring after things to come, or other secret things, by fortune-tellers, or superstitious practices.

134. What else?
All charms, spells, and heathenish observations of omens, dreams, and such like fooleries.

135. Does this commandment forbid the making of images?
It forbids the making of them, so as to adore and serve them; that is, it forbids making them our gods.

136. Does this commandment forbid all honor and veneration of the saints and angels?
No. We are to honor them as God's special friends and servants; but not with the honor which belongs to God.

137. And is it allowable to honor relics, crucifixes, and holy pictures?
Yes, with an inferior and relative honor, as they relate to Christ and his saints, and are memorials of them.

138. May we then pray to relics, or images?
No, by no means, for they have no life or sense to hear or help us.

139. What is the second commandment?
Thou shalt not take the name of the Lord, thy God, in vain.

140. What are we commanded by the second commandment?
To speak with reverence of God and all holy things, and to keep our lawful oaths and vows.

141. What are we forbid by it?
All false, rash, unjust, and unnecessary oaths; as also cursing, blaspheming, and profane words.

142. What is the third commandment?
Remember that thou keep holy the sabbath-day.

143. What are we commanded by this?
To spend the Sunday in prayer and other religious duties.

144. What do you mean by religious duties?
Hearing Mass, going to the sacraments, and reading good books.

145. What are we forbid by this commandment?
All unnecessary work, and sinful profanation of the Lord's day.

146. What is the fourth commandment?
Honor thy father, and thy mother.

147. What are we commanded by the fourth commandment?
To love, honor, and obey our parents in all that is not sin.

148. Are we commanded to obey only our father and mother?
Not only them, but also our bishops, pastors, magistrates, and masters.

149. What is forbidden by this commandment?
All contempt, stubbornness, and disobedience to our lawful superiors.

150. And what is the duty of parents and other superiors?
To take proper care of all under their charge; and to bring their children up in the fear of God.

151. What is the fifth commandment?
Thou shalt not kill.

152. What are we forbidden by the fifth commandment?
All willful murder, hatred, and revenge.

153. Does it forbid striking?

Yes, as also anger, quarrelling, and injurious words.

154. What else?

Giving scandal, and bad example.

155. What is the sixth commandment?

Thou shalt not commit adultery.

156. What is forbidden by this?

All kinds of sins of uncleanness with another's wife or husband; and all other kinds of immodesties, by kisses, touches, looks, words, or actions.

157. And what do you think of immodest plays and comedies?

They are also forbidden by this commandment; and it is sinful to be present at them.

158. What is the seventh commandment?

Thou shalt not steal.

159. What is forbidden by this commandment?

All unjust taking away, or keeping what belongs to others.

160. What else?

All manner of cheating in buying or selling; or any other way wronging our neighbor.

161. Must we restore ill-gotten goods?

Yes, if we are able, or else the sin will not be forgiven. We must also pay our debts.

162. What is the eighth commandment?

Thou shalt not bear false witness against thy neighbor.

163. What is forbidden by this commandment?

All false testimonies, rash judgments, and lies.

164. What else?

All backbiting and detraction, or any words and speeches, by which our neighbor's honor or reputation is any ways hurt.

165. What is he bound to do, who has injured his neighbor by speaking ill of him?

He must make him satisfaction, and restore his good name as far as he is able.

166. What is the ninth commandment?

Thou shalt not covet thy neighbor's wife.

167. What is forbidden by this?

All lustful thoughts and desires, and all willful pleasure in the irregular motions of the flesh.

168. What is the tenth commandment?

Thou shalt not covet thy neighbor's goods.

169. What is forbidden by this?

All covetous thoughts, and unjust desires of our neighbor's goods and profits.

Chapter 5

The Commandments of the Church

170. Are we bound to obey the commandments of the Church?
Yes, because Christ has said to the pastors of his Church: "He that heareth you, heareth me; and he that despiseth you, despiseth me."[7]

171. How many are the commandments of the Church?
Chiefly six.

172. Which be they?
1. To keep certain appointed days holy, with obligation of hearing Mass, and resting from servile works.
2. To fast Lent, the four Ember weeks, the vigils, and the Fridays according to the custom of England; and to abstain from flesh on Saturdays and other days of abstinence.
3. To pay tithes to our pastor.
4. To confess our sins to our pastor, at least once a year.
5. To receive the Blessed Sacrament once a year, and that at Easter, or thereabouts.
6. Not to solemnize marriage at certain times; nor within certain degrees of kindred, nor privately without witnesses.

173. Why does the Church command us to fast?
That by fasting we may satisfy God for our sins.

174. At what age do persons begin to be obliged to confession?
When they come to the use of reason; so as to be capable of

[7] Lk 10:16

mortal sin; which generally is supposed to be about the age of seven years.

175. And at what time do they begin to be obliged to Communion?
When they are sufficiently capable of being instructed in these sacred mysteries, and of discerning the body of our Lord.

Chapter 6

The Sacraments

176. What is a sacrament?
An outward sign of inward grace; or a sacred and mysterious sign and ceremony ordained by Christ, by which grace is conveyed to our souls.

177. Do all the sacraments give grace?
Yes, if we are duly prepared.

178. Whence have the sacraments the power of giving grace?
From Christ's precious blood.

179. Is it a great happiness to receive the sacraments worthily?
Yes, it is the greatest happiness in the world.

180. How many sacraments are there?
These seven: Baptism, confirmation, Holy Eucharist, penance, extreme unction, order, and matrimony.

181. What is baptism?
It is a sacrament by which we are made Christians, children of

God, and heirs of heaven; and are cleansed from original sin, and actual, if we be guilty of any.

182. How is baptism given?

By pouring water on the child, with the words ordained by Christ.

183. What are those words?

"I baptize thee in the name of the Father, and of the Son, and of the Holy Ghost." Which words ought to be said at the same time the water is poured.

184. What do we promise in baptism?

To renounce the devil, with all his works and pomps.

185. What is confirmation?

It is a sacrament, in which, by the imposition of hands of the bishop, we receive the Holy Ghost, in order to make us strong and perfect Christians, and soldiers of Jesus Christ.

186. How does the bishop administer this sacrament?

He prays that the Holy Ghost may come down upon us; and makes the sign of the cross with chrism on our foreheads.

187. What is the Holy Eucharist?

It is the true body and blood of Christ, under the appearances of bread and wine.

188. Why has Christ given himself to us in this sacrament?

To feed and nourish our souls, and to enable us to perform all Christian duties.

189. How is the bread and wine changed into the body and blood of Christ?
By the power of God, to whom nothing is hard or impossible, and by the words of *Jesus Christ* spoken by the priest in the Mass.

190. How must we prepare ourselves to receive the Blessed Sacrament?
We must be in the state of grace; and be fasting from midnight.

191. Is it a great sin to receive unworthily?
Yes it is. For, "he that eats and drinks unworthily, eats and drinks judgment to himself."[8]

192. What is it to receive unworthily?
To receive in mortal sin.

193. What is the Mass?
It is the unbloody sacrifice of the body and blood of Christ.

194. What are the ends for which we are to offer up this sacrifice?
First, for God's honor and glory. Secondly, in thanksgiving for all his benefits, and as a perpetual memorial of the passion and death of his Son. Thirdly, for obtaining pardon for our sins. And fourthly, for obtaining of all graces and blessings through Jesus Christ.

195. How must we hear Mass?
With very great devotion and attention.

196. What is the sacrament of penance?
It is a sacrament, in which, by the priest's absolution, joined

---

[8] 1 Cor 11:29

with contrition, confession, and satisfaction, the sins are forgiven which we have committed after baptism.

197. How do you prove that the priest hath power to absolve sinners, if they be truly penitent?
From the words of Christ, "Whose sins you shall forgive, they are forgiven."[9]

198. What are the parts of penance?
Contrition, confession, and satisfaction.

199. What is contrition?
A hearty sorrow for our sins by which we have offended so good a God, with a firm purpose of amendment.

200. What is a firm purpose of amendment?
It is a resolution, by the grace of God, not only to avoid sin, but also the occasions of it.

201. Why are we to be sorry for our sins?
The chiefest and best motive to be sorry for our sins is for the love of God, who is infinitely good in himself, and infinitely good to us; and therefore, we ought to be exceedingly grieved for having offended him.

202. What other motives have we to be sorry for our sins?
Because by them we lose heaven and deserve hell.

203. How may we obtain this hearty contrition and sorrow for our sins?
We must earnestly beg it of God; and make use of such considerations and meditations as may move us to it.

[9] Jn 20:23

204. What is confession?

It is to accuse ourselves of all our sins to a priest.

205. What if one willfully conceals a mortal sin in confession?

He commits a great sin, by telling a lie to the Holy Ghost, and makes his confession worth nothing.

206. What must we do, that we may leave out no sin in confession?

We must carefully examine our conscience upon the ten commandments, and the seven deadly sins.

207. How many things then have we to do by way of preparation for confession?

Four things: First, we must heartily pray to God for his grace to help us. Secondly, we must carefully examine our consciences. Thirdly, we must beg pardon of God, and be very sorry from our hearts for offending him. And fourthly, we must resolve to renounce our sins, and begin a new life for the future.

208. What is satisfaction?

It is doing the penance given by the priest.

209. What is an indulgence?

It is a releasing of temporal punishment which often remains due to sin, after the guilt has been remitted by the sacrament of penance.

210. What is extreme unction?

It is the anointing of the sick, with prayer, for the forgiveness of their sins.

211. When is this sacrament given?

When we are in danger of death by sickness.

212. What scripture have you for this sacrament?

"Is any one sick among you? Let him bring in the priests of the church; and let them pray over him, anointing him with oil in the name of the Lord. And the prayer of faith shall save the sick man; and the Lord shall raise him up; and if he be in sins, they shall be forgiven him."[10]

213. What is order?

It is a sacrament by which bishops, priests, etc. are ordained, and receive grace and power to perform the duties belonging to their charge.

214. What is matrimony?

It is a sacrament which gives grace to the married couple to love one another, and breed up their children in the fear of God.

Chapter 7

Of the Virtues and Vices, Etc.

215. How many are the theological virtues?

Three: Faith, hope, and charity.

216. What does faith help us to do?

It helps us to believe, without doubting, all that God has taught, and the Church proposes.

---

[10] Jas 5:14-15

217. What does hope help us to do?
To put our trust in God, that he will give us all things necessary for our salvation, if we do what he requires of us.

218. What does charity help us to do?
It helps us to love God above all things, and our neighbors as ourselves.

219. How many are the cardinal virtues?
Four: Prudence, justice, fortitude, and temperance.

220. How many are the gifts of the Holy Ghost?
Seven: Wisdom, understanding, counsel, fortitude, knowledge, godliness, and the fear of our Lord.

221. How many are the fruits of the Holy Ghost?
Twelve: Charity, joy, peace, patience, benignity, goodness, longanimity, mildness, faith, modesty, continency, and chastity.

222. Which are the two precepts of charity?
1) Thou shalt love the Lord thy God, with thy whole heart, with thy whole soul, with all thy strength, and with all thy mind;
2) And thy neighbor as thyself.

223. Say the seven corporal works of mercy.
1. To feed the hungry.
2. To give drink to the thirsty.
3. To clothe the naked.
4. To visit and ransom captives.
5. To harbor the harborless.
6. To visit the sick.
7. To bury the dead.

224. Say the seven works of mercy spiritual.
1. To convert the sinner.
2. To counsel the doubtful.
3. To comfort the sorrowful.
4. To bear wrongs patiently.
5. To forgive injuries.
6. To pray for the living and the dead.

225. Say the eight beatitudes.
1. Blessed are the poor in spirit, for theirs is the kingdom of heaven.
2. Blessed are the meek, for they shall possess the land.
3. Blessed are they that mourn, for they shall be comforted.
4. Blessed are they that hunger and thirst after justice, for they shall be filled.
5. Blessed are the merciful, for they shall find mercy.
6. Blessed are the clean of heart, for they shall see God.
7. Blessed are the peacemakers, for they shall be called the children of God.
8. Blessed are they that suffer persecution for justice sake, for theirs is the kingdom of heaven.

226. Say the seven deadly sins.
1. Pride. (vs. humility)
2. Covetousness. (vs. liberality)
3. Lust. (vs. chastity)
4. Anger. (vs. meekness)
5. Gluttony. (vs. temperance)
6. Envy. (vs. brotherly love)
7. Sloth. (vs. diligence)

227. Say the six sins against the Holy Ghost.
1. Presumption of God's mercy.
2. Despair.

3. Impugning the known truth.

4. Envy at another's spiritual good.

5. Obstinacy in sin.

6. Final impenitence.

228. **Say the four sins crying to heaven for vengeance.**

1. Willful murder.

2. Sodomy.

3. Oppression of the poor.

4. Defrauding laborers of their wages.

229. **Say the nine ways of being accessory to another person's sins.**

1. By counsel.

2. By command.

3. By consent.

4. By provocation.

5. By praise or flattery.

6. By concealment.

7. By partaking.

8. By silence.

9. By defense of the ill done.

230. **Say the three eminent good works.**

1. Almsdeeds.

2. Prayer.

3. Fasting.

231. **Say the evangelical counsels.**

1. Voluntary poverty.

2. Perpetual chastity.

3. Entire obedience.

232. **Say the four last things to be remembered.**

1. Death.

2. Judgment.
3. Hell.
4. Heaven.

Chapter 8

The Christian's Rule of Life

233. Who was the founder of the Christian religion?
Jesus Christ the Son of God, who came down from heaven, to teach us the way to heaven.

234. What rule of life then must the Christian follow, if he hopes to be saved?
He must follow the rule of life taught by Jesus Christ.

235. What is the Christian to do by this rule?
He must always hate sin, and love God.

236. How is he to hate sin?
Above all other evils; so as to be resolved never to commit a willful sin, for the love or fear of anything whatsoever.

237. How is he to love God?
Above all things, and with his whole heart.

238. How is he to learn to love God?
He must beg of God to teach him: "O my God, teach me to love thee."

239. What else must he do?

He must often think how good God is; often speak to him in his heart; and always seek to please him.

240. And does not Jesus Christ also teach us to love one another?

Yes, he commands us to love all persons without exception, for his sake.

241. In what manner are we to love one another?

In God, and for God; so as to wish well to all, and to pray for all, and never to allow ourselves any thought, word, or deed, to the prejudice of anyone.

242. And are we also to love our enemies?

Yes, we are; not only by forgiving them from our hearts, but also by wishing them well, and praying for them.

243. What other rules does Jesus Christ give, to all that desire to be his disciples?

To deny ourselves, to take up our cross, and to follow him.[11]

244. What is meant by denying ourselves?

The renouncing our own will; and going against our own humors, inclinations, and passions.

245. Why are we bound to deny ourselves in this manner?

Because our natural inclinations are prone to evil from our childhood, and if not curbed and corrected by self-denial, will infallibly carry us to hell.

[11] Cf. Mt 16:24

246. What is meant by taking up our cross?

Patiently submitting to, and willingly embracing the labors and sufferings of this short life.

247. And what is meant by following Christ?

To follow Christ is to walk in his footsteps, by an imitation of his virtues.

248. What are the virtues we are to learn of him?

To be meek and humble of heart; to be obedient unto death; and to seek to do in all things the will of his Father.

249. Which are the enemies the Christian must fight against all the days of his life?

The devil, the world, and the flesh.

250. Whom do you mean by the devil?

Satan and all his wicked angels, who are ever seeking to draw us into sin, that we may be damned with them.

251. Whom do you mean by the world?

All wicked company; and all such as love the vanities, riches, and pleasures of this world better than God.

252. Why do you number these amongst the enemies of the soul?

Because they are always seeking, by word or example, to carry us along with them in the broad road that leads to damnation.[12]

253. And what do you mean by the flesh?

Our own corrupt inclinations and passions; which are the most dangerous of all our enemies.

---

[12] Cf. Mt 7:13

254. What must we do to hinder these enemies from dragging us along with them to hell?
We must always watch, pray, and fight, against all their suggestions and temptations.

255. Whom must we depend upon in this warfare?
Not upon ourselves, but upon God alone.

Chapter 9

The Christian's Daily Exercise

256. What is the first thing you should do in the morning?
Make the sign of the cross, and offer my heart and soul to God.

257. What must you do next?
Rise diligently; dress myself modestly; and entertain myself with good thoughts, particularly by considering the goodness of God, who gives me this day, to labor in it for the salvation of my soul, and that perhaps this may be my last.

258. And what do you do, after you have put on your clothes?
I kneel down to my prayers, and perform my morning exercise.

259. What is your morning exercise?
First, I bow down my whole soul and body to adore my God; and I offer myself to his divine service. Secondly, I give him thanks for his infinite goodness to me, and to all his creatures; and desire to join with all the angels and saints in blessing and praising him. Thirdly, I crave pardon from my heart, for all my sins; and beg that I may rather die than offend my God any

more. Fourthly, I offer up to God all my thoughts, words, and actions of the day; and beg his blessing on them.

260. And what prayers do you say after this?
I say the Our Father, the Hail Mary, and the Apostles' Creed; and I make acts of faith, hope, and love of God.

261. Do you do anything else?
I pray for my friends, and for my enemies; for the living and for the dead; and I beg mercy, grace, and salvation for all. Then I conclude, by desiring our Blessed Lady to be a mother to me; and by recommending myself to my good angel, and to all the court of heaven.

262. Is this all that a good Christian should do, by way of morning exercise?
No. For he ought also, if he has time and opportunity, to meditate in the morning on his last end, or some other devout subject, and to hear Mass with attention and devotion.

263. What ought you to do at the beginning of every work or employment?
I ought to offer it up to God's service; and to think that I will do it, because it is his will, and in order to please him.

264. And what are you to do as to your eating, drinking, sleeping, and diversion?
All these things I must use with moderation; and do them, because such is the will of God; and with a good intention to please him.

265. By what other means must you sanctify your ordinary actions, and employments of the day?
By often raising up my heart to God whilst I am about them, and saying some short prayer to him.

266. What do you do as often as you hear the clock strike?
I turn myself to God, and I say to him: "O my God, teach me to love thee, in time and eternity."

267. What do you do as often as you receive any blessing from God?
I endeavor immediately to make him a return of thanksgiving and love.

268. And what do you do when you find yourself tempted to sin?
I make the sign of the cross upon my heart, and I call upon God as earnestly as I can: "Lord save me, or I perish."

269. And what if you have fallen into any sin?
I cast myself in spirit at the feet of Christ, and humbly beg his pardon, saying: "Lord be merciful to me, a sinner."

270. And what do you say when God sends you any cross, or suffering, or sickness, or pain?
I say: "Lord, thy will be done. I take this for my sins."

271. And what other little prayers do you say to yourself, from time to time, in the day?
Lord what wilt thou have me to do? O teach me to do thy holy will in all things. Lord, keep me from sin. May the name of our Lord be forever blessed. Come my dear Jesus, and take full possession of my soul. Glory be to the Father, etc.

272. What is your evening exercise?
I say the Our Father, Hail Mary, and Creed, together with the acts of faith, hope, and love of God, etc., as I did in the morning.

273. And don't you also join with the family in saying the litanies and other evening prayers, which are usually said in Catholic families?
Yes, as also in the daily examination of conscience.

274. How do you make this daily examination of conscience?

First, I place myself in the presence of God (as I usually do at the beginning of all my prayers) and I beg his light and help, to know my sins and to be sorry for them. Secondly, I consider how I have spent the day from morning until night; in what manner I have performed my prayers and all other duties; what blessings I have received from God; and what offences I have been guilty of against him, by commission or omission. Thirdly, I give thanks to God for all his blessings, and beg pardon for all my sins, endeavoring to make a hearty act of contrition for them. Fourthly, I commend my soul into the hands of God, with the best dispositions I can of love and conformity to his blessed will, as if I were to die that night.

275. How do you finish the day?

I observe due modesty in going to bed, entertaining myself with the thoughts of death. And I endeavor to compose myself to rest at the foot of the cross, and to give my last thoughts to my crucified Savior.

276. How do you make an act of faith?

O eternal truth, who hast revealed thyself to men, one God in three Persons, Father, Son, and Holy Ghost, I believe in thee. O Jesus Christ, the Son of God, my Savior and Redeemer, who hast died for us all, I believe in thee. I believe all the divine truths which thou my God hast taught us by thy word, and by thy Church, because thou hast taught them, who art the sovereign Truth; and I had rather die, than call in question any of these truths.

277. How do you make an act of hope?

O my God, who art infinitely powerful and infinitely good and merciful; who hast made me for thyself, and redeemed me by the blood of thy Son, and promised us all good through him; I firmly hope for mercy, grace, and salvation from thee, through the same Jesus Christ my Savior; resolving, on my part, to do all that thou requirest of me.

278. How do you make an act of the love of God?

O my God and my all, infinitely good in thyself, and infinitely good to me, I desire to praise thee, bless thee, glorify thee, and love thee forever. O take possession of my whole soul, and make me forever a servant of thy love.

279. And how do you make an act of the love of your neighbors?

O my God, thou hast commanded me to love every neighbor as myself, for thy sake. O give me grace to fulfill this commandment. I desire to love every neighbor, whether friend or enemy, in thee and for thee. I renounce every thought, word, or deed that is contrary to this love. I forgive all that have in any way offended me, and I beg thy mercy, grace, and salvation for all the world.

280. How do you make an act of contrition for your sins?

O my God, who art infinitely good, and always hatest sin; I beg pardon from the bottom of my heart, for all my offences against thee. I detest them all, and am heartily sorry for them, because they offend thy infinite goodness; and I beg I may rather die than be guilty of them anymore.

FINIS.

THE
CATHOLICK CHRISTIAN
INSTRUCTED

In the Sacraments, Sacrifice, Ceremonies,
and Obſervances of the CHURCH.

By Way of
QUESTION and ANSWER.

By *R..... C.......*

LONDON:
Printed in the YEAR MDCCXXXVII.

Original Title Page
(1737)

The
Catholick Christian
Instructed

In the Sacraments, Sacrifice, Ceremonies,
and Observances of the CHURCH.

By Way of
QUESTION and ANSWER.

By *R* . . . . .   C . . . .

LONDON:
Printed in the YEAR 1737

Chapter 1

Of the Sign of the Cross

1. Why do you treat of the sign of the cross, before you begin to speak of the sacrament?

Because this holy sign is made use of in all the sacrament, to give us to understand, that they all have their whole force and efficacy from the cross, that is, from the death and passion of Jesus Christ. "What is the sign of Christ," says St. Augustine, "which all know, but the cross of Christ, which sign, if it be not applied to the foreheads of the believers, to the water with which they are baptized, to the chrism with which they are anointed, to the sacrifice with which they are fed, none of these things is duly performed?"[1]

2. But did the primitive Christians only make use of the sign of the cross in the administration of the sacrament?

Not only then, but also upon all other occasions. "At every step," says the ancient and learned Tertullian, "at every coming in and going out, when we put on our clothes or shoes, when we wash, when we sit down to table, when we light a candle, when we go to bed . . . whatsoever conversation employs us, we imprint on our foreheads the sign of the cross."[2]

3. What is the meaning of this frequent use of the sign of the cross?

It is to show that we are not ashamed of the cross of Christ; it is to make an open profession of our believing in a crucified God; it is to help us to bear always in mind his death and passion;

---

[1] Augustine, *Tractate 118*, n. 5
[2] Tertullian, *Liber de Corona Militis*, Ch. 3

and to nourish thereby in our souls the three divine virtues of faith, hope, and charity.

4. How are these three divine virtues exercised in the frequent use of the sign of the cross?

First, faith is exercised, because the sign of the cross brings to our remembrance the chief article of the Christian belief, viz. the Son of God dying for us upon the cross. Second, our hope is thereby daily nourished and increased; because this holy sign continually reminds us of the passion of Christ, on which is grounded all our hope for mercy, grace and salvation. Third, charity, or the love of God is excited in us by that sacred sign; by representing to us the love which God has showed us in dying upon the cross for us.

5. In what manner do you make the sign of the cross?

In blessing ourselves, we form the sign of the cross, by putting our right hand to the forehead, and so drawing, as it were, a line down to the breast or stomach, and then another line crossing the former, from the left shoulder to the right: and the words that we pronounce at the same time are these: "In the name of the Father, and of the Son, and of the Holy Ghost"; by which we make a solemn profession of our faith in the Blessed Trinity. But in blessing other persons or things we form the cross in the air, with the right hand extended towards the thing we bless.

6. Have you anything more to add in favor of the cross, and the use of signing ourselves with the sign of the cross?

Yes, the cross is the standard of Christ, and is called by our Lord himself, the "sign of the Son of man."[3] It is the badge of all good Christians, represented by the letter *tau*, ordered to be set as a mark upon the foreheads of those that were to escape

---

[3] Mt 24:30

the wrath of God.[4] It was given by our Lord to Constantine, the first Christian emperor, as a token and assurance of victory, when he and his whole army, in their march against the tyrant Maxentius, saw a cross formed of pure light above the sun, with this inscription: "By this conquer"; which account the historian Eusebius, in his first book of the life of Constantine, declares he had from that emperor's own mouth. To which we may add that the sign of the cross was used of old by the holy fathers as an invincible buckler against the devil, and a powerful means to dissipate his illusions; and that God has often made it an instrument in their hands of great and illustrious miracles, of which there are innumerable instances in ancient church history and in the writings of the fathers, which it would be too tedious here to recount.

---

[4] Cf. Ez 9:4; Jerome, *Commentary on Ezekiel*

Chapter 2

Of the Sacrament of Baptism

7. What do you mean by a sacrament?
An outward sign or ceremony of Christ's institution, by which grace is given to the soul of the worthy receiver.

8. What are the necessary conditions for a thing to be a sacrament?
These three: First, it must be a sacred sign, and consequently, as to the outward performance, it must be visible or sensible. Second, this sacred sign must have annexed unto it a power of communicating grace to the soul. Third, this must be by virtue of the ordinance or institution of Christ.

9. How then do you prove that baptism is a sacrament, since the scripture nowhere calls it so?
Because it has these three conditions: First, it is an outward visible sign consisting in the washing with water, with the form of words prescribed by Christ. Second, it has a power of communicating grace to our souls in the way of a new birth; whence it is called by the apostle, "The laver or washing of regeneration and renewing of the Holy Ghost."[5] Third, we have the ordinance and institution of Christ, "Go teach all nations, baptizing them in the name of the Father, and of the Son, and of the Holy Ghost,"[6] and "except a man be born again of water and the Holy Ghost, he cannot enter into the kingdom of God."[7]

---

[5] Ti 3:5
[6] Mt 28:19
[7] Jn 3:5

10. In what manner must baptism be administered, so as to be valid?
It must be administered in true natural water, with this or the like form of words: *I baptize thee in the name of the Father, and of the Son, and of the Holy Ghost*; which words ought to be pronounced at the same time as the water is applied to the person that is baptized, and by the same minister.

11. What if the words "I baptize thee," or any one of the names of the three Persons should be left out?
In that case it would be no baptism.

12. What if the baptism should be administered in rosewater, or any of the like artificial waters?
It would be no baptism.

13. Ought baptism to be administered by dipping, or by pouring of the water, or by sprinkling with the water?
It may be administered validly any of these ways; but the custom of the Church is to administer this sacrament either by dipping in the water, which is used in the East, or by pouring of the water upon the person baptized, which is more customary in these parts of Christendom. Moreover, it is the custom in all parts of the Catholic Church, and has been so from the apostles' days, to dip or pour three times at the names of the three divine Persons; though we don't look upon this as so essential that doing otherwise would render the baptism invalid.

14. What think you of those that administer baptism so slightly, that it is doubtful whether it may in any sense be called an ablution or washing; as for instance, those that administer it only with a flick of a wet finger?
Such as these expose themselves to the danger of administering no baptism.

15. What do you think of baptism administered by heretics or schismatics?

The Church receives their baptism, if they observe the Catholic matter and form. That is, if they baptize with true natural water, pronouncing at the same time these words: *I baptize thee in the name of the Father, and of the Son, and of the Holy Ghost.*

16. What think you of baptism administered with the due form of words, but without the sign of the cross?

The omission of this ceremony does not render the baptism invalid.

17. What is your judgment of the baptism said to be administered by some modern Arians, *In the name of the Father, through the Son, in the Holy Ghost?*

Such a corruption of the form makes the baptism null and invalid.

18. What is the doctrine of the Church as to baptism administered by a layman or woman?

If it be attempted without necessity, it is a criminal presumption; though even then the baptism is valid, and is not to be reiterated. But in a case of necessity, when a priest cannot be had, and a child is in immediate danger of death, baptism may not only validly, but also lawfully be administered by any person whatsoever. In which case a cleric, though only in lesser orders, is to be admitted preferably to a layman, and a man preferably to a woman, and a Catholic preferably to a heretic.

19. How do you prove that infants may be baptized who are not capable of being taught or instructed in the faith?

I prove it first by a tradition which the Church has received from the apostles,[8] and practiced in all ages ever since. Now as none were more likely or better qualified than the apostles to understand the true meaning of the commission given them by their master to baptize all nations, so none were more diligent than they to execute faithfully this commission according to his meaning, and to teach their disciples to do the same.[9] So that what the Church has received by tradition from the apostles and their disciples was undoubtedly agreeable to the commission of Christ.

Secondly, I prove it by comparing together two texts of scripture, one of which declares that without baptism no one can enter into the kingdom of heaven: "Except a man be born again of water and the Holy Ghost, he cannot enter into the kingdom of God."[10] The other text declares that infants are capable of this kingdom: "Suffer little children to come unto me and forbid them not; for of such is the kingdom of God,"[11] and consequently they must be capable of baptism.

Thirdly, circumcision, in the old law, corresponded to baptism in the new law, and was a figure of it.[12] But circumcision was administered to infants.[13] Therefore, baptism in like manner is to be administered to infants.

Fourthly, we read in scripture of whole families baptized by St. Paul.[14] Now it is probable that in so many whole families there were some infants.

Fifthly, as infants are not capable of helping themselves by faith and repentance, were they not capable of being helped by the sacrament of baptism, they could have no share in Christ

---

[8] Cf. Irenaeus, *Against Heresies*, Bk. 2, Ch. 22; Origen, *Commentary on Romans* 5:9; Cyprian, *Epistle 58*; Chrysostom, *Ad Neophytos*; Augustine, *Letter 166*, Ch. 3

[9] Cf. Mt 28:20

[10] Jn 3:5

[11] Lk 18:16

[12] Cf. Col 2:11-12

[13] Cf. Gn 17

[14] Cf. Acts 16:15, 33; 1 Cor 1:16

THE CATHOLICK CHRISTIAN INSTRUCTED

and no means to be delivered from original sin; and conse-quently, almost one half of mankind dying before the use of reason must inevitably perish, if infants were not to be baptized.

Sixthly, if infants' baptism were invalid, the gates of hell would have long since prevailed against the Church; yea, for many ages there would have been no such thing as Christians upon earth, since for many ages before the Anabaptists arose, all persons had been baptized in their infancy: which baptism, if it were null, they were no Christians, and consequently there was no Church. Where then was that promise of Christ, "Upon this rock I will build my Church, and the gates of hell shall not prevail against it"?[15] And "Lo, I am with you always, even to the end of the world"?[16]

Besides, if infants' baptism be null, the first preachers of the Anabaptists had never received baptism, or had received it from those who never had been baptized. A likely set of men for bringing back God's truth banished from the world, who had not so much as received the first badge or character of a Christian; and who, so far from having any orders or mission, had not so much as baptism.

20. How do you prove against the Quakers that all persons ought to be baptized?

From the commission of Christ, "Go teach all nations, baptiz-ing them in the name of the Father, and of the Son, and of the Holy Ghost."[17] From that general sentence of our Lord, "Except a man be born again of water and the spirit, he cannot enter into the kingdom of God."[18] From the practice of the apostles and of the first Christians, who were all baptized. Thus we read, with relation to the first converts to Christianity at Jerusalem,

[15] Mt 16:18
[16] Mt 28:20
[17] Mt 28:19
[18] Jn 3:5

when they asked of the apostles what they should do, that Peter
said unto them: "Repent and be baptized every one of you in the
name of Jesus Christ . . . then they that gladly received his word
were baptized."[19] Thus we read of the Samaritans converted by
Philip, that "they were baptized both men and women," and
that "Simon [Magus] himself also believed and was baptized,"[20]
as was also the eunuch of Queen Candace.[21] Thus we find Paul
baptized by Ananias,[22] Cornelius and his friends by order of
St. Peter,[23] Lydia and her household by St. Paul,[24] etc. In fine,
from the perpetual belief and practice of the whole Church
ever since the apostles' days, which in all ages and all nations
has ever administered baptism in water to all her children, and
never looked upon any to be rightly Christians until they were
baptized. Now "if a person will not hear the church, let him be
to thee as a heathen and a publican."[25]

**21. How do you prove from scripture that the apostles gave baptism
in water?**

From Acts 8: "See here is water," said the eunuch to St. Philip,
"what does hinder me to be baptized? . . . and they both went
down into the water, both Philip and the eunuch, and he baptized him."[26] And, "Can any man forbid water," said St. Peter,
"that these should not be baptized, who have received the Holy
Ghost as well as we? And he commanded them to be baptized
in the name of the Lord."[27] Where we see that even they who
received the Holy Ghost, and consequently had been baptized

---

[19] Acts 2:38, 41
[20] Acts 8:12, 13
[21] Cf. Acts 8:36-38
[22] Cf. Acts 9:18
[23] Cf. Acts 10:47-48
[24] Cf. Acts 16:15
[25] Mt 18:17
[26] Acts 8:36, 38
[27] Acts 10:47-48

by the Spirit, were nevertheless commanded to be baptized in water. Hence St. Paul tells us that "Christ loved the church and gave himself for it, that he might sanctify it, cleansing it by the laver of water, in the word of life."[28] And, "Let us draw near with a true heart . . . having our hearts sprinkled from an evil conscience, and our bodies washed with pure water."[29]

22. What are the effects of the sacrament of baptism?

First, it washes away original sin, in which we are all born, by reason of the sin of our first father, Adam. Second, it remits all actual sins, which we ourselves have committed (in case we have committed any before baptism), both as to the guilt and pain. Third, it infuses the habit of divine grace into our souls, and makes us the adopted children of God. Fourth, it gives us a right and title to the kingdom of heaven. Fifth, it imprints a character or spiritual mark in the soul. Sixthly, in fine, it lets us into the Church of God, and makes us children and members of the Church.

23. How do you prove that all sins are remitted in baptism?

From Acts 2: "Repent and be baptized every one of you in the name of Jesus Christ for the remission of sins."[30] "Arise and be baptized," says Ananias to Paul, "and wash away thy sins [in the Greek, *be washed from thy sins*], calling upon the name of the Lord,"[31] "I will pour clean water upon you, and you shall be cleansed from all your filthiness."[32] Hence, in the Nicene Creed we confess one baptism unto the remission of sins.

---

[28] Eph 5:25-26
[29] Heb 10:22
[30] Acts 2:38
[31] Acts 22:16
[32] Ez 36:25

24. **May not a person obtain the remission of his sins and eternal salvation without being actually baptized?**

In two cases, he may. The first is when a person not yet baptized, but heartily desiring baptism, is put to death for the faith of Christ before he can have this sacrament administered to him; for such a one is baptized in his own blood. The second case is when a person that can by no means procure the actual administration of baptism has an earnest desire of it, joined with a perfect love of God and repentance of his sins, and dies in this disposition; for this is called the baptism of the Holy Ghost, *baptismus flaminis*.

25. **From whence has baptism the power of conferring grace, and washing away our sins?**

From the institution of Christ, and in virtue of his blood, passion and death, from whence also all the other sacraments have their efficacy. For there is no obtaining mercy, grace, or salvation, but through the passion of Jesus Christ.

26. **In what manner must a person that is come to years of discretion prepare himself for the sacrament of baptism?**

By faith and repentance; and therefore it is necessary that he be first well instructed in the Christian doctrine, and that he firmly believe all the articles of the Catholic faith. Second, that he be heartily sorry for all his sins, firmly resolving to lead a good Christian life, to renounce all sinful habits, and to make full satisfaction to all whom he has in any way injured.

27. **But what if a person should be baptized without being in these dispositions?**

In that case he would receive the sacrament and character of baptism, but not the grace of the sacrament, nor the remission of his sins, which he cannot obtain until by a sincere repentance he detests and renounces all his sins.

28. **Is it necessary for a person to go to confession before he receives the sacrament of baptism?**

No, it is not, because the sins committed before baptism are washed away by baptism, and not by the sacrament of penance; and therefore there is no need of confessing them.

29. **What think you of those that put off for a long time their children's baptism?**

I think they are guilty of a sin, in exposing them to the danger of dying without baptism; since, as daily experience ought to convince them, young children are so quickly and so easily snatched away by death.

Chapter 3

Of the Ceremonies of Baptism

30. **Why does the Church make use of so many ceremonies in baptism?**

First, to render thereby this mystery more venerable to the people. Second, to make them understand the effects of this sacrament, and what the obligations are which they contract in this sacrament.

31. **Are the ceremonies of baptism very ancient?**

They are all of them very ancient, as may be demonstrated from the writings of the holy fathers; and as we know no beginning of them, we have reason to conclude that they come from apostolical tradition.

32. In what places does the Church administer the sacrament of baptism?

Regularly speaking and excepting the case of necessity, she does not allow baptism to be administered anywhere else but in the churches which have fonts; the water of which by apostolical tradition is solemnly blessed every year on the Vigils of Easter and Whit-Sunday.

33. What is the meaning of having godfathers and godmothers in baptism?

First, that they may present to the Church the person that is to be baptized and may be witnesses of his baptism. Second, that they may answer in his name, and be sureties for his performance of the promises which they make for him.

34. What is the duty of godfathers and godmothers?

To see, as much as lies in them, that their godchildren be brought up in the true faith and in the fear of God; that they be timely instructed in the whole Christian doctrine, and that they make good those engagements which they have made in their name.

35. May all sorts of persons be admitted for godfathers and godmothers?

No, but only such as are duly qualified for discharging the obligations of a godfather or godmother. Upon which account none are to be admitted that are not members of the Catholic Church, none whose lives are publicly scandalous, none who are ignorant of the Christian doctrine, etc.[33]

---

[33] Cf. *Rituale Romanum*

36. How many godfathers and godmothers may a person have in the Catholic Church?

The Council of Trent orders that no one should have any more than one godfather and one godmother; that the spiritual kindred, which the child and its parents contract with the godfathers and godmothers and which is an impediment of marriage, may not be extended to too many persons.[34]

37. In what order or manner does the Catholic Church proceed in the administration of baptism?

First, the priest having asked the name of the person that is to be baptized (which ought not to be any profane or heathenish name, but the name of some saint, by whose example he may be excited to a holy life and by whose prayers he may be protected), inquires of him: "N. what dost thou demand of the Church of God?" To which the person himself, if at age (or the godfather and godmother for him), answers, "Faith"; by which is meant not the bare virtue, by which we believe what God teaches, but the whole body of Christianity, as comprehending both belief and practice; into which the faithful enter by the gate of baptism. The priest goes on and asks, "What does faith give thee?" R: "Life everlasting." V: "If thou wilt enter into life, keep the commandments: Thou shalt love the Lord thy God with thy whole heart, and with thy whole soul, and with thy whole mind; and thy neighbor as thyself."

After this, the priest blows three times upon the face of the person that is to be baptized, saying, "Depart out of him or her, O unclean spirit, and give place to the Holy Ghost, the Comforter." This ceremony was practiced by the universal Church long before St. Augustine's days,[35] and it is used in contempt of

---

[34] Cf. Council of Trent, Session 24

[35] Who calls it a most ancient tradition: Augustine, *De Nuptiis Et Concupiscentia*, Bk. 2, Ch. 33, 50.

Satan, and to drive him away by the Holy Ghost, who is called the Spirit or Breath of God.

Then the priest makes the sign of the cross on the forehead and on the breast of the person that is to be baptized, saying: "Receive the sign of the cross upon thy forehead and in thy heart; receive the faith of the heavenly commandments, and let thy manners be such, that thou mayest now be the temple of God." This sign of the cross upon the forehead is to give us to understand that we are to make open profession of the faith of a crucified God, and never to be ashamed of his cross; and the sign of the cross upon the breast is to teach us that we are always to have Christ crucified in our hearts.

After this, there follow some prayers for the person that is to be baptized, to beg of God to dispose his soul for the grace of baptism. Then the priest blesses some salt, and puts a grain of it in the mouth of the person that is to be baptized. By which ancient ceremony we are admonished to procure and maintain in our souls true wisdom and prudence, of which salt is an em-blem or figure, inasmuch as it seasons and gives a relish to all things. Upon which account it was commanded in the law that salt should be used in every sacrifice or oblation made to God; to whom no offering can be pleasing where the salt of discretion is wanting.[36] We are also admonished by this ceremony so to season our souls with the grace of God, as to keep them from the corruption of sin, as we make use of salt to keep things from corrupting.

Then the priest proceeds to the solemn prayers and exor-cisms, used of old by the Catholic Church in the administration of baptism, to cast out the devil from the soul, under whose power we are born by original sin. "I exorcise thee," says he, "O unclean spirit, in the name of the Father, + and of the Son, + and of the Holy Ghost, + that thou mayest go out, and depart

[36] Cf. Lv 2:13

from this servant of God, N. For he commands thee, O thou cursed and condemned wretch, who with his feet walked upon the sea, and stretched forth his right hand to Peter that was sinking. Therefore, O accursed devil, remember thy sentence, and give honor to the living and true God. Give honor to Jesus Christ his Son, and to the Holy Ghost, and depart from this servant of God, N. For our God and Lord Jesus Christ has vouchsafed to call him to his holy grace and blessing and to the font of baptism." Then he signs the forehead with the sign of the cross, saying, "And this sign of the holy cross, which we imprint on his forehead, mayest thou, O cursed devil, never dare to violate, through the same Christ our Lord, Amen."

All that has been hitherto set down of the prayers and ceremonies of baptism is usually performed in the porch or entry of the church, to signify that the catechumen, or person that is to be baptized is not worthy to enter into the church, until the devil first be cast out of his soul. But after these prayers and exorcisms the priest reaches forth the extremity of his stole to the catechumen, or if it be an infant, lays it upon him, and so introduces him into the church, saying, "N. come into the temple of God, that thou mayest have part with Christ unto everlasting life, Amen."

Being come into the church, the priest, jointly with the party that is to be baptized (or, if it be an infant, with the godfather and godmother), recites aloud the Apostles' Creed and the Lord's Prayer, then reads another exorcism over the catechumen, commanding the devil to depart, in the name and by the power of the most Blessed Trinity. After which, in imitation of Christ who cured with his spittle the man that was deaf and dumb,[37] he wets his finger with his spittle, and touches first the ears of the catechumen, saying "Ephpheta," that is, *be thou opened*, then his nostrils, adding these words: "unto the odor

[37] Cf. Mk 7:32ff

61

of sweetness." "But be thou put to flight, O devil, for the judgment of God will be at hand," by which ceremony the Church instructs her catechumens to have their ears open to God's truth, and to smell its sweetness; and begs this grace for them.

Then the priest asks the person that is to be baptized, "N. Dost thou renounce Satan?" To which the person himself, if at age (otherwise the godfather and godmother in his name), answer: "I renounce him." The priest goes on, "And all his works?" R: "I renounce them." V: "And all his pomps?" R: "I renounce them."

This solemn renouncing of Satan, and of his works, and of his pomps, in the receiving of baptism, is a practice as ancient as the Church itself, and in a particular manner requires our attention: Because it is a promise and vow that we make to God, by which we engage ourselves to abandon the party of the devil, to have nothing to do with his works, that is, with the works of darkness and sin, and to cast away from us his pomps, that is, the maxims and vanities of the world. It is a covenant we make with God by which we, on our parts, promise him our allegiance, and to fight against his enemies; and he, on his part, promises us life everlasting, if we are faithful to our engagements. But in the moment we break this solemn covenant by willful sin, we lose both the grace of baptism, and all that title to an eternal inheritance which we received in baptism, together with the dignity of children of God; and become immediately slaves of the devil, and children of hell.

After this renouncing of Satan and declaring war against him, to give us to understand what kind of arms we are to procure in this spiritual conflict, the priest anoints the catechumen upon the breast and between the shoulders with holy oil, which is solemnly blessed by the bishop every year on Maundy-Thursday; which outward unction is to represent the inward anointing of the soul by divine grace, which, like a sacred oil, penetrates our hearts, heals the wounds of our souls, and fortifies them against our passions and concupiscences. Where note, that the anointing of the breast is to signify the necessity of fortifying the heart with heavenly courage, to act manfully, and to do our duty in all things; and the anointing between the shoulders is to signify the necessity of the like grace to bear and support all the adversities and crosses of this mortal life. The words which the priest uses at this conjuncture are: "I anoint thee with the oil of salvation in Christ Jesus our Lord, that thou mayest have eternal life, Amen."

Then the priest asks the catechumen: "N. Dost thou believe in God the Father Almighty, Creator of heaven and earth?" **R**: "I believe." **V**: "Dost thou believe in Jesus Christ, his only Son, our Lord, who was born and who suffered for us?" **R**: "I believe." **V**: "Dost thou believe in the Holy Ghost, the holy Catholic Church, the communion of saints, the forgiveness of sins, the resurrection of the body, and life everlasting?" **R**: "I believe." Which answers are made either by the catechumen himself, if able, or by the godfather and godmother; and imply another part of the covenant of baptism, viz. the covenant of faith by which we oblige ourselves to a steady and sincere profession of the great truths of Christianity, and that not by words alone, but by the constant practice of our lives.

After this the priest asks: "N. will thou be baptized?" **R**: "I will." Then the godfather and godmother both holding or touching their godchild, the priest pours the water upon his head three times in the form of a cross, or where the custom is to dip, dips him three times, saying at the same time these words: "N. I baptize thee in the name of the Father, and of the Son, and of the Holy Ghost." Which words are pronounced in such manner that the three pourings of the water concur with the pronouncing of the three names of the divine Persons, for the form is to be pronounced but once. But if there be a doubt whether the person has been baptized before or not, then the priest makes use of this form: "N. If thou art not already baptized, I baptize thee in the name of the Father, and of the Son, and of the Holy Ghost."

Then the priest anoints the person baptized on the top of the head in the form of a cross with holy chrism, which is a compound of oil and balm, solemnly consecrated by the bishop. Which ceremony comes from apostolical tradition, and gives us to understand, first, that in baptism we are made partakers with Christ (whose name signifies *anointed*) and have a share in his unction and grace. Second, that we partake also in some manner in his dignity of king and priest, as all Christians are called by St. Peter a royal or kingly priesthood,[38] and therefore we are anointed in this way, as kings and priests are anointed. Third, that we are consecrated to God by baptism, and therefore are anointed with holy chrism, which the Church is accustomed to make use of in anointing all those things which she solemnly consecrates to the service of God. The prayer which the priest recites on this occasion is as follows: "May the Almighty God, the Father of our Lord Jesus Christ, who has regenerated thee of water and the Holy Ghost, and who has given thee the remission of all thy sins +, anoint thee with the chrism of salvation in the same Christ Jesus our Lord, unto life everlasting. Amen." Then the priest says, "Peace be to thee." **R:** "And with thy spirit."

After which the priest puts upon the head of the person that has been baptized, a white linen cloth, commonly called the chrism, in place of the white garment with which the new Christians used formerly to be clothed in baptism, to signify the purity and innocence which we receive in baptism and which we must take care to preserve until death. In putting on this white linen, the priest says: "Receive this white garment, which thou mayest carry unstained before the judgment seat of our Lord Jesus Christ, that thou mayest have eternal life, Amen."

[38] Cf. 1 Pt 2:9

Then he puts a lighted candle into the hand of the person baptized, or of the godfather, saying: "Receive this burning light, and keep thy baptism without reproof; observe the commandments of God, that when our Lord shall come to his nuptials, thou mayest meet him together with all the saints in the heavenly court, and mayest have life eternal and mayest live forever and ever, Amen." Which ceremony alludes to the parable of the ten virgins who took their lamps and went forth to meet the bridegroom,[39] and admonishes us to keep the light of faith ever burning by the oil of good works, that whensoever our Lord shall come, we may be found with our lamps burning, and may go in with him into the eternal life of his heavenly kingdom.

Lastly, the priest, addressing himself to the person baptized, says: "N. Go in peace, and the Lord be with thee, Amen." Then he admonishes as well the parents as the godfather and godmother of their respective duty with regard to the education and instruction of their child, and of the care which the Church requires of the parents, not to let the child lie in the same bed with them or with the nurse, for fear of its being overlaid. And lastly, the priest informs them of the spiritual kindred which is contracted between the godparents and the child, as also between the godparents and the parents of the child, which makes it unlawful for them afterwards to marry those to whom they are thus spiritually allied.

[39] Cf. Mt 25

Chapter 4

Of the Sacrament of Confirmation

38. What do you mean by confirmation?
A sacrament by which the faithful after baptism receive the
Holy Ghost, by the imposition of the hands of the bishop and
prayer, accompanied with the unction or anointing of their
foreheads with holy chrism.

39. Why do you call it confirmation?
From its effect, which is to confirm or strengthen those that receive it in the profession of the true faith, to make them soldiers
of Christ and perfect Christians, and to arm them against their
spiritual enemies.

**40. How do you prove from scripture, that the apostles practiced
confirmation?**
I prove it from where we read of St. Peter and St. John confirm-
ing the Samaritans. "They prayed for them that they might
receive the Holy Ghost . . . then laid they their hands on them,
and they received the Holy Ghost."[40] "They were baptized in
the name of the Lord Jesus. And when Paul had laid his hands
upon them, the Holy Ghost came on them."[41] It is of confirmation also that St. Paul speaks, "Not laying again the foundation
. . . of the doctrine of baptism, and of laying on of hands."[42]
And "Now he which confirmeth us with you in Christ, and

[40] Acts 8:15, 17
[41] Acts 19:5-6
[42] Heb 6:1-2

hath anointed us, is God: who hath also sealed us, and given the earnest of the Spirit in our hearts."[43]

41. How do you prove that confirmation is a sacrament?

First, because it is plain from Acts 8 that the visible sign of the imposition of hands has annexed to it an invisible grace, viz. the imparting of the Holy Ghost. Consequently, confirmation is a visible sign of invisible grace, and therefore is a sacrament. Second, because the Church of God from the apostles' days has always believed it to be a sacrament, and administered it as such.[44]

42. Who is the minister of this sacrament?

The ordinary minister of this sacrament is a bishop only.

43. Can this sacrament be received any more than once?

No, because, like baptism, it imprints a character or spiritual mark in the soul, which always remains. Hence, those that are to be confirmed are obliged to be so much the more careful to come to this sacrament worthily, because it can be received but once, and if they then receive it unworthily, they have no share in the grace which is thereby communicated to the soul; instead of which, they incur the guilt of a grievous sacrilege.

---

[43] 2 Cor 1:21-22

[44] Cf. Dionysius, *On the Ecclesiastical Hierarchy*, Ch. 4; Tertullian, *On Baptism*, Ch. 7, *On the Resurrection of the Flesh*, Ch. 8, *Prescription against Heretics*, Ch. 4; Cornelius, *Epistola ad Fabium Antiochensem Episcopum, apud Eusebium*, Bk. 6, Ch. 43; Cyprian, *Epistle 69, Epistle 73, Epistle 74*; Synod of Elvira, Can. 38; Synod of Laodicea, Can. 48; Cyril of Jerusalem, *Catechetical Lecture 21*; Pacian, *Epistle 1, 3 ad Sympronianum, Sermone de Baptismo*; Ambrose, *On the Mysteries*, Ch. 6-7, *Treatise on the sacrament* (attributed to Ambrose) Bk. 3, Ch. 2; Optatus of Milevis, *Against the Donatists*; Jerome, *Dialogue Against the Luciferians*; Innocent I, *Epistle 9 ad Decentium*; Augustine, *Tractate 6 on John, Contra Literas Peliliani*, Ch. 24; Cyril of Alexandria, *ad Joelis 2. v. 24*; Leo the Great, *Sermon 24*; Theodoret, *Commentary on the Song of Songs 1 v. 3*; Gregory the Great, *Homily 17 on the gospels*.

44. In what disposition is a person to be, in order to approach worthily to the sacrament of confirmation?
He must be free from mortal sin and in the state of grace, for the Holy Ghost will never come into a soul which Satan possesses by mortal sin.

45. In what manner then must a person prepare himself for the sacrament of confirmation?
First, he must examine his conscience, and if he finds it charged with willful sin, he must take care to purge it by a good confession. Second, he must frequently and fervently call upon God, to dispose his soul for receiving the Holy Ghost.

46. What kind of grace does this sacrament communicate to the soul?
It communicates to the soul the fountain of all grace, the Holy Ghost, with all his gifts; but more in particular, a fortifying grace to strengthen the soul against all visible and invisible enemies of the faith.

47. Is then this sacrament absolutely necessary to salvation?
It is not so necessary, but that a person may be saved without it. Yet it would be a sin to neglect it when a person might conveniently have it, and a crime to contemn or despise it.

48. What kind of persons stand most in need of the grace of this sacrament?
Those that are the most exposed to persecutions upon account of their religion, or to temptations against faith.

49. At what age may a person be confirmed?
Ordinarily speaking, the Church does not give confirmation until a person is come to the use of reason, though sometimes she confirms infants; in which case great care must be taken

that they be put in mind, when they come to the use of reason, that they have received this sacrament.

50. What is the obligation that a Christian takes upon him in confirmation?

He lists himself there for a soldier of Christ, and consequently is obliged, after having received this sacrament, to fight manfully the battles of his Lord.

51. May a person have a godfather or godmother in confirmation?

He may, by way of an instructor and an encourager in the spiritual warfare; and this godfather or godmother contracts the like obligations as in the sacrament of baptism, and the same spiritual kindred.

52. May a person that is confirmed take a new name?

It is usual so to do, not by way of changing one's name of baptism, but by way of adding to it another name of some saint, to whom one has a particular devotion, and by whose prayers he hopes to acquit himself more faithfully of the obligations of a soldier of Christ.

53. Is a person obliged to receive this sacrament fasting?

No, he is not, though it is advisable so to receive it.

54. In what manner is the sacrament of confirmation administered?

First, the bishop turning towards those that are to be confirmed, with his hands joined before his breast, says: "May the Holy Ghost come down upon you, and the power of the Most High keep you from all sins." R: "Amen." Then signing himself with the sign of the cross, he says, "Our help is in the name of the Lord." R: "Who made heaven and earth." Then, extending his hands towards those that are to be confirmed (which is what the ancients call the imposition of hands), he prays that they may receive the Holy Ghost:

Let us pray. O Almighty, everlasting God, who hast vouchsafed to regenerate these thy servants by water and the Holy Ghost; and who hast given them the remission of all their sins; send forth upon them thy sevenfold Holy Spirit, the Comforter from heaven.

R: Amen.

The Spirit of wisdom and of understanding.

R: Amen.

The Spirit of counsel and of fortitude.

R: Amen.

The Spirit of knowledge and of piety.

R: Amen.

Replenish them with the Spirit of thy fear, and sign them with the sign of the cross + of Christ, in thy mercy, unto life everlasting. Through the same Jesus Christ thy Son our Lord, who liveth and reigneth with thee in the unity of the same Holy Spirit, one God, forever and ever. Amen.

Then the bishop makes the sign of the cross with holy chrism upon the forehead of each one of those that are to be confirmed, saying, "N. I sign thee with the sign of the cross, I confirm thee with the chrism of salvation, in the name of the Father, and of the Son, and of the Holy Ghost, Amen." After which he gives the person confirmed a little blow on the cheek, saying, *Pax tecum*, that is, "peace be with thee."

Then the bishop, standing with his face towards the altar, prays for those that have been confirmed, that the Holy Ghost may ever dwell in their hearts and make them the temple of his glory. And then dismisses them with this blessing: "Behold thus shall every man be blessed, who feareth the Lord. May the Lord bless you from Sion, that you may see the good things of

Jerusalem all the days of your life; and may have life everlasting. Amen."

**55. I would willingly be instructed in the meaning of these cere-
monies; therefore pray tell me first why the Church makes use
of chrism in confirmation, and what this chrism is?**

Chrism is a compound of oil of olives and balm of Gilead, solemnly consecrated by the bishop on Maundy-Thursday; and the unction, or outward anointing of the forehead with chrism, is to represent the inward anointing of the soul in this sacrament with the Holy Ghost. The oil, whose proper-ties are to fortify the limbs and to give a certain vigor to the body, to assuage our pains, etc., represent the like spiritual effects of the grace of this sacrament in the soul. And the balm, which is of a sweet smell, represents the good odor or sweet savor of Christian virtues and an innocent life, with which we are to edify our neighbors after having received this sacrament.

**56. Why is this unction made on the forehead, and in form of the
cross?**

To give us to understand that the effect of this sacrament is to arm us against worldly fear and shame: and therefore we receive the standard of the cross of Christ upon our foreheads, to teach us to make an open profession of his doctrine and maxims; and not to flinch from this profession, for fear of anything that the world can either say or do.

**57. What is the meaning of the bishop's giving a little blow on the
cheek to the person that is confirmed?**

It is to imprint in his mind that from this time forward he is to be ready, like a true soldier of Jesus Christ, to suffer patiently all kinds of affronts and injuries for his faith.

58. And why does the bishop, at the same time as he gives the blow, say, "peace be with thee"?
To signify that the true peace of God, which, as St. Paul says, exceeds all understanding,[45] is chiefly to be found in patient suffering for God and his truths.

Chapter 5

Of the Sacrament of the Eucharist

59. What you mean by the sacrament of the Eucharist?
The sacrament which our Lord Jesus Christ instituted at his last supper, in which he gives us his body and blood under the forms or appearance of bread and wine.

60. Why do you call this sacrament the Eucharist?
Because the primitive Church and the holy fathers have usually called it so:[46] for the word *eucharist* in the Greek signifies *thanksgiving*, and is applied to this sacrament because of the thanksgiving which our Lord offered in the first institution of it.[47] And because of the thanksgiving with which we are obliged to offer and receive this great sacrament and sacrifice, which contains the abridgment of all God's wonders, the fountain of all grace, the standing memorial of our redemption, and the pledge of a happy eternity. This Blessed Sacrament is also called the Holy Communion, because it unites the faithful with one

[45] Cf. Phil 4:7
[46] Cf. Justin Martyr, *First Apology*, Ch. 66; Irenaeus, *Against Heresies*, Bk. 4, Ch. 34; Tertullian, *Liber de Corona Militis*, Ch. 3; Cyprian, *Epistle 53*; First Council of Nicea, Can. 18
[47] Cf. Mt 26:27; Mk 14:23; Lk 22:19; 1 Cor 11:24

another, and with their head Christ Jesus.[48] And it is called the supper of our Lord, because it was first instituted by Christ at his last supper.

61. What is the faith of the Catholic Church concerning this sacrament?

That the bread and wine are changed by the consecration into the real body and blood of Christ.

62. Is it then the belief of the Church that Jesus Christ himself, true God and man, is truly, really, and substantially present in the Blessed Sacrament?

It is. For where the body and blood of Christ are, there his soul also, and his divinity must needs be; and consequently, there must be the whole Christ, God and man. There is no taking him in pieces.

63. Is that which we receive in this sacrament the same body as that which was born of the Blessed Virgin, and which suffered for us upon the cross?

It is the same body, for Christ never had but one body. The only difference is that then, his body was mortal and passible; it is now immortal and impassible.

64. Then the body of Christ in the sacrament cannot be hurt or divided, neither is it capable of being digested or corrupted?

No, certainly: for though the sacramental species, or the outward forms of bread and wine, are liable to these changes, the body of Christ is not.

65. Is it then a spiritual body?

It may be called a spiritual body in the same sense as St. Paul,

---

[48] Cf. 1 Cor 10:16-17

speaking of the resurrection of the body, says, "It is sown a natural body, it is raised a spiritual body."[49] Not, but that it still remains a true body, as to all that is essential to a body, but that it partakes in some measure of the qualities and properties of a spirit.

First Proof of the Real Presence

66. How do you prove the real presence of the body and blood of Christ in this sacrament?

I prove it first from the express and plain words of Christ himself, the eternal truth, delivered at the time of the first institution of this Blessed Sacrament, and recorded in no less than four different places in the new testament. In all these places, Christ himself assures us that what he gives us in the Blessed Sacrament is his own body and blood: "Take, eat; this is my body. . . . This is my blood of the new testament, which is shed for many for the remission of sins."[50] "Take, eat; this is my body. . . . This is my blood of the new testament, which is shed for many."[51] "This is my body which is given for you. . . . This cup is the new testament in my blood which is shed for you."[52] "This is my body which is broken (*sacrificed*) for you. . . . This cup is the new testament in my blood."[53] Now the body which was given and sacrificed for us, the blood of the new testament which was shed for us, is without all doubt the real body and blood of Christ. Therefore, what Christ gives us in this Blessed Sacrament is his real body and blood: nothing can be more plain.

[49] 1 Cor 15:44
[50] Mt 26:26, 28
[51] Mk 14:22, 24
[52] Lk 22:19-20
[53] 1 Cor 11:24-25

67. Why do you take these words of Christ at his last supper according to the letter, rather than in the figurative sense?

You might as well ask a traveler why he chooses the highway, rather than to go by bypaths with evident danger of losing his way. We take the words of Christ according to their plain, obvious, and natural meaning, agreeable to that general rule acknowledged by our adversaries[54] that in interpreting scripture, the literal sense of the words is not to be forsaken, and a figurative one followed, without necessity; and that the natural and proper sense is always to be preferred, where the case will admit it. It is not therefore incumbent upon us to give a reason why we take these words of Christ according to their natural and proper sense; but it is our adversaries' business to show a necessity of taking them otherwise. The words themselves plainly speak for us, for Christ did not say, "this is a figure of my body, and this is a figure of my blood"; but he said, "this is my body, and this is my blood." It is their duty, as they tender the salvation of their souls, to beware of offering violence to texts so plain, and of wresting them from their evident meaning.

However, we have many reasons to offer, why we take the words of Christ (which he spoke at his last supper in the institution of the Blessed Sacrament) in their most plain, natural, and obvious meaning. First, because he was then all alone with his twelve apostles, his bosom friends and confidants, to whom he was always accustomed to explain in clear terms whatever was obscure in his parables or other discourses to the people. "To you," says he to his disciples, "it is given to know the mystery [the secrets] of the kingdom of God, but unto them that are without, all things are done in parables."[55] And "Without a parable spoke he not unto them [the people], but when they were alone, he expounded all things to his disciples."[56] "Hence-

---

[54] Cf. Dr. Harris' *Sermon on Transubstantiation*, p. 7, 8
[55] Mk 4:11
[56] Mk 4:34

forth I call you not servants; for the servant knoweth not what
his lord doth: but I have called you friends, for all things that
I have heard of my Father, I have made known unto you."[57]
How then is it likely that in this most important occasion of
all, when, the very night before his death, he was taking his last
leave and farewell of these his dear friends, he should deliver
himself to them in terms which, if they are not to be taken according to the letter, are obscure beyond all example, and not
anywhere to be paralleled?

Secondly, he was at that time making a covenant which
was to last as long as time itself should last. He was enacting a
law, which was to be forever observed in his Church. He was
instituting a sacrament, which was to be frequented by all the
faithful until he should come. He was, in fine, making his last
will and testament, and therein bequeathing to his disciples and
to us all, an admirable legacy and pledge of his love. Now such
is the nature of all these things, viz. of a covenant, of a law, of
a sacrament, of a last will and testament, that as he that makes
a covenant, a law, etc., always designs that what he covenants,
appoints, or ordains should be rightly observed and fulfilled.
So, of consequence, he always designs that it should be rightly
understood; and therefore always expresses himself in plain
and clear terms in his covenants, laws, etc. This is what all
wise men ever observe in their covenants, laws, and last wills:
industriously avoiding all obscure expressions, which may give
occasion to their being misunderstood, or to contentions and
lawsuits about their meaning. This is what God himself observed in the old covenant, in all the ceremonial and moral
precepts of the law, in all the commandments, in the institution
of all the legal sacraments, etc. All are expressed in most clear
and plain terms. It can then be nothing less than impeaching
the wisdom of the Son of God, to imagine that he should make

[57] Jn 15:15

his new law and everlasting covenant in figurative and obscure terms, which he knew would be misunderstood by the greatest part of Christendom; or to suppose that he should institute the chief of all his sacrament under such a form of words, which in their plain, natural, and obvious meaning, imply a thing so widely different from what he gives us therein, as his own body is from a bit of bread; or, in fine, to believe that he would make his last will and testament in words affectedly ambiguous and obscure; which, if taken according to that sense which they seem evidently to express, must lead his children into a pernicious error concerning the legacy that he bequeaths them.

In effect, our Lord certainly foresaw that his words would be taken according to the letter by the bulk of all Christendom, that innumerable of the most learned and most holy would understand them so, and that the Church even in her general councils would interpret his words in this sense. It must be then contrary to all probability that he who foresaw all this would affect to express himself in this manner, in his last will and testament, had he not meant what he said; or that he should not have somewhere explained himself in a more clear way, to prevent the dreadful consequence of his whole Church's authorizing an error in a matter of so great importance.

68. **Have you any other reason to offer for taking the words of the institution according to the letter, rather than in a figurative sense?**

Yes, we have for so doing, as I have just now hinted, the authority of the best and most authentic interpreter of God's word, viz. his holy Church; which has always understood these words of Christ in their plain literal sense, and condemned all those that have presumed to wrest them to a figure. Witness the many synods held against Berengarius, and the decrees of the general councils of Lateran, Constance, and Trent. Now against this authority, hell's gates shall never prevail,[58] and with this inter-preter Christ has promised that both he himself and the Holy Ghost, the Spirit of truth, should abide forever.[59]

69. But are not many of Christ's sayings to be understood figura-tively, as when he says that he is a door, a vine, etc.? And why then may not also the words of the institution of the Blessed Sacrament be understood figuratively?

It is a very bad argument to pretend to infer that because some of Christ's words are to be taken figuratively, therefore all are to be taken so; that because in his parables or similitudes his words are not to be taken according to the letter, therefore we are to wrest to a figurative sense the words of the institution of his solemn covenant, law, sacrament, and testament at his last supper; that because he has called himself a door or a vine in circumstances in which he neither was, nor ever could be misunderstood by anyone (he having taken so much care in the same places to explain his own meaning), therefore he would call bread and wine his body and blood, in circumstances in which it was natural to understand his words according to the letter, as he foresaw all Christendom would understand them, and yet has taken no care to prevent this interpretation of them.

There is therefore a manifold disparity between the case of the expressions you mention (viz. "I am the door," "the vine," etc.), and the words of the last supper, "This is my body, this is my blood." First, because the former are delivered as parables and similitudes, and consequently as figures; the latter are the words of a covenant, sacrament, and testament, and therefore are to be understood according to their most plain and obvious meaning. Second, because the former are explained by Christ himself in the same places in a figurative sense; the latter are

[58] Cf. Mt 16:18
[59] Cf. Mt 28:20; Jn 14:16-17

not. Third, because the former are worded in such a manner as to carry with them the evidence of a figure, so that no man alive can possibly misunderstand them or take them in any other than a figurative meaning; the latter are so expressed, and so evidently imply the literal sense, that they that have been the most desirous to find a figure in them have been puzzled to do it,[60] and all Christendom has for many ages judged without the least scruple that they ought to be taken according to the letter. Fourth, because the Church of God has authorized the literal interpretation of the words of the institution of the Blessed Sacrament; not so of those other expressions.

In fine, because according to the common laws and customs of speech a thing may indeed, by an elegant figure, be called by the name of that thing of which it has the qualities or properties. And thus Christ, by having in himself the property of a door, inasmuch as it is by him that we must enter into his sheepfold,[61] and the property of the vine, in giving life and fruit to its branches,[62] might according to the usual laws of speech, elegantly call himself a door and a vine. But it would be no elegant metaphor to call bread and wine, without making any change in them, his body and blood; because bread and wine have in themselves neither any similitude, nor quality, nor property of Christ's body and blood; as it would be absurd, for the same reason, to point at any particular door or vine, and say, "this is Jesus Christ."

---

[60] It was the case of Luther himself, as we learn from his epistle to his friends at Strasburg (see Tom. 5. fol. 502); and of Zwingli, and as we learn from his epistle to Pomeranus (see fol. 256).

[61] Cf. Jn 10:9

[62] Cf. Jn 15:1

70. But may not the sign or figure, according to the common laws of speech, be called by the name of the thing signified? And have we not instances of this nature in scripture; as when Joseph interpreting the dream of Pharaoh, says, "the seven good cows are seven years";[63] and our Lord interpreting the parable of the sower, says, "the seed is the word of God";[64] and St. Paul says, "the rock was Christ"?[65]

In certain cases, when a thing is already known to be a sign or figure of something else, which it signifies or represents, it may indeed, according to the common laws of speech and the use of the scripture, be said to be such or such a thing, as in the interpretation of dreams, parables, ancient figures, and upon such like occasions; where, when a thing is said to be this or that, the meaning is evident; viz. that it signifies or represents this or that. But it is not the same in the first institution of a sign or figure; because, when a thing is not known beforehand to be a sign or representation of some other thing, to call it abruptly by a foreign name would be contrary to all laws of speech, and both absurd and unintelligible. As for instance, if a person by an art of memory had appointed within himself that an oak tree should be a sign or memorandum of Alexander the Great, and pointing to the tree, should gravely tell his friends (who were not acquainted with his design), "this is that hero that overcame Darius." Such a proposition as this would justly be censured as nonsensical and unworthy of a wise man; because such a figure of speech would be contrary to all laws of speech, and unintelligible.

Just so would it have been, if our Savior at his last supper, without giving his disciples any warning beforehand of his meaning to speak figuratively, and without their considering beforehand the bread and wine as signs and representations

[63] Gn 41:26
[64] Lk 8:11
[65] 1 Cor 10:4

of anything else, should have abruptly told them, "This is my body, this is my blood," had he not meant that they were so indeed. For abstracting from the change which Christ was pleased to make in the elements by his almighty word, a bit of bread has no more similitude to the body of Christ than an oak tree has to Alexander the Great. So that nothing but the real presence of Christ's body and blood could verify his words at his last supper, or vindicate them from being highly absurd and unworthy the Son of God.

71. But do not those words which our Lord spoke, "This do in remembrance of me,"[66] sufficiently clear up the difficulty and determine his other words to a figurative sense?

These words, "Do this in remembrance of me," inform us indeed of the end for which we are to offer up and to receive the body and blood of Christ, viz. for a perpetual commemoration of his death,[67] but they no way interfere with those other words, "this is my body, and this is my blood," so as to explain away the real presence of Christ's body and blood. For why should Christ's body and blood be less present in the sacrament, because we are commanded in the receiving of them to remember his death? Certainly St. Matthew and St. Mark, who in their gospels have quite omitted those words, "Do this in remembrance of me," never looked upon them as a necessary explication of the words of the institution, or as any ways altering or qualifying the natural and obvious meaning of these words, "this is my body, this is my blood."

72. But does not the remembrance of a thing suppose it to be absent; for otherwise, why should we be commanded to remember it?

Whatsoever things we may be liable to forget, whether really

---

[66] Lk 22:19
[67] Cf. 1 Cor 11:26

present or really absent, may be the object of our remembrance; and thus we are commanded in scripture to remember God,[68] though "in him we live, move and have our being."[69] So that this command of remembering Christ is no ways opposite to his real presence. The most that can be inferred from it is that he is not visibly present, which is very true; and therefore, lest we should forget him, this remembrance is enjoined. Besides, if we hearken to the apostle,[70] he will inform us that what we are commanded to remember is the death of Christ; now the death of Christ is not a thing really present, but really past, and therefore a most proper subject for our remembrance.

Second Proof of the Real Presence

73. What other proof have you for the real presence of Christ's body and blood in the sacrament of the Eucharist, besides the words of the institution, "this is my body, and this is my blood"?
We have a very strong proof in the words of Christ, spoken to the Jews in John 6. Where, upon occasion of the miracle of feeding the multitude with five loaves, having spoken of the necessity of believing in him who is the living bread that came down from heaven, he passes from this discourse concerning faith, to speak of this sacrament:

> "I am the living bread that came down from heaven: if any man eat of this bread, he shall live forever, and the bread that I will give is my flesh, which I will give for the life of the world." The Jews therefore strove amongst themselves, saying: "How can this man give us his flesh to eat?" Then Jesus said unto them, "Verily, verily I say unto you, except ye eat the flesh of

---

[68] Cf. Dt 8:18; Eccles 12:1
[69] Acts 17:28
[70] Cf. 1 Cor 11:26

the Son of man, and drink his blood, you have no life in you. Whoso eateth my flesh and drinketh my blood, hath eternal life, and I will raise him up at the last day: for my flesh is meat indeed, and my blood is drink indeed. He that eateth my flesh and drinketh my blood, dwelleth in me, and I in him. As the living Father hath sent me, and I live by the Father: so he that eateth me, even he shall live by me. This is that bread which came down from heaven, not as your fathers did eat manna, and are dead, he that eateth of this bread shall live forever."[71]

In which words the eating of Christ's flesh and the drinking his blood is so strongly, so clearly, and so frequently inculcated, and we are so plainly told that the bread which Christ was to give is that very flesh which he gave for the life of the world, that one must be resolved to keep one's eyes shut against the light, if one will not see so plain a truth.

74. How do you prove that Christ in this place is speaking of the Blessed Sacrament?

By comparing the words which he spoke upon this occasion with those which he delivered at his last supper in the institution of the Blessed Sacrament. In the one place he says, "the bread that I will give is my flesh, which I will give for the life of the world," in the other, taking bread and distributing it, he says, "this is my body which is given for you." Where it is visible that the one is a promise which the other fulfils, and consequently that both the one and the other have relation to the same sacrament. Hence we find that the consensus of the holy fathers has always explained these verses of John 6 as spoken of the sacrament.[72]

[71] Jn 6:51-59
[72] Cf. Irenaeus, *Against Heresies* Bk. 5, Ch. 2; Origen, *Homily 16 on Numbers*; Cyprian, *Treatise 4*; Hilary, *On the Trinity*, Bk. 8; Basil, *The Morals*, reg. 1, c. 1; Cyril of Jerusalem, *Catechetical Lecture 22*; Ambrose, *On the Mysteries*, Ch. 8.; Epiphanius, *Haeresi 55*;

75. But does not Christ promise eternal life to everyone that eateth of that bread of which he is there speaking[73] which promise cannot be understood with relation to the sacrament, which many receive to their own damnation?[74]

He promises eternal life to everyone that eateth of that bread; but this is to be understood, provided that he eat it worthily and that he persevere in the grace which he thereby receives. And in this sense it is certain that this sacrament gives eternal life; whereas the manna of old had no such power.[75] In like manner our Lord promises that "everyone that asketh shall receive,"[76] and yet many ask and receive not, because they ask not as they ought.[77] Thus St. Paul tells us that "whosoever shall call upon the name of the Lord shall be saved,"[78] which also certainly must be understood, provided they do it worthily and perseveringly; lest this text contradict that other: "Not everyone that saith to me Lord, Lord, shall enter into the kingdom of heaven: but he that doeth the will of my Father which is in heaven."[79] Thus, in fine, Christ tells us "He that believeth and is baptized shall be saved,"[80] and yet many believe and are baptized, like Simon Magus, who for want of a true change of heart or of perseverance in good, are never saved.[81]

Theodoret, *Ecclesiastical History*, Bk. 4, Ch. 10. See also John Chrysostom, Augustine, and Cyril of Alexandria writing upon the sixth chapter of St. John.

[73] Cf. Jn 6:52, 55, 59
[74] Cf. 1 Cor 11:29
[75] Cf. Jn 6:59
[76] Mt 7:8
[77] Cf. Jas 4:3
[78] Rom 10:13
[79] Mt 7:21
[80] Mk 16:16
[81] Cf. Acts 8:13

76. **But if those words of Christ be understood of the sacrament, will it not follow that no one can be saved without receiving this sacrament, and that also in both kinds, contrary to the belief and practice of the Catholic Church; since our Lord tells us, "Verily, verily, I say unto you, except you eat of the flesh of the Son of man, and drink his blood, you have [or you shall have] no life in you"?**[82]

It follows from those words that there is a divine precept for the receiving this Blessed Sacrament, which if persons willfully neglect, they cannot be saved. So that the receiving this sacrament either actually, or in desire, is necessary for all those that are come to the years of discretion (not for infants, who are not capable of discerning the body of the Lord[83]). But that this sacrament should be received by all in both kinds is not a divine precept, nor ever was understood to be such by the Church of God, which always believed that under either kind Christ is received whole and entire, and consequently that under either kind we sufficiently comply with the precept of receiving his flesh and blood.

77. **Why may not those words of Christ be taken figuratively, so as to mean no more than the believing in his incarnation and death?**

Because it would be too harsh a figure of speech, and unbecoming the wisdom of the Son of God, to express the believing in him by such strange metaphors as eating his flesh and drinking his blood, such as no man ever used before or since. And to repeat and inculcate these expressions, so often to the great offence both of the Jews and even of his own disciples, who upon this account went back and walked no more with him,[84] when he might so easily have satisfied both the one and the other by

---

[82] Jn 6:54
[83] Cf. 1 Cor 11:29
[84] Cf. Jn 6:61, 67

telling them that he meant no more by all that discourse than that they should believe in him.

78. **Did then the Jews and those disciples who cried out, "This is a hard saying, and who can hear it?"[85] understand our Savior right, or did they mistake his meaning?**
They understood him right, so far as relates to the real receiving his flesh and blood. But as to the manner of receiving, they understood him not; since they had no thoughts of his giving himself whole and entire, veiled in a sacrament, but apprehended the eating of his flesh, cut off from his bones, and drinking of his blood, according to the vulgar manner of other meat and drink, which we digest and consume. However, their not understanding him seems not to have been so faulty as their refusing to believe him: hence our Lord reprehends not their want of understanding, but their not believing.[86] And Peter, in the name of the apostles, in opposition to those disciples that had fallen off, says, "Lord, to whom shall we go? thou hast the words of eternal life. And we believe and are sure that thou art Christ the Son of the living God."[87] So that these people ought, like the apostles, to have submitted themselves to believe what as yet they understood not; and not to have run away from him, who by his evident miracles proved himself to be the Son of God, and consequently incapable of an untruth. By which example, we may see how much more wisely Catholics act (who in this mystery, like the apostles, submit themselves to believe what they cannot comprehend, because they know that Christ has the words of eternal life) than those who like the apostate disciples cry out: "This is a hard saying, and who can hear it?"[88] and thereupon will walk no more with Christ and his Church.

[85] Jn 6:61
[86] Cf. Jn 6:65
[87] Cf. Jn 6:69-70
[88] Jn 6:61

79. What did our Lord say to his disciples, who were offended with his discourse concerning the eating of his flesh?
He said unto them, "Doth this offend you? what, and if ye shall see the Son of man ascend up where he was before?"[89] Which words are variously interpreted, and may either be understood to signify that they who made a difficulty of believing that he could give them his flesh to eat then whilst he was visible amongst them, would have much more difficulty of believing it after he was gone from them by his ascension; or else Christ, by mentioning his ascension, would correct their mistaken notion of his giving them his flesh and blood in that gross manner which they apprehended; or, in fine, he mentioned his ascension into heaven to convince their incredulity by the evidence of so great a miracle, which at once was to demonstrate both his almighty power and the truth of his words.

80. What is the meaning of the following words: "It is the spirit that quickeneth, the flesh profiteth nothing; the words that I speak unto you, they are spirit and they are life"?[90]
The meaning is that the flesh separated from the spirit, in the manner which the Jews and incredulous disciples apprehended, would profit nothing: for what would it avail us to feed upon dead flesh, separated from the soul and divinity, and consequently from the life-giving spirit? But then it would be blasphemy to say that the flesh of Christ, united to his spirit (in that manner in which the Catholic Church believes his flesh to be in the Blessed Sacrament accompanied with his soul and divinity), profits nothing: for if the flesh of Christ were of no profit, he would never have taken flesh for us, and his incarnation and death would be unprofitable to us. Which is the height of blasphemy to affirm.

[89] Jn 6:62-63
[90] Jn 6:64

"What means, 'the flesh profits nothing'?" says St. Augustine, writing upon this text in *Tractate 27*:

> It profits nothing, as they understood it; for they understood flesh as it is torn in pieces in a dead body, or sold in the shambles; and not as it is animated by the spirit. Wherefore it is said, 'the flesh profits nothing,' in the same manner as it is said, 'knowledge puffeth up.' Must we then fly from knowledge? God forbid: what then means 'knowledge puffeth up'? That is, if it be alone without charity; therefore the apostle added, 'but charity edifieth.' Join therefore charity to knowledge, and knowledge will be profitable, not by itself, but through charity: So here also the flesh profiteth nothing, viz. the flesh alone: let the spirit be joined with the flesh, as charity is to be joined with knowledge, and then it profits much. For if the flesh profiteth nothing, the Word would not have been made flesh, that he might dwell in us.[91]

So far St. Augustine.

Besides, according to the usual phrase of scripture, flesh and blood are often taken for the corruption of our nature, as for man's natural sense and apprehension, etc.; as when it is said that "flesh and blood cannot inherit the kingdom of God,"[92] and "flesh and blood hath not revealed it unto thee,"[93] etc. And in this sense the flesh profiteth nothing, but it is the Spirit and grace of God that quickeneth and giveth life to our souls. And as the words which our Lord had spoken to them tended to insinuate to them so great a sacrament, in which they should receive this Spirit, grace, and life in its very fountain, therefore he tells them, "the words that I speak unto you, they are spirit, and they are life."

---

[91] Augustine, *Tractate 27*, n. 5
[92] 1 Cor 15:50
[93] Mt 16:17

Other Proofs of the Real Presence

81. **Have you any other proofs from scripture of the real presence of the body and blood of Christ in the Blessed Sacrament?**
   Yes. 1 Corinthians 10, where the apostle, to discourage Christians from having anything to do with the sacrifices offered to idols, tells them that the cup of blessing which we bless is "the communion of the blood of Christ," and the bread which we break is "the communion of the body of Christ."[94] Secondly, "Wherefore whosoever shall eat this bread, or drink this cup of the Lord unworthily, shall be guilty of the body and blood of the Lord."[95] How so, if what the unworthy receiver takes be no more than bread and wine? Thirdly, "He that eateth and drinketh unworthily, eateth and drinketh damnation to himself, not discerning the body of our Lord."[96] How shall he discern it, if it be not there really present?

82. **Have you anything more to add by way of proof out of scripture?**
   Yes, from the ancient figures of the Eucharist, which demonstrate that there is something more noble in it than bread and wine taken only in remembrance of Christ.

83. **What are those ancient figures?**
   There are many, but I shall take notice chiefly of three, viz. the paschal lamb, the blood of the testament, and the manna from heaven.

84. **How do you prove that these three were figures of the Eucharist?**
   I prove it with regard to the paschal lamb (which is acknowledged at all hands to have been a type of Christ) because it is visible, that the rites and ceremonies of it prescribed had chiefly

[94] 1 Cor 10:16
[95] 1 Cor 11:27
[96] 1 Cor 11:29

relation to the eating of it;[97] and consequently to this typical lamb in the old testament corresponds in the new testament the Lamb of God, as eaten by his people in this sacrament: which for this reason was instituted immediately after our Lord had eaten the Passover with his disciples, that the figure might be both explained and accomplished, and might make way for the truth.[98]

Secondly, that the blood of the testament with which Moses sprinkled the people, saying, "This is the blood of the testament which God hath enjoined to you,"[99] was a figure of the blood of Christ in this sacrament, as our Lord himself sufficiently declared by evidently alluding to this figure when he gave the cup to his disciples, saying, "This is my blood of the new testament,"[100] or, "This cup is the new testament in my blood."[101]

Thirdly, that the manna was a figure of this sacrament, appears from John 6, "Your fathers did eat manna and are dead, he that eateth of this bread shall live forever";[102] and from 1 Corinthians 10, where the apostle, speaking of the figures of our sacrament in the old law, and taking notice of the cloud and the passage of the Red Sea as figures of baptism,[103] in the third and fourth verses, gives the manna and the water from the rock as figures of the Eucharist.[104] The same is the continuous doctrine of the holy fathers, and is sufficiently demonstrated

---

[97] Cf. Ex 12

[98] Concerning this figure, see the continuous sense of the fathers in Tertullian, *Against Marcion*, Bk. 4; Cyprian, *Treatise I*; Jerome, *Commentary on Matthew*; Chrysostom, *Homily on the Betrayal of Judas*; Augustine, *Contra Literas Petiliani*, Bk. 2, Ch. 37; Gaudentius, *Tractate 2 on Exodus*; Cyril of Alexandria, *Contra Nestorium*; Theodoret, *Commentary on 1 Corinthians*, Ch. 10; Leo the Great, *Sermon 58*; Hesychius, *Commentary on Leviticus*, Ch. 23; Gregory the Great, *Homily 22 on the gospels*.

[99] Ex 24:8; Heb 9:20

[100] Mt 26:28; Mk 14:24

[101] Lk 22:20; 1 Cor 11:25

[102] Jn 6:59

[103] Cf. 1 Cor 10:1-2

[104] Cf. 1 Cor 10:3-4

from the analogy which is found between the manna and this Blessed Sacrament.[105]

85. How do you prove from these ancient figures the real presence of Christ's body and blood in this sacrament?

Because if in this sacrament there were nothing more than bread and wine taken in remembrance of Christ, and as types and figures of his body and blood, then the figures of the old law would equal the sacrament of the new law, yea, far excel them. For who does not see that the paschal lamb was a more noble type, and far better representing Christ than bread and wine? Who does not perceive that the blood of victims solemnly sacrificed to God was a better figure of Christ's blood than the juice of the grape? Who can question but the heavenly manna, which is called the bread of angels, and was so many ways miraculous, was far beyond the bread of men? Who will not acknowledge that it is something more excellent and divine to foretell things to come, than only to commemorate things past? It must therefore be visible to every Christian that if the paschal lamb, the blood of the testament, and the manna were types of Christ, given to us in this sacrament, then this sacrament itself must be something more than a type, figure or remembrance of Christ; and consequently must contain and exhibit him really to us.

86. But why may not a person suppose that the figures of the old testament might equal or excel the sacrament of the new?

No one that pretends to the name of Christian can suppose this, since the apostle assures us that the old law had nothing but "a shadow of the good things to come,"[106] that all its sacrifices and sacraments were but weak and beggarly elements,[107] and that it was annulled by reason of the weakness and the

---

[105] For which see the annotations in the *Doway Bible* upon Exodus 16.
[106] Heb 10:1
[107] Cf. Gal 4:9

unprofitableness thereof.[108] And does not the very nature of the thing assure us that the figure must be inferior to the thing prefigured?

87. Have you any other argument from scripture in favor of the real presence of our Lord's body in the Blessed Sacrament?
Yes: Those innumerable texts of scripture, which prove the unerring authority of the Church of Christ and the indispensable obligation of the faithful to follow the judgment of the Church and to rest in her decisions, plainly demonstrate that to be truth which the Church has so long ago declared with relation to this controversy, and that all Christians are obliged to yield to this decision.

88. When did the Church decide this matter?
As soon as ever it was called in question, that is, about seven hundred years ago, in the days of Berengarius, who was the first that openly attacked the doctrine of the real presence, and was thereupon condemned by the whole Church in no less than fourteen councils held during his lifetime in divers parts of Christendom; and the determination of these councils was afterwards confirmed by the general councils of Lateran, Constance, and Trent.

89. What scripture do you bring to show that all Christians are obliged to submit to these decisions of the councils and pastors of the Church?
"If he neglect to hear the church, let him be to thee as a heathen and a publican."[109] "He that heareth you heareth me, and he that despiseth you, despiseth me, and he that despiseth me, despiseth him that sent me."[110] "As my Father hath sent me,

[108] Cf. Heb 7:18
[109] Mt 18:17
[110] Lk 10:16

even so I send you."[111] "Remember them which have the rule over you, who have spoken unto you the word of God, whose faith follow. . . . Obey them that have the rule over you and submit yourselves."[112] "He that knoweth God heareth us [the pastors of the Church], he that is not of God heareth not us: by this we know the spirit of truth and the spirit of error."[113] And what wonder that Christ should require this submission to his Church and her pastors and teachers, whom he has given for the perfecting of the saints, "that we henceforth be no more children tossed to and fro, and carried about with every wind of doctrine";[114] since even in the old law he required, under pain of death, a submission to the synagogue and her ministers in their decisions relating to the controversies of the law.[115]

90. What scripture do you bring to show that the Church is not liable to be mistaken in these decisions?

This is evidently proved from a great many texts both of the old and new testaments, in which we are assured, first, that the Church is the pillar and ground of the truth,[116] and consequently not liable to error. Second, that Christ has built his Church upon a rock, and that the gates of hell [the powers of darkness and error] shall not prevail against her.[117] Third, that Christ, who is "the way, the truth, and the life,"[118] will always be with the teachers of his Church, "even to the end of the world."[119] Fourth, that the Holy Ghost, the Spirit of truth, shall abide forever with these same teachers of the Church,[120] and "guide them into all

[111] Jn 20:21
[112] Heb 13:7, 17
[113] 1 Jn 4:6
[114] Eph 4:14
[115] Cf. Dt 17:8ff
[116] Cf. 1 Tm 3:15
[117] Cf. Mt 16:18
[118] Jn 14:6
[119] Mt 28:20
[120] Cf. Jn 14:16

truth."[121] Fifth, that God has made a covenant with the Church; that his Spirit, and his words, which he has put in her mouth at the time when our Redeemer came, should not depart out of her mouth, nor out of the mouth of her seed, nor out of the mouth of her seed's seed, from henceforth and forever.[122] Sixthly, that God has made a solemn oath to his Church, like that which he made to Noah, that he would not be wrathful with her, nor rebuke her;[123] that he has promised to be her "everlasting light,"[124] and to set his sanctuary in the midst of her forevermore;[125] all which is inconsistent with her being led astray by damnable errors. And thus the scripture, by plainly giving testimony to the Church and Church authority, plainly also gives testimony to the truth of Christ's real presence in the Eucharist, which has been so often declared by that authority.

91. Besides these arguments from scripture and Church authority, have you anything else to allege in proof of the real presence?
Yes. First, the authority of all the ancient fathers, whose plain testimonies may be seen in an appendix to a book entitled *A Specimen of the Spirit of the Dissenting Teachers.*[126]

Secondly, the perpetual consent of the Greeks and all the oriental Christians, demonstrated by Monsieur Arnauld and the Abbe Renaudot,[127] confirmed by the authentic testimonies[128] of their patriarchs, archbishops, bishops, abbots, etc.,

---

[121] Jn 16:13

[122] Cf. Isa 59:20-21

[123] Cf. Isa 54:9-10

[124] Isa 60:19

[125] Cf. Ez 37:26

[126] The author here references his own pseudonymous work: Philalethes, *A Specimen of the Spirit of the Dissenting Teachers* (London: Meighan, 1736).

[127] See their books bearing the title *La Perpétuité de la Foy*, etc.

[128] See the testimony of seven archbishops of the Greek Church in Antoine Arnauld, *La Perpétuité de la Foy*, vol. 3 (Paris: Savreux, 1674), 569; as also the testimonies of the archbishops and clergy of the isles of the archipelago (Ibid., 572ff), of diverse abbots and religious (Ibid., Ch. 4, 5), of four patriarchs of Constantinople, of the patriarch of

by the decrees of their synods against Cyril Lucar,[129] by the writings of their ancient and modern divines,[130] and by all their liturgies; and acknowledged by many protestant witnesses.[131]

Alexandria, and of thirty-five metropolitans or archbishops in AD 1672 (Ibid., Ch. 6), of the Churches of Georgia and Mingrelia (Ibid., Ch. 7), of the patriarch of Jerusalem and of several other archbishops, abbots, etc. (Ibid., 703), of Macarius and Neophytus, patriarchs of Antioch (Ibid., 723), of Methodius, patriarch of Constantinople (see Antoine Arnold, *Reponse Generale* [Paris: Savreux, 1671], 151). See also the orthodox confession of the oriental Church, signed by the four patriarchs and many other bishops (Ibid., 138). That the same is the faith of the Armenians, is proved by the testimonies of Haviadour, an Armenian prelate of Uscanus, bishop of St. Sergius; also of David the patriarch, and other bishops and priests of the Armenians given at Aleppo in AD 1668 (see Antoine Arnold, *La Perpétuité de la Foy*, vol. 1 [Paris: Savreux, 1669], Appendix, 73, 81-82), of James, patriarch of the greater Armenia, and many other bishops and priests (*Reponse Generale*, 283ff), of the archbishops of the Armenians in Constantinople, Adrianople, and Amasæa (Ibid.), of Cruciadorus, patriarch of the lesser Armenia, with other bishops and priests in AD 1672 (*La Perpétuité*, vol. 3, 774), of the Armenians of Grand Cairo, AD 1671, and of several bishops at Ispahan in the same year (Ibid., 775-778). See also in the first and third volume of Arnold's *La Perpétuité*, and in the *Reponse Generale*, many other attestations of the belief of the Muscovites, Jacobites or Surians, Cophts, Maronites and Nestorians, touching the real presence and transubstantiation.

[129] See the *Acts* of the Synod of Constantinople under the patriarch Cyril of Beraea (1639), the synod under the patriarch Parthenius (1642), and the Synod of Cyprus (1668).

[130] See (besides the testimonies of the Greek fathers of the first six centuries) Anastasius of Sina, in his *Odegos*; Germanus patriarch of Constantinople, in his *Theoria*; St. John Damascene, *Orat. 3 de Imaginibus, Lib. 2. Paralel. c. 5.; L. 4. Fidei Orthodoxæ*, c. 13; the second Council of Nicea of 350 bishops Act. 6.; *Elias Cret. Comment in Orat. 1.; St. Greg. Naz.*; Nicephorus, Patriarch of Constantinople, *Antirhetico 2.*; Theodorus Studites, *Antirhetico 1. Num. 10. Theophylactus ad Cap. 26. St. Matthaei. Euthymius*, in *Matt. 26.*; Samonas, bishop of Gaza, in *Discept. contra Achmed Saracenum*; Nicholas of Methone, *de Corp. et Sang. Christi.*; Nicholas Cabasilas.; Mark of Ephesus and *Bessarion*; *qui omnes in suis opusculis*, says Bishop Forbes *de Euch. L.I. c3., apertissime transubstantiationem confitentur.* Jeremias Patriarcha, in *Resp. 1* and *2 ad Lutheranos*. Gabriel Philadelph. *de Sacrament*. The Greeks of Venice, in *Resp. ad Cardinal. Guis. Agapius*, etc. See also in the two additional volumes of Renaudot to the *Perpétuité de la Foy*, etc. the concurrent testimonies of the divines of the other *oriental sects*, and of all their liturgies.

[131] Sir Edwin Sandy's *Relation of the Religions of the West*, p. 233. Dr. Potter's *Answer to Charity Mistaken*, p. 225. Bishop Forbes *de Euch.* Bk. 1. Ch. 3. p. 412. Crusius in *Germano-græcia*. Bk. 5. p. 226. Danawerus, *L. de Eccles. Græc.-hodierna*, p. 46, etc. Hence Dr. Philip Nicholai a protestant, in his first book of the *Kingdom of Christ*, p. 22, writeth thus: "Let my Christian readers be assured, that not only the Churches of the Greeks, but also the Russians, and the Georgians, and the Armenians, and the Indians, and the Ethiopians, as many of them as believe in Christ, hold the true and real presence of the body and blood of the Lord," etc.

Now what can be a more convincing evidence of this doctrine's having been handed down by tradition from the apostles, than to see all sorts of Christians, which have any pretensions to antiquity, all agreeing in it?

Thirdly, both ancient and modern Church history furnish us with many instances of miracles the best attested, which from time to time have been wrought in testimony of this same truth; of which in diverse parts of Christendom there are standing monuments to this day. It would be too tedious to descend to particulars, and so much the less necessary, because all the miracles of Jesus Christ himself, as they prove that he could not be a liar, so they demonstrate that what he gives us in this sacrament is verily and indeed his body and blood, as he has so clearly told us.

Transubstantiation Proved, Objections Answered

92. What do you understand by transubstantiation?
That the bread and wine in the Blessed Sacrament are truly, really, and substantially changed by consecration into the body and blood of Christ.

93. In what then does the Catholic doctrine of transubstantiation differ from the consubstantiation maintained by the Lutherans?
It differs in this, that Luther and his followers maintain the real presence of the body and blood of Christ in the bread and wine, or with the bread and wine: whereas the Catholic Church believes that the bread and wine are converted into the body and blood of Christ, so that there remains nothing of the inward substance of the bread and wine after consecration, but only the outward appearances or accidents.

THE CATHOLICK CHRISTIAN INSTRUCTED

94. How do you prove this transubstantiation?

First, from the texts of scripture above quoted, especially from the words of the institution[132] and from the words of Christ.[133] For our Lord, when he first gave the Blessed Sacrament, did not say, "in this, or with this, is my body and blood"; but he said, "this is my body, and, this is my blood." Neither did he say, "in the bread that I will give, will I give you my flesh," but he said, "the bread that I will give is my flesh, which I will give for the life of the world." Secondly, from the tradition of the ancient fathers, whose doctrine may be seen in the books above quoted. Thirdly, from the authority and decision of the Church of God in her general councils of Lateran, Constance, and Trent. And indeed, supposing that the words of Christ in the institution of the Blessed Sacrament are to be taken according to the letter (as both Catholics and Lutherans agree), the most learned protestants have often urged against Luther and his followers that the Catholic transubstantiation is more agreeable to the letter of Christ's words than the Lutheran consubstantiation.[134]

95. But does not St. Paul, speaking of the sacrament after consecration, call it bread?[135]

He does, and so do we. First, because it is the bread of life, the food and nourishment of the soul. Second, because it still retains the qualities and accidents of bread, and has the whole outward appearance of bread; and therefore, according to the scripture phrase is called bread, as angels appearing in the shape of men are oftentimes in scripture called men.[136] Third, because it was consecrated from bread, and therefore, according to the method of speaking usual in scripture, is called bread because

---

[132] Cf. Mt 26:26ff
[133] Cf. Jn 6:52ff
[134] Cf. Bossuet, *Histoire des Variations des Églises Protestantes*, Bk. 2, n. 31-33
[135] Cf. 1 Cor 10:16
[136] Cf. Lk 24:4; Acts 1:10

it was made from bread; as man is called dust because made out of dust,[137] and the serpent is called a rod because made from a rod,[138] etc. Besides, we have two very good interpreters that inform us what this bread is, of which St. Paul is there speaking, viz. the same apostle, when he tells us that the bread which we break is "the communion of the body of Christ,"[139] and our Savior himself, when he tells us, "the bread that I will give is my flesh, which I will give for the life of the world."[140]

96. But what will you say to our Savior's calling the sacrament the "fruit of the vine"?[141]

If it were certain our Savior had so called the consecrated wine of the Blessed Sacrament, it would prove no more than St. Paul's calling the other kind bread. That is, it would only show that the name of wine, or the fruit of the vine, might be given to it, from having the accidents and appearance of wine, and having been consecrated from wine. But there is all the reason in the world to think that this appellation of the fruit of the vine was given by our Savior, not to the consecrated cup or chalice, but to the wine of the paschal supper, which they drank before the institution of the sacrament. This appears evident from St. Luke, who thus relates the whole manner:

> When the hour was come, he sat down, and the twelve apostles with him. And he said to them: With desire I have desired to eat this pasch with you, before I suffer. For I say to you, that from this time I will not eat it, till it be fulfilled in the kingdom of God. And having taken the chalice, he gave thanks, and said: Take, and divide it among you: For I say to you, that I

[137] Cf. Gn 3:19
[138] Cf. Ex 7:12
[139] 1 Cor 10:16
[140] Jn 6:52
[141] Mt 26:29

will not drink of the fruit of the vine, till the kingdom of God come. And taking bread, he gave thanks, and brake; and gave to them, saying: This is my body, which is given for you. Do this for a commemoration of me. In like manner the chalice also, after he had supped, saying: This is the chalice, the new testament in my blood, which shall be shed for you. But yet behold, the hand of him that betrayeth me is with me on the table.[142]

Where it is visible, that it was not the sacramental cup, but that which was drunk with the Passover, to which our Savior gives the name of the fruit of the vine.

97. But if the bread and wine do not remain after consecration, what then becomes of them?

They are changed by the consecration into the body and blood of Christ.

98. How can bread and wine be changed into the body and blood of Christ?

By the almighty power of God, to whom nothing is hard or impossible, who formerly changed water into blood and a rod into a serpent,[143] and water into wine,[144] and who daily changes bread and wine by digestion into our body and blood.

99. But do not all our senses bear testimony that the bread and wine still remain?

No, they only bear testimony that there remains the color and taste of bread and wine, as indeed there does; but as to the inward substance, this is not the object of any of the senses, nor can be perceived by any of them.

[142] Lk 22:14-21
[143] Cf. Ex 7:9-10, 17-21
[144] Cf. Jn 2:6-10

100. Are not our senses then deceived in this case?

Properly speaking they are not, because they truly represent what is truly there, viz. the color, shape, taste, etc. of bread and wine. But it is the judgment that is deceived when upon account of this color, shape, taste, etc., it too hastily pronounces that this is bread and wine.

101. But are we not sufficiently authorized, by the testimony of the senses, to make a judgment of a thing's being in effect, that which it has all the appearances of?

Regularly speaking we are, when neither reason nor divine authority interposes itself to oblige us to make another judgment. And thus, the miracles and resurrection of Christ were demonstrated to the apostles by the testimony of their senses. But the case would have been altered if God himself assured them that what appeared to be flesh and bones was indeed another thing: for in such a case they ought certainly to have believed the testimony of God, rather than their own senses.

102. Can you give me any instances in which the testimony of man's senses has represented one thing, and the divine authority of God's word has assured us that it was not indeed what it appeared to be, but quite another thing?

Yes, we have many such instances in scripture; as when angels have appeared in the shape of men,[145] and the Holy Ghost, in the shape of a dove.[146]

103. Is there not then any of our senses that we may trust to, in relation to the judgment that we are to make concerning the inward part of the sacrament of the Eucharist?

Yes, we may safely trust to the sense of hearing; which informs

---

[145] Cf. Gn 19; Mt 28; Mk 16
[146] Cf. Lk 3:22

us by the word of God, and the authority of the Church of God, that what appears to be bread and wine in this sacrament, is indeed the body and blood of Christ. Now "faith comes by hearing," saith St. Paul, "and hearing by the word of God."[147]

104. But if the substance of the bread and wine be not there, what is it then that gives nourishment to our bodies, when we receive this sacrament?

This sacrament was not ordained for the nourishment of the body, but of the soul: though I do not deny but the body also is nourished when we receive the Blessed Eucharist, not by the substance of bread and wine, which is not there, nor by the body and blood of Christ, which is incorruptible and therefore cannot be digested for our corporal nourishment; but by the quantity and other accidents of the bread and wine (if with the Aristotelian philosophers you suppose them really distinguished from matter and substance), or by another substance which the Almighty substitutes, when by the ordinary course of digestion the sacramental species are changed, and the body and blood of Christ cease to be there.

105. But how can the accidents of bread and wine remain without the substance?

By the almighty power of God: which answer if it satisfy you not, I remit you to the Cartesian philosophers, who will tell you that as the body and blood of Christ in the sacrament are contained precisely in the same circumscription and dimensions as the bread and wine were before the consecration, it follows of course that they must affect our senses in the same manner. Now color, taste, etc. according to modern philosophy are nothing but the affections of our senses.[148]

---

[147] Rom 10:17
[148] Cf. Purchot, *Part* 1. *Phys.* Sect. 5. Cap. 1

106. How can the whole body and blood of Christ be contained in so small a space as that of the host; nay, even in the smallest sensible particle of it?

By the same almighty power by which a camel can pass through the eye of a needle: "with men this is impossible," says our Savior, but not with God; for "with God all things are possible."[149]

107. How can the body of Christ be both in heaven, and at the same time in so many places upon earth?

By the same almighty power of God which we profess in the very first article of our Creed, when we say, "I believe in God the Father Almighty." So that it is a question better becoming an infidel than a Christian to ask, "how this can be?" when we are speaking of a God to whom nothing is impossible; and who would not be God indeed, if he could not do infinitely more than we can conceive. It is like the Jewish question, "How can this man give us his flesh to eat?"[150] As if the power of God were not as incomprehensible as himself; and as if it were not worse than madness for weak mortals to pretend to fathom this immense depth of the power of the Almighty, by the short line and plummet of human reason.

108. But is it not an evident contradiction for the same body to be at once in two places?

Not at all; no more than for one God to subsist in three distinct Persons; or one Person in two natures; or one soul to be at once both in the head and in the heart; or two bodies to be at once in the selfsame place, as when Christ's body came in to the disciples, the doors being shut;[151] or the same body, after having returned to dust, to be many ages after restored at the resurrection.

[149] Mt 19:26; Mk 10:27
[150] Jn 6:52
[151] Cf. Jn 20:26

109. How do you prove there is no evident contradiction in any of all these things?

Because thousands of as good philosophers and divines as any are, cannot see any such contradiction: which is a plain demonstration there is no evidence in the case; and consequently, it would be the highest rashness to deny the possibility of these things to the power of the Almighty.

110. But what need was there that Christ should leave us his real body and blood in this sacrament, since without this real presence, he might have bequeathed the selfsame graces to our souls?

He might indeed, if so he had pleased; as he might also have brought about the salvation of mankind, if he had so pleased, without becoming man himself and dying upon a cross for us. But he chose these wondrous ways as most suitable to his love, and most proper to excite us to love him. And who shall presume to call him to an account why he has condescended so far?

111. But are not the body and blood of Christ liable to be hurt and abused in the sacrament?

The body and blood of Christ is now immortal, impassible, and incorruptible, and consequently not liable to be hurt, nor divided, nor corrupted; though it may be said indeed to be abused by the unworthy communicant, and upon that account St. Paul says that such a one is "guilty of the body and blood of Christ."[152] But this abuse no more hurts the immortal body of Christ, than this or any other crime can hurt or violate his divinity.

---

[152] 1 Cor 11:27

Of the Bread and Wine

112. What kind of bread does the Church make use of for the sacrament of the Eucharist?

The Church of Rome makes use of wafers of unleavened bread; that is, of bread made of fine wheaten flour with no other mixture but pure water.

113. Why does not the Church make use of common bread for this sacrament?

Because she follows the example of Christ, who at his last supper, when he first instituted and gave the Blessed Sacrament to his disciples, made use of unleavened bread.

114. How do you prove that?

I prove it, because the day in which Christ first gave the Blessed Sacrament was, according to St. Matthew, St. Mark, and St. Luke, the first day of unleavened bread.[153] Now upon that day, and for the whole following week, there was no other bread to be found in Israel; and it was even death to use any other but unleavened bread, as we learn from Exodus 12: "Seven days shall ye eat unleavened bread, even the first day ye shall put away leaven out of your houses: for whosoever eateth leavened bread from the first day until the seventh day, that soul shall be cut off from Israel. . . . Seven days shall there be no leaven found in your houses,"[154] etc. So that it is plain that our Savior made use of unleavened bread at his last supper, and that there was no other bread used at that time.

---

[153] Cf. Mt 26:17; Mk 14:12; Lk 22:7
[154] Ex 12:15, 19

115. Is there any other reason why we should prefer unleavened bread?

Yes, unleavened bread is an emblem or symbol of sincerity and truth. Hence St. Paul admonishes us to "purge out the old leaven" of malice and wickedness, and to feast with "the unleavened bread of sincerity and truth."[155]

116. What kind of wine do you make use of for this sacrament?

Wine of the grape, with which by apostolical tradition we mingle a little water.

117. Has the practice of mingling water with wine been always observed from the apostles' days?

It certainly has, and that throughout the whole Church.[156]

118. Did Christ, when he gave the cup to his disciples, mingle water with the wine?

It is probable he did, though the scripture neither mentions the water nor the wine, but only speaks of his giving them the cup. However, the ancient and universal practice of the Church in all probability comes originally from the example of Christ.

119. Is there not some mystery or secret meaning in the mingling of the water with the wine in the chalice?

Yes. It represents to us, first the union of the human and divine nature in the Person of the Son of God; Second, the union of the faithful with Christ their head; Third, the water and blood that flowed from the side of Christ.

[155] 1 Cor 5:7-8
[156] Cf. Justin Martyr, *Second Apology*; Irenaeus, *Against Heresies*, Bk. 5, Ch. 2; Cyprian, *Epistle 62*

120. Why did our Lord appoint bread and wine for the matter of this sacrament?

First, because bread and wine being most nourishing to the body, were the most proper to represent the grace of this sacrament, which is the food and nourishment of the soul. Second, because bread and wine are both composed of many individuals (viz. grains or grapes), made one by a perfect union of them all; and therefore, as the holy fathers take notice, are a most proper type or symbol of Christ's mystical body the Church, and of that unity which our Lord would recommend to the faithful by this sacrament, according to that of St. Paul: "We being many are one bread, and one body, for we are all partakers of that one bread."[157]

121. What other things are signified or represented by the outward forms of bread and wine in this sacrament?

They are chiefly designed to signify or represent to us three things: the one now past, viz. the passion of Christ, of which they are the remembrance; another really present, viz. the body and blood of Christ, of which they are the veil; a third to come, viz. everlasting life, of which they are the pledge.

Of Communion in One Kind

122. Why don't the faithful in the Catholic Church receive under the form of wine, as well as under the form of bread?

The Catholic Church has always looked upon it to be a thing indifferent, whether the faithful receive in one kind or in both; because she has always believed that they receive Jesus Christ himself, the fountain of all grace, as much in one kind as in both. But her custom and discipline for many ages has been

---

[157] 1 Cor 10:17

to administer this sacrament to the laity only in one kind, viz. under the form of bread, by reason of the danger of spilling the blood of Christ, if all were to receive the cup; which discipline was confirmed by the general Council of Constance in opposition to the Hussites, who had the rashness to condemn in this point, the practice of the universal Church.

123. Did the Catholic Church never allow of the Communion in both kinds?
She did, and may again, if she pleases; for this is a matter of discipline, which the Church may regulate or alter, as she shall see most expedient for the good of her children.

124. What do you mean when you say, "this is a matter of discipline"; I thought Communion in one kind had been looked upon in the Catholic Church as a matter of faith?
You must distinguish in this case between that which is of faith, and that which is of discipline only. It is a matter of faith that under one kind we receive Christ whole and entire, and the true sacrament; and that there is no command of Christ for all the faithful to receive in both kinds: so far both is and ever was the faith of the Catholic Church, for her faith is unalterable. But then, whether the Blessed Sacrament should actually be administered to the laity in one kind or in both, that is to say, what is most proper or expedient for the Church to practice or ordain in this particular, considering the circumstances of time, place, etc.; this is what I call a matter of discipline, which may be different in different ages, without any alteration of the faith of the Church.

125. But did not Christ command the receiving in both kinds: "Drink ye all of it"?[158]

These words were addressed to the twelve apostles, who were all that were then present, and the precept was by them all fulfilled: "And they all drank of it."[159] Now it is certain that many things were spoken in the gospel to the apostles in quality of pastors of the Church, which were not directed to the laity; as when they were commissioned to preach and baptize,[160] and to absolve sinners;[161] and upon this very occasion to do what Christ had done, that is, to consecrate and administer this sacrament in remembrance of him.[162] And consequently, it is no argument that all are obliged to drink of the cup because Christ commanded all the apostles to drink of it, no more than that all are obliged to consecrate the sacrament because Christ commanded all the apostles to do it. For both these commands were delivered at the same time, upon the same occasion, and to the same persons.

126. But why should the apostles and their successors, the bishops and priests of the Church, be commanded to drink of the cup rather than the laity? Or why should Christ, at the first institution of the sacrament, consecrate and give it in both kinds, if all Christians were not always to receive it in both kinds?

To satisfy both these queries at once, you are to take notice that the Blessed Eucharist, according to the faith of the Catholic Church and as we shall show hereafter, is a sacrifice as well as a sacrament; and of this sacrifice, by the institution of Christ, the apostles and their successors, the bishops and priests of the Church, are the ministers whom he has commanded to

---

[158] Mt 26:27
[159] Mk 14:23
[160] Cf. Mt 28:19-20
[161] Cf. Jn 20:23
[162] Cf. Lk 22:19

offer it in remembrance of his death.[163] Now this sacrifice in remembrance of Christ's death, for the more lively representing the separation of Christ's blood from his body, requires the separate consecration of both kinds, and therefore the priests that are the ministers of this sacrifice receive at that time in both kinds; and Christ, in the first institution of this sacrifice, consecrated and gave both kinds, designing without doubt that it should be so received, at least by the ministers.

127. But why should not the nature of the sacrament as much require both kinds to be received by all, as the nature of the sacrifice requires both kinds to be consecrated?

Because the nature of the sacrament consists in being the sign and cause of grace, now under either kind there is both a sufficient sign of grace, viz. of the nourishment of the soul, and at the same time the fountain and cause of all grace, by the real presence of Christ, in whom are locked up all the treasures of grace: so that the nature of the sacrament sufficiently subsists in either kind. But the nature of the sacrifice particularly requires exhibiting to God the body and blood of his Son, under the veils that represent the shedding of his blood, and his death. Therefore, the nature of the sacrifice requires the separate consecration of both kinds, which being consecrated, must be received by someone, and by no one more properly than by the minister.

128. Does not Christ say, "Except ye eat of the flesh of the Son of man, and drink his blood, ye have no life in you"?[164]

He does, and in the same chapter he tells us, "He that eateth me, even he shall live by me"; and, "he that eateth of this bread, shall live forever."[165] Which texts are easily reconciled if we

---

[163] Ibid.
[164] Jn 6:54
[165] Jn 6:58, 59

consider that, according to the Catholic doctrine and according
to the truth, whosoever receives the body of Christ most certainly receives his blood at the same time; since the body which
he receives is a living body (for Christ can die no more[166]),
which cannot be without the blood. There is no taking Christ
by pieces; whoever receives him, receives him whole.

**129. But are not the faithful deprived of a great part of the grace of
this sacrament, by receiving only in one kind?**
No. Because the grace of this sacrament being annexed to the
real presence of Christ, who is the fountain of all grace, and
Christ being as truly and really present in one kind as in both,
consequently he brings with him the same grace to the soul
when received in one kind, as he does when received in both.

**130. Is it not then a privilege, granted to the priests above the laity,
to receive in both kinds?**
No. Their receiving in both kinds, as often as they say Mass,
is no privilege, but the consequence of the sacrifice which they
have been offering, as you may gather from what I have told
you already. For, as for other times, when they are not saying
Mass, no priest, bishop, or pope, even upon his deathbed, ever
receives otherwise than in one kind.

**131. Have you anything more to add in favor of Communion in one
kind?**
Yes. First, that the scripture in many places, speaking of the
Holy Communion, makes no mention of the cup.[167] Second,
that the scripture promises life eternal to them that receive in
one kind.[168] Third, that the ancient Church most certainly allowed of Communion in one kind, and practiced it on many

---

[166] Cf. Rom 6:9
[167] Cf. Lk 24:30-31; Acts 2:42, 46, 20:7; 1 Cor 10:17
[168] Cf. Jn 6:52-59

occasions.[169] Fourth, that many learned protestants have acknowledged that there is no command in scripture for all to receive in both kinds.[170]

132. But what would you say further to a scrupulous soul, which, through the prejudice of a protestant education, could not be perfectly easy upon this article?

I should remit such a person to the Church and her authority, and to all those divine promises recorded in scripture, by which we are assured, that in hearing the Church and her pastors, we are secure; that Christ and his Holy Spirit shall be always with them, to guide them into all truth; and that the gates of hell shall never prevail against this authority. So that a Christian soul has nothing to fear in conforming herself to the authority and practice of the Church of God, but very much in pretending to be wiser than the Church, or making a scruple to hear and obey her spiritual guides.

Of the Manner of Administering

133. In what manner is the Blessed Eucharist administered to the people?

After the Communion of the priest in the Mass, such of the people as are to communicate go up to the rail before the altar, and there kneel down; and taking the towel, hold it before their breasts, in such manner that if in communicating, it should happen that any particle should fall, it may not fall to

---

[169] Cf. Tertullian, *Ad Uxorem*, Bk. 2, Ch. 5; Denys of Alexandria, *Epistola ad Fabium Antiochensem Episcopum, apud Eusebium*, Bk. 6, Ch. 43; Cyprian, *Treatise 3*; Basil, *Letter 93*; Ambrose, *de Satyro Fratre*; Paulinus, *Vita Ambrosii*.

[170] Cf. Luther in his epistle to the Bohemians, *Spalatensis de Rep. Eccles.* L. 5, c. 6; Bishop Forbes, *L. 2 de Eucharist*, c. 1, 2; White, bishop of Ely, *Treatise on the Sabbath*, p. 97; Bishop Montagu, *Orig.* p. 97.

the ground, but be received upon the towel. Then the clerk, in the name of all communicants, says the confiteor, or the general form of confession by which they accuse themselves of all their sins to God, to the whole court of heaven, and to God's minister; and crave mercy of God, and the prayers and intercession of both the triumphant and militant Church. After which the priest, turning towards the communicants, says: "May the Almighty God have mercy on you, and forgive you your sins, and bring you to everlasting life. Amen. May the almighty and merciful Lord grant you pardon, absolution, and remission of all your sins. Amen."

Then the priest, taking the particles of the Blessed Sacrament which are designed for the communicants, and holding one of them, which he elevates a little over the pyx or paten, pronounces the following words: *Ecce Agnus Dei*, etc., that is, "Behold the Lamb of God; behold he who taketh away the sins of the world." Then he repeats three times, *Domine non sum dignus*, etc., that is, "Lord, I am not worthy that thou shouldst enter under my roof: speak but only the word, and my soul shall be healed." After which he distributes the Holy Communion, making the sign of the cross with the consecrated particle upon each one, and saying to each one, "The body of our Lord Jesus Christ preserve thy soul unto life everlasting. Amen."

134. In what manner is the Blessed Sacrament administered to the sick?

The Catholic Church has always practiced the reserving some consecrated particles of the Blessed Eucharist for communicating the sick; and where she enjoys free exercise of religion, takes care that this Blessed Sacrament be carried to them with a religious solemnity, attended with lights, etc. When the priest comes into the chamber where the sick person lies, he says, "Peace be to this house." R: "And to all that dwell therein." Then setting down the pyx with the Blessed Sacrament upon the table, which must be covered with a clean linen cloth, he takes holy water and sprinkles the sick person and the chamber, saying, *Asperges*, etc., "Thou shalt sprinkle me, O Lord, with hyssop, and I shall be cleansed: thou shalt wash me, and I shall be made whiter than snow." Then Psalm 1: "Have mercy on me, O God, according to thy great mercy. Glory be to the Father," etc. Then he again repeats the anthem, "Thou shalt sprinkle me," etc., after which he adds:

V: Our help is in the name of the Lord.
R: Who made heaven and earth.
V: O Lord hear my prayer.
R: And let my cry come to thee.
V: The Lord be with you.
R: And with thy spirit.

Let us pray. O Holy Lord, Almighty Father, everlasting God, graciously hear us; and vouchsafe to send thy holy angel from heaven, to guard, cherish, protect, visit, and defend all that dwell in this habitation, through Christ our Lord. Amen.

Then the priest coming to the sick person, endeavors to dispose him and to prepare him for receiving the Blessed Sacrament; and, if he has any sin upon his conscience, hears his confession and absolves him. After which the sick person, or some other in his name, says the confiteor, and the priest says, "May the Almighty God have mercy on thee," etc. as above. "Behold the Lamb of God," etc. "Lord I am not worthy," etc. And in giving the Blessed Sacrament, if it be by way of viaticum, or preparation for death, he says, "Receive, brother (or sister), the viaticum of the body of our Lord Jesus Christ, who may guard thee from the wicked enemy, and bring thee to everlasting life, Amen." But if the sick person be not in danger of death, the priest, in giving the Blessed Sacrament, pronounces the usual form: "May the body of our Lord Jesus Christ preserve thy soul to life everlasting. Amen." After which the priest says the following prayer:

O holy Lord, Almighty Father, eternal God, we beseech thee with faith, that the sacred body of our Lord Jesus Christ thy Son may be available to this our brother (or sister) that has received it as a medicine to eternity, both for body and soul; through the same Lord Jesus Christ thy Son, who liveth and reigneth with thee in the unity of the Holy Ghost, forever and ever. Amen.

Then, if there remain in the pyx any other particles of the Blessed Sacrament, the priest gives the benediction therewith to the sick person. Otherwise, he pronounces the usual blessing, making the sign of the cross, and saying, "May the blessing of the Almighty God, Father, Son, and Holy Ghost descend upon thee, and remain always with thee. Amen."

135. **In what disposition of soul is a person obliged to be, in order to receive worthily the Blessed Sacrament?**
He is obliged to be in the state of grace, and free at least from the guilt of mortal sin; that is to say, from the guilt of any willful transgression in any matter of weight, of the commandments of God or his Church. The reason of this is because a soul that is under the guilt of mortal sin is an enemy to God, and a slave of the devil; and therefore it would be a grievous crime for a soul in that state to presume to receive the body and blood of Christ, which, according to the doctrine of St. Paul, would be receiving damnation to herself.[171]

---

[171] Cf. 1 Cor 11:29

136. What then is a person to do in order to prevent so great an evil?
Saint Paul tells you, that he is to "try himself";[172] that is, to search and examine diligently his own conscience before he ventures to approach to this Blessed Sacrament.

137. And what if, upon examination, he finds his conscience charged with any weighty matter?
He must take care to discharge it in the manner that Christ has appointed, viz. by a hearty repentance and sincere confession; laying open the state of his soul to those sacred judges to whom Christ said, "Whose sins you shall forgive, they are forgiven; and whose sins you shall retain, they are retained."[173]

138. What else is required of a person that is to receive the Blessed Sacrament?
He must be fasting, at least from midnight; for so the Church commands, agreeably to a most ancient and apostolical tradition. So that if through inadvertence a person has taken anything, though it were no more than one drop or crumb, after twelve o'clock at night, he must by no means receive that day; it would be a crime to attempt it.

139. Is there no exception from this rule?
Yes, the case of danger of approaching death is excepted; for then persons are permitted to receive the Blessed Sacrament by way of viaticum, though they are not fasting.

140. What kind of devotion do you recommend to a Christian that is preparing himself for the Holy Communion?
Besides the clearing his conscience from sin by a good confession, I recommend to him, first, to think well on the great work

[172] 1 Cor 11:28
[173] Jn 20:23

he has in hand, to consider attentively who he is, and who it is that he is preparing to receive, and earnestly to beg of God to make him worthy. Second, to propose to himself a pure intention, viz. the honor of God, and the health of his own soul; and in particular, that by worthily receiving Christ he may come to a happy union with him, according to that of St. John: "He that eateth my flesh, and drinketh my blood, dwelleth in me, and I in him."[174] Third, to meditate on the sufferings and death of his Redeemer, in compliance with that command of our Lord, "Do this in remembrance of me."[175] Fourth, to prepare himself by acts of virtue, more especially of faith, love, and humility; that so he may approach to his Lord with a firm belief of his real presence in this sacrament, and of his death and passion; with an ardent affection of love to him who has so much loved us, and with a great sentiment of his own unworthiness and sins, joined with a firm confidence in the mercies of his Redeemer.

141. What ought to be a Christian's behavior at the time of receiving this Blessed Sacrament?

As to the interior, he ought to have his soul at that time full of the sentiments we have just now mentioned of faith, love, and humility. And as to the exterior, he ought to have his head erect, his eyes modestly cast down, his mouth moderately open, and his tongue a little advanced on his lower lip, that so the priest may conveniently put the sacred host on his tongue which he must gently convey into his mouth, and after having moistened it for a moment or two on his tongue, swallow it as soon as he can. In all which he is carefully to avoid: First, putting his mouth to the towel; Second, chewing with his teeth, or raising the host to the roof of his mouth; Third, letting the sacred particle quite dissolve in his mouth; Fourth, spitting soon

[174] Jn 6:57
[175] Lk 22:19

after Communion. But if the particle should happen to stick to the roof of his mouth, let him not be disturbed, nor put his finger in his mouth to remove it; but gently remove it with his tongue as soon as he can, and so convey it down.

142. What devotion do you recommend after Communion?

First, adoration, praise, and thanksgiving, in order to welcome our dear Savior upon his coming under our roof. Here then let the soul cast herself at the feet of her Lord: let her, like Magdalen, wash them in spirit with her tears: or, if she dares presume so high, let her embrace him with the spouse in the Canticles, and say, "I have found him whom my soul loves; I will hold him, and will not let him go."[176] Let her, like the royal prophet, invite all heaven and earth to join with her in praising her Lord, and let her excite all her powers to welcome him. Second, I recommend to the devout communicant to make a present or offering to Christ, in return for his having given himself. The present that he expects is our heart and soul, which, with all its faculties, ought on this occasion to be offered and consecrated to our Lord. Third, at this time the soul ought to lay all her necessities before her Redeemer, and not neglect so favorable a conjuncture of suing for his mercy and grace, both for herself and the whole world; for those more especially whom she is in particular obliged to pray for; and above all things, let her pray that nothing in life or death may ever separate her from the love of him whom she has here received, and chosen for her Lord and spouse forever.

143. What do you think of those that spend little or no time in recollection and devotion after Communion?

I think they put an affront upon Christ, in so quickly turning their backs upon him; and that they wrong their own souls,

---

[176] Cant 3:4

which by this neglect are robbed of those graces and comforts which they would have received, if they had stayed in his company.

144. Have you anything more to recommend after Communion?
I have this to recommend with regard to the whole following day, that a person take care to be more than ordinarily recollected, and very much upon his guard against the snares of the enemy, who is never more busy than upon this occasion to fling some temptation or provocation in a Christian's way, by which he may disturb the soul and rob her of the treasure which she has received; and therefore it behooves Christians to be cautious against this wicked enemy and all his stratagems, lest by putting us into a passion, or otherwise drawing us into sin, he quickly drive Christ out of our souls. If you desire to be more perfectly instructed in what relates to this Blessed Sacrament and the devotion that is proper before and after Communion, I refer you to Fr. Lewis de Granada's *Memorial of a Christian Life, Book III*; Dr. Gobinet's second volume of the *Instruction of Youth*; or Mr. Gother's little book of *Instructions and Devotions for Confession and Communion*.

145. Are all Christians that are come to the years of discretion under an obligation of receiving this sacrament?
They certainly are. First, by a divine precept or commandment of Christ, "Except you eat the flesh of the Son of man, and drink his blood, you shall have no life in you,"[177] which precept obliges to the receiving sometime at least in our life, and at our death. Second, by a precept or commandment of the Church published in the great Council of Lateran IV, by which all the faithful are obliged to receive at least once a year, and that within the Easter-time (which begins on Palm-Sunday and

---

[177] Jn 6:54

lasts until Low-Sunday); except the person, by the advice of his pastor, should, for some just reason, be permitted to put off his Communion until another time.

146. What is the penalty imposed by this council on such as neglect their Easter Communion?
The council orders that such offenders should be excluded from the Church, and if they die in this transgression, be deprived of Christian burial.

147. Are persons then actually excommunicated that neglect their Easter Communion?
No, they are not, until superiors pronounce the sentence of excommunication against them: because the council does not actually inflict this penalty, but only orders or authorizes the inflicting of it.

148. If a person has passed by the time of Easter, or was hindered from communicating at that time, is he obliged to communicate afterwards, as soon as he can?
Yes, he is; at least if you speak of one that has been a whole year without communicating; for the Church precept obliges to the receiving at least once a year. For the same reason, a person that has not been at Communion within the year, and foresees that he shall be hindered at Easter, ought to anticipate his paschal Communion by receiving beforehand.

149. And what if a person has made a sacrilegious Communion at Easter, has such a one satisfied the precept of the Church?
No, certainly.[178] And therefore such a one remains obliged to

---

[178] See the proposition condemned by Pope Innocent XI in *Sanctissimus Dominus* (1679), n. 55.

Communion, in the same manner as if he had not communicated at all.

150. At what age are Christians obliged by the precept of the Church to communicate?

As soon as they come to the years of discretion, as it is expressed in the Council of Lateran IV: that is, when they have that perfect use of reason, and are so well instructed in their duty as to be able to discern the body of the Lord, and to receive it with due reverence and devotion. Now this happens in some earlier, in others later, but seldom earlier than about ten years of age.

151. But what if a child, that is between seven and ten years of age, should be in evident danger of death?

Many divines are of opinion, if such a one be come to the use of reason (which is commonly presumed after seven years of age), that he may or even ought to receive, because of the command of Christ.[179] So Suarez, Navarrus, etc.

152. What are the effects of this Blessed Sacrament in the worthy receivers?

It is the food, nourishment, strength, and life of the soul; by supplying it with sanctifying grace, by repairing its forces, by arming it against its passions and concupiscences, by maintaining it at present in the life of grace, and bringing it to life and glory everlasting, according to that of St. John: "The bread that I will give is my flesh, for the life of the world. . . . He that eateth of this bread, shall live forever."[180]

---

[179] Cf. Jn 6:54; thus Suarez, Navarrus, etc.
[180] Jn 6:52, 59

Of the Worship of Christ in This Sacrament

153. What kind of honor is due to this Blessed Sacrament?

Divine honor and adoration, inasmuch as it contains truly and really the divine Person of Jesus Christ, the Son of God; who, as he is truly God, ought most certainly to be adored, wheresoever he is.

154. Is there no danger of idolatry in this practice?

No, certainly; because this honor is not paid to the outward veil, or the sacramental signs, but to Jesus Christ, who lies hidden there: now Jesus Christ is no idol, but the true and living God.

155. But if the doctrine of the real presence and transubstantiation should not be true, should we not then at least be guilty of idolatry?

We are as positively certain, by divine faith, of the truth of the doctrine of the real presence and of transubstantiation, as protestants can be of the divinity of Jesus Christ. And therefore, we are as much out of the reach of the danger of idolatry in worshipping Christ in this sacrament, as they are in worshipping him in heaven. I shall add, for their further satisfaction, that some of their best divines have discharged us from all danger of idolatry in worshipping Christ in this sacrament; as they may find in Dr. Jeremy Taylor's *Liberty of Prophesying,* and Mr. Thorndike's *Just Weights and Measures.*[181] Dr. Taylor's words on this subject deserve to be remarked. He writes as follows:

> Idolatry is a forsaking the true God, and giving divine worship to a creature, or to an idol; that is, to an imaginary God. . . .

[181] Cf. Herbert Thorndike, *Just Weights and Measures,* 2nd ed. (London: Roycroft, 1680), 125ff.

Now it is evident that the object of their [the Catholics] adoration in the Blessed Sacrament, is the only true and eternal God,
hypostatically joined with his holy humanity, which humanity
they believe actually present, under the veil of the sacramental
signs. And if they thought him not present, they are so far
from worshipping the bread in this case, that themselves profess it idolatry to do so. Which is a demonstration that their
soul has nothing in it that is idolatrical . . . the will has nothing
in it but what is a great enemy to idolatry; and nothing burns
in hell but proper will.[182]

So far this learned protestant prelate.

156. Why does the Catholic Church reserve the Blessed Sacrament in her churches?

She reserves the Blessed Sacrament in tabernacles upon her
altars, partly that she may have it there to carry to the sick at all
hours, whenever they shall be in need of it; and partly for the
comfort of her children, who by this means have Jesus Christ
always amongst them, and may come when they please to visit
him. This custom of reserving the Blessed Sacrament is as ancient as Christianity, as appears from the most certain monuments of antiquity.[183] And it is upon account of the Blessed
Sacrament reserved in the tabernacle that a lamp hangs before
the altar to burn there day and night, and that we kneel as often
as we pass before the tabernacle.

157. Why is the Blessed Sacrament, upon certain days, exposed to the view of the people in a remonstrance set up upon the altar?

It is to invite the people to come there to adore Jesus Christ, and

---

[182] Jeremy Taylor, A Discourse of the Liberty of Prophesying (London: Royston, 1647), 258.

[183] Cf. Tertullian, Ad Uxorem, Bk. 2, Ch. 5; Cyprian, Treatise 3

to excite in them a greater devotion by the sight of their Lord, veiled in these sacred mysteries.

158. What is the meaning of the benediction given on certain days?
It is a devotion practiced by the Church, in order to give adoration, praise, and blessing to God for his infinite goodness and love, testified to us in the institution of this Blessed Sacrament, and to receive at the same time the benediction or blessing of our Lord here present.

159. Why is the Blessed Sacrament sometimes carried in solemn procession through the streets?
To honor our Lord there present with a kind of triumph, and thereby to make him some sort of amends for the injuries and affronts which are so frequently offered to this divine sacrament; and to obtain his blessing for all those places through which he passes.

Chapter 6

Of the Sacrifice of the Mass

160. What do you mean by the Mass?
The Mass is the liturgy of the Catholic Church, and consists in the consecration of the bread and wine into the body and blood of Christ, and the offering up of this same body and blood to God, by the ministry of the priest, for a perpetual memorial of Christ's sacrifice upon the cross, and a continuation of the same to the end of the world.

161. Why is this liturgy called the Mass?

Some think this word is derived from the Hebrew word *missach*[184] which signifies a voluntary offering; others are of opinion that it is derived from the *missa,* or *missio,* that is, from the dismissal of the catechumens and others who were not permitted anciently to be present at this sacrifice. But be this as it will, the name is of very ancient use in the Church.[185]

162. Is the Mass properly a sacrifice?

Yes, it is.

163. What do you mean by a sacrifice?

A sacrifice, properly so called, is an oblation or offering of some sensible thing made to God by a lawful minister, to acknowledge by the destruction or other change in the thing offered, the sovereign power of God and to render him the homage due to his supreme Majesty.

164. How then is the Mass a sacrifice?

Because it is an oblation of the body and blood of Jesus Christ, offered under the outward and sensible signs of bread and wine to God, by the ministry of the priests of the Church, lawfully consecrated and empowered by Christ; and this oblation is accompanied with a real change and destruction of the bread and wine, by the consecration of them into the body and blood of Christ, and a real exhibiting of Christ our victim, heretofore immolated upon the cross, and here mystically dying in the separate consecration of the two different species; and this oblation is made to God to acknowledge his sovereign power, to render him our homage, and for all the other ends for which the sacrifice is offered to His Divine Majesty.

[184] Cf. Dt 16:10
[185] As appears from Ambrose, *Letter 20*; Leo the Great, *Epist. 81 ad Dioscorum*; Gregory the Great, *Homily 6 on the gospels.*

165. What are the ends for which sacrifice of old was offered, and is still to be offered to God?
For these four ends: First, for God's own honor and glory, by acknowledging his sovereignty and paying him our homage; Second, to give God thanks for all his blessings; Third, to beg pardon for our sins; Fourth, to obtain grace and all blessings from His Divine Majesty.

166. Have the servants of God, from the beginning of the world, been always accustomed to honor him with sacrifices?
Yes they have. Witness the sacrifice of Abel,[186] the sacrifice of Noah,[187] the sacrifice of Melchisedech,[188] the sacrifices of Abraham,[189] the sacrifices of Job,[190] and the many different kinds of sacrifices prescribed in the law of Moses. Of these ancient sacrifices some were holocausts, or whole burnt offerings, in which the victim or host was wholly consumed by fire, and thereby given fully to God without reserve for the more perfect acknowledgement of his sovereignty. Others were sin offerings or sacrifices offered for sin. Others were pacific or peace offerings, and these were either offered in thanksgiving for blessings received, or for obtaining of graces and favors from the Divine Majesty. Again, some were bloody sacrifices, in which the victim was slain; others unbloody, as the sacrifice of Melchisedech which was bread and wine,[191] the sacrifices of fine flour with oil and frankincense,[192] of unleavened cakes,[193] of the scape goat,[194] etc.

[186] Cf. Gn 4:4
[187] Cf. Gn 8:20-22
[188] Cf. Gn 14:18-20
[189] Cf. Gn 15, 22
[190] Cf. Jb 1:5, 42:8-9
[191] Cf. Gn 14:18
[192] Cf. Lv 2:1
[193] Cf. Lv 2:4
[194] Cf. Lv 16

167. Were these sacrifices, of the law of nature and of the law of Moses, agreeable to the Divine Majesty?

They were, as often as they were accompanied with the inward sacrifice of the heart; not for any virtue or efficacy that they had in themselves, as being but weak and needy elements, but in view of the sacrifice of Christ, of which they all were types and figures, and in consideration of the faith of those that offered them, by which they believed in a Redeemer to come, whose blood alone was capable to reconcile them to God.

168. Why are all these sacrifices now abolished?

Because they were but figures of the sacrifice of Christ, and therefore were to give place to his sacrifice, as figures to the truth.

169. How do you prove that these ancient sacrifices had no power nor efficacy of themselves, and were to make way for another sacrifice, viz. that of Christ?

This is evident from many texts of scripture; I shall only allege one at present, viz. Psalm 39, spoken in the Person of Christ to his Father: "Sacrifice and oblation thou wouldst not; but ears thou hast perfected to me [or as St. Paul reads it, "a body thou hast prepared for me"[195]], holocaust and sin offering thou didst not require; then said I, behold I come."[196]

170. What is then the sacrifice of Christians under the new law?

We have no other sacrifice but that of Christ, which he once offered upon the cross, and daily offers by the ministry of his priests upon the altar in the Eucharist.

[195] Heb 10:5
[196] Ps 39:7-8

171. Is the sacrifice of the cross and that of the Eucharist the same sacrifice, or two distinct sacrifices?
It is the same sacrifice; because the victim is the selfsame Jesus Christ, and the priest or principal offerer is also the selfsame Jesus Christ; it was he that offered himself upon the cross, it is he that offers himself upon the altar. The only difference is in the manner of the offering; because in the sacrifice of the cross, Christ really died, and therefore that was a bloody sacrifice; in the Sacrifice of the Altar, he only dies mystically, and therefore this is an unbloody sacrifice. I say he dies mystically, inasmuch as his death is represented in the consecrating apart the bread and wine, to denote the shedding of his sacred blood from his body at the time of his death.

172. Why do you say that Jesus Christ is the priest that offers the Sacrifice of the Altar, since there is always another priest to perform this office?
Because the priest that officiates in the Mass, officiates as Christ's vicegerent, and in his Person; and therefore when he comes to the consecration of the elements, in which this sacrifice essentially consists, he speaks not in his own name, but in the name and Person of Christ, saying, "This is my body, this is the chalice of my blood," etc. So that Christ himself is the principal priest; the officiant only acts by his authority, in his name and Person.

173. But what need was there of the Sacrifice of the Altar, since we were fully redeemed by the sacrifice of the cross?
First, that we might have in the Sacrifice of the Altar a standing memorial of the death of Christ. Second, that by the Sacrifice of the Altar, the fruit of his death might daily be applied to our souls. Third, that his children might have, till the end of the world, an external sacrifice in which they might join together in the outward worship of religion, as the servants of God from

the beginning of the world had always done. Fourth, that in and by this sacrifice they might unite themselves daily with their high priest and victim Christ Jesus, and daily answer the four ends of sacrifice.

174. What proofs have you that the Mass is properly a sacrifice?

Because as we learn from many plain texts of scripture quoted in the foregoing chapter, and from the perpetual tradition of the universal Church, in the consecration of the Holy Eucharist, the bread and wine are really changed into the body and blood of Christ; and consequently in and by this consecration, the real body and blood of Christ our victim, which for us was immolated upon the cross, is in the Mass exhibited and presented to God. Therefore the Mass is properly a sacrifice, and the same sacrifice as that which Christ offered upon the cross. And that this sacrifice is propitiatory for the obtaining of the remission of our sins, we learn from the very words of Christ our Lord, at the first institution of it at his last supper, when in the consecration of the elements, speaking in the present tense, he tells us (as his words are in the original Greek), "This is my body which is broken [or sacrificed] for you,"[197] "This is my blood of the new testament, which is shed for many for the remission of sins,"[198] or, "This cup is the new testament in my blood, which [cup] is shed for you,"[199] viz. for the remission of your sins.

175. Have you any other texts of scripture for the sacrifice of the Mass?

Yes, besides many figures of this sacrifice in the old testament (of which the most evident is that of the bread and wine offered by Melchisedech, the priest of the Most High God,[200] accord-

[197] 1 Cor 11:24
[198] Mt 26:28; Mk 14:24
[199] Lk 22:20
[200] Cf. Gn 14:18-20

ing to whose order Christ is said to be a priest forever,[201] and that, as the holy fathers take notice, by reason of this Sacrifice of the Eucharist[202]) we have the prophecy of Malachi; where God, rejecting the Jewish sacrifices, declares his acceptance of the sacrifice or pure offering which should be made to him in every place among the gentiles;[203] which text the ancient fathers, both Greek and Latin, urge to show that the Eucharist is a sacrifice.[204]

In the new testament, we have Hebrews 13, where the apostle tells us that under the new law "we have an altar [and consequently a sacrifice], whereof they have no right to eat who serve the tabernacle";[205] that is, they who continue in the service of the old law. The same apostle makes a parallel between the partakers of the Christian sacrifice and those that partake of the Jewish or heathenish victims,[206] so as evidently to suppose that the Christian table which he mentions is an altar, where Christ is mystically immolated and afterwards eaten by the faithful, as in the Jewish and heathenish sacrifices the victim was first offered on the altar, and then eaten by the people. From whence the apostle infers that they who were partakers of this great sacrifice of the body and blood of Christ ought not to be partakers with devils, by eating of the meats sacrificed to idols. The Sacrifice of the Mass is also mentioned in Chapter 13 of the Acts of the Apostles, where what we read in the protestant testament as, "they ministered to the Lord and fasted" etc., in the Greek original is: "as they were sacrificing to the Lord, and

201 Cf. Ps 109:4

202 Cf. Cyprian, *Epistle 62*; Chrysostom, *Homily 35 on Genesis*; Epiphanius, *Haeresi 55*; Jerome, *Epistle 126 ad Evagrius*; Augustine, *Exposition on Psalm 33*, *City of God*, Bk. 15, Bk. 18; Cyril of Alexandria, *Glaphyra on the Pentateuch*, Bk. 2; Theodoret, *Questions on Genesis*, n. 64.

203 Cf. Mal 1:10-11

204 Cf. Justin Martyr, *Dialogue with Trypho*; Irenaeus, *Against Heresies*, Bk. 4, Ch. 18; Chrysostom, *Commentary on Psalm 92*; Augustine, *City of God*, Bk. 18.

205 Heb 13:10

206 Cf. 1 Cor 10:14-21

fasting, the Holy Ghost said, separate me Barnabas and Saul for the work whereunto I have called them."[207] Where the word which we have rendered in English as *sacrificing* is the selfsame which to this day is used by the Greeks to express the Sacrifice of the Mass.

Besides these arguments from scripture for the sacrifice offered to God in the Blessed Eucharist, we have the authority and the perpetual tradition of the Church of God, from the days of the apostles. Witness the most ancient liturgies of all the churches and nations, Latins, Greeks, Goths Syrians, Armenians, Egyptians, Ethiopians, Indians, etc. Witness the manifold testimonies of councils and fathers of all ages. Witness the frequent use in all Christian antiquity of the names of altar, sacrifice, oblation, priest, etc. Witness, in fine, the universal consent of Christians of all denominations before Luther's time, in offering up the Eucharist as a sacrifice; which is a matter of fact that cannot be contested. To which, if we add another truth, no less notorious, viz. that no one of our adversaries can pretend to assign the time in which the use of this sacrifice first begun, we cannot have a more certain proof of an apostolical tradition. It is the rule which St. Augustine gives, by which to discern apostolical traditions.[208]

176. But does not St. Paul say that Christ, by one offering, viz. that of the cross, hath perfected forever them that are sanctified?[209] What room then can there be for the Sacrifice of the Mass?
What the apostle says is certainly true, that the sacrifice of Christ upon the cross is that one offering by which we are perfected forever; because the whole world was redeemed by that one sacrifice, and all other means of our sanctification or salvation have their force and efficacy from that one offering. Yet as

[207] Acts 13:2
[208] Cf. Augustine, *De Baptismo*, Bk. 4, Ch. 24
[209] Cf. Heb 10:14

that one offering, by which Christ has perfected forever them that are sanctified, is no way injured by his supplications which, as man, he makes for us to his Father in heaven, where, as the same apostle tells us, "He ever liveth to make intercession for us,"[210] so neither is it any ways injured, but highly honored by the representing of the same offering to God in the Sacrifice of the Altar.

177. But the apostle tells us that Christ does not offer himself often,[211] what say you to this?
He speaks there of offering himself in a bloody manner, by dying for the redemption of the world, which was to be but once. But though the price of our redemption was to be paid but once, yet the fruit of it was to be daily applied to our souls, by those means of grace which Christ has left in his Church that is, by his sacrament and sacrifice.

Chapter 7

Of Hearing Mass

178. Are the faithful obliged to be present at the Sacrifice of the Mass?
They are obliged by a precept of the Church to be present thereat upon all Sundays and holy days.

[210] Heb 7:25
[211] Cf. Heb 9:25

179. Why does the Church oblige all her children to assist at the Sacrifice of the Mass upon all Sundays and holy days?

That as Sundays and holy days are particularly set apart for the worship of God and the sanctification of their souls, they may answer these ends by assembling together on these days to commemorate the death of Christ, and to offer to God this most solemn worship of sacrifice, by the hands of the priest and of their high priest Christ Jesus: First, in testimony of God's sovereignty, and as a homage due to His Divine Majesty; Second, to give thanks for all his blessings general and particular; Third, to beg mercy and pardon for all their sins; Fourth, to obtain all necessary graces from the fountain of all grace.

180. Why might not this as well be done without going to hear Mass?

Because, as we have seen in the foregoing chapter, the Mass is a sacrifice instituted by Christ to be offered for all those ends. And as in this sacrifice Christ himself is both the priest and the victim, who here presents to his eternal Father that same body and blood by which we were redeemed. It must be evident that there can be no better means of adoring God and offering our homage to him, than by uniting ourselves to this sacrifice of his only Son; no more acceptable thanksgiving than that which is here offered by and through Jesus Christ; no means of obtaining mercy and pardon comparable to this oblation of the blood of the Lamb; in fine, no more seasonable time for obtaining the favors of heaven, than when we appear before the throne of grace with him, and through him, in whom his Father is always well pleased.

181. In what disposition of soul ought persons then to go to hear Mass?

They ought to go as if they were going to Mount Calvary, to be present at the passion and death of their Redeemer; since the Mass is indeed the same sacrifice as that which he there offered. And consequently, there can be no better devotion for the time of Mass than that which has relation to the passion of Christ, which is therein commemorated and represented to the eternal Father. And all the faithful, when they are at Mass, should endeavor to put their souls in the like dispositions of adoration, thanksgiving, love, and repentance for their sins, with which a good Christian would have assisted at the sacrifice of the cross, had he been present there.

182. What think you of those who, during the time of Mass, instead of attending to this great sacrifice, suffer themselves to be carried away with willful distractions?

Such as these don't hear Mass. That is, they don't fulfil the Church precept, nor satisfy the obligation of the day; but rather mock God, whilst outwardly they pretend to honor him, and their heart is far from him.

183. What then do you say to those who, during the time of the Mass, are laughing and talking, or pass that time in criminal amusements?

These not only are guilty, like the former, of breaking the Church precept, but also must answer for the scandal that they give by their ill example, and for their hindering others from attending to their duty; as well as for their profaning those most sacred mysteries by such an unchristian behavior at this holy time.

184. I should be glad if you would explain to me the order and ceremonies of the Mass: and first, pray what is the meaning of the priest's vestments?

The priest, in saying Mass, represents the Person of Christ, who is the high priest of the new law, and the Mass itself represents his passion; and therefore, the priest puts on these vestments to represent those with which Christ was ignominiously clothed at the time of his passion.

Thus, for instance, the amice represents the rag or clout with which the Jews muffled our Savior's face, when at every blow they bid him prophesy who it was that struck him.[212] The alb represents the white garment with which he was vested by Herod. The girdle, maniple, and stole represent the cords and bands with which he was bound in the different stages of his passion. The chasuble, or outward vestment, represents the purple garment with which he was clothed as a mock king; upon the back of which there is a cross, to represent that which Christ bore on his sacred shoulders. Lastly, the priest's tonsure, or crown, is to represent the crown of thorns which our Savior wore.

Moreover, as in the old law the priests that were to officiate in sacred functions had, by the appointment of God, vestments assigned for that purpose, as well for the greater decency and solemnity of the divine worship, as to signify and represent the virtues which God required of his ministers, so it was proper that in the Church of the new testament, Christ's ministers should, in their sacred functions, be distinguished from the laity by their sacred vestments, which might also represent the virtues which God requires in them. Thus the amice, which is first put upon the head, represents divine hope, which the apostle calls the helmet of salvation; the alb, innocence of life; the girdle (with which the loins are begirt), purity and chastity; the maniple (which is put on the left arm) patient-suffering the labors of this mortal life; the stole, the sweet yoke of Christ to be borne in this life, in order to a happy immortality in the next; in fine, the chasuble, which as uppermost, covers all the rest, the virtue of charity.

In these vestments the Church makes use of five colors: the white, on the feasts of our Lord, of the Blessed Virgin, of the angels, and of the saints that were not martyrs; the red,

---

[212] Cf. Lk 22:64

on the feasts of Pentecost, of the Invention and Exaltation of the Cross, and of the apostles and martyrs; the green, on the greatest part of the Sundays; the violet, in the penitential times of Advent and Lent, and upon vigils and Emberdays; and the black, upon Good Friday and in the Masses for the dead.

185. Why is there always a crucifix upon the altar, at the time of Mass?

That, as the Mass is said in remembrance of Christ's passion and death, the priest and people may have always before their eyes the image that represents his passion and death.

186. What is the meaning of having lighted candles upon the altar, at the time of Mass?

First, to honor the triumph of our fathers, which is there celebrated by these lights, which are tokens of our joy and of his glory. Second, to denote the light of faith, with which we are to approach him.

187. What is the meaning of making a reverence to the altar?

First, because the altar is a figure of Christ, who is not only our sacrifice and our high priest, but our altar too, inasmuch as we are to offer our prayers and sacrifices through him. Second, because the altar is the seat of the divine mysteries, and therefore deserves our reverence.

188. What is the meaning of the use of incense in the Mass and other offices of the Church?

Incense is an emblem of prayer, ascending to God from a heart inflamed with his love, as the smoke of incense ascends on high from the fire of the censer. Hence the royal prophet says, "Let my prayer, O lord, be directed like incense in thy sight."[213] And

---

[213] Ps 140:2

St. John in the Apocalypse saw the four and twenty elders and the angel offering up to God odors and incense, which were the prayers of the saints.[214] Moreover the incensing of the altar, of the priest, etc. is, according to the use of the Church, a token of honor to the thing that is incensed: not of divine honor, since we also incense the whole choir and the people, but of a due respect for the things of God, for his ministers and people.

189. What is the use of singing and of organs in the divine service?
To help to raise the heart to heaven, and to celebrate with greater solemnity the divine praises.

The Order of Mass

190. Tell me now, if you please, the different parts of the Mass and the ceremonies thereof, that I may be the better instructed in this heavenly sacrifice?
First, the priest standing at the foot of the altar, having made a low reverence, begins with the sign of the cross, saying, *In nomine Patris*, etc. "In the name of the Father, and of the Son, and of the Holy Ghost," and then recites alternately with the

---

[214] Cf. Apoc 5:8, 8:4

clerk Psalm 42, *Judica me, Deus*, etc. "Judge me, O God," etc., composed by David in the time that he was persecuted by Saul, and kept at a distance from the tabernacle or Temple of God, and expressing his ardent desires and hopes of approaching to God's altar and offering praise and sacrifice to him. And therefore this psalm is most proper here, as expressing the sentiments of soul with which we ought to come to this holy sacrifice.

Secondly, the priest, bowing down at the foot of the altar, says the confiteor, or general confession, acknowledging his sins to God, to the whole court of heaven, and to all the faithful there assembled, and begging their prayers to God for him: and the clerk repeats the same in the name of the people, to the end that both priest and people may dispose themselves for this great sacrifice by a sincere repentance for their sins. Our adversaries object against this form of confession because therein we confess our sins to the saints, as if this was giving them an honor that belongs to God alone; not considering that the confessing of our sins to any one, so far from being an honor peculiar to God, is what we are directed in scripture to do to one another.[215] And accordingly in this very form, which we call the confiteor, we not only confess our sins to God and to his saints, but the priest also confesses to the people, and the people to the priest.

Thirdly, the priest in going up to the altar begs for himself and the people that God would take away their iniquities, that they may be worthy to enter into his sanctuary. Then coming up to the altar he kisses it in reverence to Christ, of whom it is a figure; and going to the book he reads what is called the introit, or entrance of the Mass; which is different every day, and generally an anthem taken out of the scripture, with the first verse of one of the psalms, and the *Gloria Patri*, to glorify the Blessed Trinity.

[215] Jas 5:16

Fourthly, he returns to the middle of the altar, and says alternately with the clerk the *Kyrie eleison,* or "Lord, have mercy on us," which is said three times to God the Father; three times, *Christe eleison,* or "Christ have mercy on us," to God the Son; and three times again *Kyrie eleison* to God the Holy Ghost. This frequently calling for mercy teaches us the necessity of approaching to this sacrifice with a penitential spirit, and that the best devotion for this beginning of the Mass, is to offer up to God the sacrifice of a contrite and humble heart.

Fifthly, after the *Kyrie eleison,* the priest recites the *Gloria in excelsis,* "Glory be to God on high," etc., being an excellent hymn and prayer to God, the beginning of which was sung by the angels at the birth of Christ. This, being a hymn of joy, is omitted in the Masses for the dead and in the penitential times of Advent, Lent, etc. After this the priest turning about to the people, says, *Dominus vobiscum,* "The Lord be with you." **R**: *Et cum spiritu tuo,* "And with thy spirit." Then returning to the book, he says, *Oremus,* "Let us pray," and then reads the collects or prayers of that day, concluding them with the usual termination: *Per Dominum nostrum,* etc. "Through our Lord Jesus Christ," etc. with which the Church commonly concludes all her prayers, as hoping for no mercy, grace, or blessing, but through our Savior Jesus Christ.

Sixthly, after the collects is read the lesson or epistle of the day (and upon the Wednesdays and Saturdays in the Ember-weeks, several lessons or epistles), at the end of which the clerk answers, *Deo gratias,* "Thanks be to God," to give God thanks for the heavenly instructions contained in that divine lesson of holy writ. The lesson or epistle is followed by the gradual or tract, consisting of some devout verses taken out of scripture; to which are joined the alleluias, to praise God with joy, excepting the penitential time between Septuagesima and Easter; for then alleluia is not said.

Seventhly, after the epistle and gradual, the book is removed to the other side of the altar, in order to read the gospel of the day; which removal of the book represents the passing from the preaching of the old law, figured by the lesson or epistle, to the gospel of Jesus Christ, published by the preachers of the new law. The priest before he reads the gospel, makes his prayer, bowing down before the middle of the altar, that God would cleanse his heart and his lips, that he may be worthy to declare his gospel. At the beginning of the gospel both priest and people make the sign of the cross: First, upon their foreheads, to signify that they will not be ashamed of the cross of Christ and his doctrine; Second, upon their mouth, to signify that they will profess it in words; Third, upon their breast, to signify that they will always keep it in their hearts. During the gospel, the people stand, to show by this posture their readiness to go and do whatsoever they shall be commanded by their Savior in his divine word. At the end, the clerk answers in the name of the people, *Laus tibi Christe*, "Praise be to thee, O Christ"; to give praise to our Redeemer for his heavenly doctrine; and the priest kisses the book, in reverence to those sacred words which he has been reading out of it. In the High or Solemn Mass, the gospel is sung by the deacon, and lighted candles are held by the acolytes on each side, to denote the light which Christ brought us by his gospel.

Eighthly, after the gospel upon all Sundays, as also upon the feasts of our Lord, of the Blessed Virgin, of the apostles, and of the doctors of the Church, the priest standing at the middle of the altar, recites the Nicene Creed, and kneels down at these words, *Et homo factus est*, "And he was made man," in reverence to the mystery of our Lord's incarnation. Then turning about to the people, he greets them with the usual salutation, *Dominus vobiscum*, "The Lord be with you." R: *Et cum spiritu tuo*, "And with thy spirit." After which he reads a short sentence of scripture called the offertory, and then takes off the veil from the chalice, in order to proceed to offering up the bread and wine for the sacrifice.

Ninthly, he offers first the bread upon the paten, or little plate; then pours the wine into the chalice, mingling with it a little water, and offers that up in like manner, begging that this sacrifice may be accepted by the Almighty for the remission of his sins, for all there present, for all the faithful living and dead, and for the salvation of all the world. Then bowing down, he says, "In the spirit of humility, and in a contrite mind, may we be received by thee, O Lord: and so may our sacrifice be made this day in thy sight, that it may please thee, O Lord God." Then he blesses the bread and wine with the sign of the cross, invoking the Holy Ghost, saying, "Come thou, the Sanctifier, the almighty and eternal God, and bless + this sacrifice prepared for thy holy name." After this he goes to the corner of the altar, and there washes the tips of his fingers, saying, *Lavabo*, etc. "I will wash my hands among the innocent, and I will encompass thy altar, O Lord," etc. as in the latter part of Psalm 25. This washing of the fingers denotes the cleanness and purity of soul with which these divine mysteries are to be celebrated; which ought to be such as not only to wash away all greater filth, but even the dust which sticks to the tips of our fingers, by which are signified the smallest faults and imperfections.

Tenthly, after washing his fingers the priest returns to the middle of the altar, and there bowing down, begs of the Blessed Trinity to receive this oblation in memory of the passion, resurrection and ascension of our Lord Jesus Christ, and for an honorable commemoration of the Blessed Virgin and of all the saints, that they may intercede for us in heaven, whose memory we celebrate on earth. Then turning about to the people, he says, *Orate fratres*, etc. that is, "Brethren, pray that my sacrifice and yours may be made acceptable in the sight of God the Father Almighty." The clerk answers in the name of the people, "May the Lord receive this sacrifice from thy hands, to the praise and glory of his own name, and for our benefit, and that of all his holy Church."

Eleventhly, the priest says, in a low voice, the prayers called the secreta, which correspond to the collects of the day and are different every day. He concludes by saying aloud, *Per omnia saecula saeculorum*, that is, "world without end." **R**: "Amen." Then after the usual salutation, "The Lord be with you," **R**: "And with thy spirit," he admonishes the people to lift up their hearts to God *(Sursum corda)*, and to join with him in giving thanks to our Lord *(Gratias agamus Domino Deo nostro)*, to which the clerk answers, *Dignum et justum est*, "It is meet and just." Then follows the preface, so called because it serves as an introduction to the Canon of the Mass; in which, after solemnly acknowledging ourselves bound in duty ever to give thanks to God, through his Son Jesus Christ, whose majesty all the choirs of angels ever praise and adore, we humbly beg leave to have our voices admitted together with theirs in that celestial hymn, *Sanctus, sanctus, sanctus*, etc., "Holy, holy, holy, Lord God of hosts. The heavens and earth are full of thy glory. Hosanna in the highest. Blessed is he that comes in the name of the Lord. Hosanna in the highest."

Twelfthly, after the preface follows the Canon of the Mass, or the most sacred and solemn part of this divine service, which is read with a low voice, as well to express the silence of Christ in his passion and his hiding at that time his glory and his divinity, as to signify the vast importance of that common cause of all mankind, which the priest is then representing, as it were in secret to the ear of God, and the reverence and awe with which both priest and people ought to assist at these tremendous mysteries. The Canon begins by the invoking the Father of mercies, through Jesus Christ his Son, to accept this sacrifice for the holy Catholic Church, for the pope, for the bishop, for the king, and for all the professors of the Catholic and apostolic faith throughout the whole world. Then follows the *memento*, or commemoration of the living, for whom in particular the priest intends to offer up that Mass, or who have been particularly recommended to his prayers, etc. To which is subjoined a remembrance of all there present, followed by a solemn commemoration of the Blessed Virgin, the apostles and martyrs, and all the saints, to honor their memory by naming them in the sacred mysteries, to communicate with them, and to beg of God the help of their intercession, through Jesus Christ our Lord.

Then the priest spreads his hands over the bread and wine, which are to be consecrated into the body and blood of Christ (according to the ancient ceremony prescribed in the Levitical law, that the priest or persons who offered sacrifice should lay their hands upon the victim before it was immolated[216]), and he begs that God would accept of this oblation which he makes in the name of the whole Church, and that he would grant us peace in this life, and eternal salvation in the next. Then he blesses the bread and wine with the sign of the cross (a ceremony frequently repeated in the Mass in memory of Christ's passion, of which this sacrifice is the memorial; and to give us to understand that all grace and sanctity flow from the cross of Christ, that is, from Christ crucified), and he prays that God would render this oblation blessed, received, approved, reasonable, and acceptable, that it may be made to us the body and blood of his most beloved Son, our Lord Jesus Christ. Then he proceeds to the consecration, first of the bread into the body of our Lord, and then of the wine into his blood; which consecration is made by the words of Christ pronounced by the priest in his name, and as bearing his Person: and this is the chief action of the Mass, in which the very essence of this sacrifice consists. Because, by the separate consecration of the bread and wine, the body and blood of Christ are really exhibited and presented to God, and Christ is mystically immolated.

Immediately after the consecration follows the elevation, first of the host, then of the chalice, in remembrance of Christ's

---

[216] Cf. Lv 1:3-16

elevation upon the cross and that the people may adore their Lord veiled under these sacred signs. At the elevation of the chalice, the priest recites those words of Christ, "As often as you shall do these things, you shall do them in remembrance of me." Then he goes on making a solemn commemoration of the passion, resurrection, and ascension of Christ, and begging of God to accept this sacrifice, as he was pleased to accept the oblations of Abel, Abraham and Melchisedech, and to command that it may, by his holy angel, be presented upon the altar above, in presence of His Divine Majesty, for the benefit of all those that shall partake of these mysteries here below.

Then the priest makes the *memento* or remembrance for the dead; praying for all those that are gone before us with the sign of faith and rest in the sleep of peace, and in particular for those for whom he desires to offer this sacrifice, that God would grant them a place of refreshment, light and peace, through Jesus Christ our Lord. Then raising his voice at *Nobis quoque peccatoribus*, "And to us sinners," etc., he strikes his breast in token of repentance, like the humble publican in the gospel, and begs of God mercy and pardon, and to be admitted into some part and society with the holy apostles and martyrs, through Christ our Lord. He goes on: "By whom, O Lord, thou dost always create, sanctify, enliven, bless, and give us all these good things." Then kneeling down, and taking the sacred host in his hand, he makes the sign of the cross with it over the chalice, saying, "Through him, and with him, and in him, is to thee, God the Father in the unity of the Holy Ghost, all honor and glory"; which last words he pronounces elevating a little the host and chalice from the altar; and then kneels down, saying with a loud voice, *Per omnia saecula saeculorum*, "Forever and ever." R: "Amen."

Thirteenthly, after this follows the *Pater Noster*, or Lord's Prayer, which is pronounced with a loud voice; and in token of the people's joining in this prayer, the clerk in their name says aloud the last petition, *Sed libera nos a malo,* "But deliver us from evil." The priest answers "Amen," and goes on with a low voice, begging that we may be delivered from all evils past, present, and to come; and by the intercession of the Blessed Virgin, and of all the saints, be favored with peace in our days, and secured from sin and all disturbances, through Jesus Christ our Lord. Then he breaks the host, in imitation of Christ's breaking the bread before he gave it to his disciples, and in remembrance of his body being broken for us upon the cross; and puts a particle of it into the chalice, saying to the people, "The peace of the Lord be always with you." **R:** "And with thy spirit." This cere-mony of mixing a particle of the host with the species of wine in the chalice represents the reuniting of Christ's body, blood, and soul at his resurrection; and the priest's wish or prayer for peace at the time of this ceremony puts us in mind of that *Pax vobis,* or "Peace be unto you," which our Lord spoke to his disciples when he first came to them after his resurrection.[217]

Fourteenthly, then follows the *Agnus Dei,* etc. which the priest pronounces three times, striking his breast in token of repentance. The words are: "Lamb of God, who takest away the sins of the world, have mercy on us." At the third time, instead of "have mercy on us," he says, "grant us peace." After the *Ag-nus Dei* follow three prayers, which the priest says to himself by way of preparation for receiving the Blessed Sacrament. After which kneeling down, and then rising and taking up the Blessed Sacrament, he three times strikes his breast, saying, *Domine non sum dignus,* etc., "Lord I am not worthy that thou shouldst enter under my roof; but only thou say the word, and my soul shall be healed." Then receiving the sacred host he says, "The body of our Lord Jesus Christ preserve my soul to life everlasting, Amen." Having paused awhile, he proceeds to the receiving of the chalice, using the like words, "The blood of our Lord Jesus

[217] Cf. Jn 20:19-26

Christ," etc. Then follows the Communion of the people, if any are to receive.

Fifteenthly, after the Communion, the priest takes first a little wine into the chalice, which is called the first ablution, in order to consummate what remains of the consecrated species in the chalice; and then takes a little wine and water, which is called the second ablution, upon his fingers, over the chalice, to the end that no particle of the Blessed Sacrament may remain sticking to his fingers, but that all may be washed into the chalice and so received. Then wiping the chalice and covering it, he goes to the book and reads a versicle of the holy scripture called the communion, because it was used to be sung in the High Mass at the time that the people communicated. After this, he turns about to the people with the usual salutation, *Dominus vobiscum*, and then returning to the book, reads the collects, or prayers called the postcommunion; after which he again greets the people with *Dominus vobiscum*, and gives them leave to depart with *Ite Missa est*, "Go, the Mass is done." Here, bowing before the altar, he makes a short prayer to the Blessed Trinity; and then gives his blessing to all there present in the name of the same Blessed Trinity, *Benedicat vos*, etc., "May the Almighty God, Father, + Son, and Holy Ghost, bless you." He concludes by reading at the corner of the altar the beginning of the gospel according to St. John, which the people hear standing; but at the words, *Verbum caro factum est*, "The word was made flesh," both priest and people kneel in reverence to the mystery of Christ's incarnation. The clerk at the end answers, *Deo gratias*, "Thanks be to God." And then the priest departs from the altar, reciting to himself the *Benedicite*, or the canticle of the three children, inviting all creatures in heaven and earth to bless and praise our Lord.

191. In what manner ought the people to be employed during the Mass?

In such prayers and devotions as are most suitable to that holy sacrifice; which having so close a relation to the passion of Christ, is then best heard when the assistants turn the attention and affections of their souls towards the mysteries of the passion of our Lord, which are there represented.

192. Is it not a good way of hearing Mass to accompany the priest through every part of it, so as to accommodate one's devotion to what he is then about?

It is a very good and profitable way; Not that the very prayers of the priest, especially in the Canon and consecration, are always proper for the people, but that in every part of the Mass it is proper that the people should use such prayers as are adapted to what the priest is then doing.

193. What kind of prayers and devotions then do you esteem the best adapted to the several parts of the Mass?

I should recommend:

+ **In the beginning of the Mass,** an earnest application of the soul to God, by way of begging his divine grace for the worthily and profitably assisting at this sacrifice.
+ **At the confiteor,** and what follows until the *Kyrie eleison* inclusively, I should advise the assistants to a humble confession of their sins to God, with a most hearty repentance and earnestly begging his mercy.
+ **At the *gloria in excelsis*,** let them join in that heavenly hymn, and excite their souls to the affections expressed therein.
+ **At the collects,** let them recommend to God their own necessities and those of the whole Church.
+ **At the epistle, gradual, and gospel,** either let them attend to the heavenly lessons contained in them; or, if they have not the

convenience for this, let them employ themselves in giving thanks to God for revealing to us his divine truths, and instructing us not only by his servants the prophets and apostles, but also by his Son; and begging of God that their lives may be always conformable to the maxims of his gospel.

+ **At the *credo*,** let them recite it to themselves, with a lively faith of those great truths contained in it.

+ **At the offertory,** let them join with the priest in offering up first the host, and then the chalice, for themselves and for the whole Church; but let them at the same time unite themselves closely with their high priest, Christ Jesus, and with him, through him, and in him, offer up their hearts and souls to God, to be consecrated to his divine service and change into him; and in particular at the mingling of the water with the wine in the chalice, let them pray for this happy union with God.

+ **At the *lavabo*,** when the priest washes his fingers at the corner of the altar, let them excite in their souls a hearty act of repentance, and beg to be washed from their sins in the blood of the Lamb.

+ **When the priest turns about** and says, *Orate fratres*, let them pray that God would accept that oblation for his own honor and their salvation.

+ **At the preface,** let them raise up their hearts to God at *Sursum corda*, and pour forth their souls in thanksgiving to him; joining themselves with the heavenly choirs, and with them humbly and fervently pronouncing that sacred hymn, *Sanctus*, "Holy, holy, holy, Lord God of hosts," etc.

+ **During the Canon** of the Mass, let them, together with the priest and together with the invisible priest, Christ Jesus, offer up the sacrifice for the four ends of sacrifice: 1) For God's honor, adoration, and glory. 2) In thanksgiving for all his benefits, and especially for our redemption through Jesus Christ. 3) To obtain mercy and pardon through him for all their sins.

4) To obtain all graces and blessings of which they stand in need. Let them also join in the solemn commemoration that is here made of the passion, resurrection, and ascension of the Son of God, and of the glory of his Church triumphant in heaven.

+ **At the *memento* for the living**, let them earnestly recommend to God their parents, friends, benefactors, etc.; their superiors, spiritual and temporal; those that have particularly desired their prayers; those that are in their agony or other great necessity, temptation, or affliction; those to whom they have given scandal or ill example; their enemies, and all unbelievers and sinners, that God may convert them; in fine, all true servants of God, and all such for whom God would have them to pray.

+ **At the consecration** and elevation, let them again offer themselves to God with and through Christ, and with all the reverence of their souls, adore their Lord there really present under the sacramental veils.

+ **At the *memento* for the dead**, let them represent to the eternal Father this victim which takes away the sins of the world, in behalf of all the faithful departed in the communion of the Church, and particularly of their relations, friends, etc., and those who stand most in need of prayers, or for whom God is best pleased that they should pray.

+ **At the *Pater Noster***, let them join in that heavenly prayer; begging in the first petition ("hallowed be thy name"), the honor and glory of God's name; in the second petition, the propagation of his kingdom here upon earth, and that they may have a share in his kingdom in heaven; in the third petition, the perfect accomplishment of his will by all and in all; in the fourth, the participation of the bread of life; in the fifth, the forgiveness of their sins; in the sixth, the grace of God against temptations; and in the seventh, a deliverance from all evils.

+ **At the breaking of the host**, let them remember Christ's body broken for them upon the cross, and let them pray for that peace which the priest wishes them, with God, with their neighbors, and with themselves.

+ **At *Agnus Dei***, let them, in the spirit of humility and contrition, beg mercy and pardon for their sins.

+ **During the following prayers** and whilst the priest is receiving, let them make a spiritual communion: 1) By a lively faith of the real presence of the Lamb of God slain for our sins, and of the abundance of grace which he brings to those that receive him worthily. 2) By an ardent desire of partaking of this life-giving food. 3) By humbly acknowledging at the *Domine non sum dignus*, and heartily bewailing their unworthiness and sins, which hinder them from daring to approach to this heavenly table. 4) By fervent prayer, begging that Christ would communicate to them some share in those graces which he brings with him to the worthy receiver, and that he would come at least spiritually to their souls, and take possession of them, and unite them to himself by an indissoluble band of love.

+ **After the communion**, let them return thanks to God for the passion and death of his Son, and for having been permitted to assist at these divine mysteries; let them receive with humility the benediction given by the priest in the name of the Blessed Trinity; let them beg pardon for their negligences and distractions; and so offering themselves and all their undertakings to God, depart in peace.

194. **What advice would you give to those who through indisposition, or other unavoidable impediments, are not able to assist at Mass upon a Sunday or holy day?**

I would advise them to endeavor to hear Mass at least in spirit, according to the method prescribed by Mr. Gother for the absent, in the little book of instructions and devotions for hearing Mass.

195. **What if a person, through the absolute necessity of his unhappy circumstances, should be tied to a place where he can never hear Mass; do you think he might not then be allowed to join in prayer with those of another communion, by way of supplying this defect?**

No, certainly. It is a misfortune, and a great misfortune, to be kept like David when he was persecuted by Saul, at a distance from the Temple of God and his sacred mysteries; but it would be a crime to join one's self upon that account with an heretical or schismatic congregation, whose worship God rejects as sacrilegious and impious. In such a case, therefore, a Christian must serve his God alone to the best of his power, by offering to him the homage of prayer, adoration, contrition, etc. And must frequently hear Mass in spirit, by joining himself with all the faithful throughout the earth, wherever they are offering to God that divine sacrifice; ever sighing after these heavenly mysteries, and praying for his delivery from that Babylon, which keeps him at a distance from the temple of God.

Chapter 8

Of Saying Mass in Latin

196. **Is it not a great prejudice to the faithful that the Mass is said in Latin, which is a language that the generality of them do not understand?**

It is no prejudice to them at all, provided they be well instructed in the nature of this sacrifice, and taught (as we have explained above) how to accompany the priest with prayers and devotions adapted to every part of the Mass, such as they commonly have in their manuals or other prayer books. Hence it is visible to any unprejudiced eye that there is far more devotion amongst Catholics at Mass, than there is at protestants' Common Prayer.

197. But is not the Mass also a common prayer, that ought to be said alike by all the faithful?

It is a common sacrifice that is offered for all, and in some manner by all; but as for the particular form of prayers used by the priest in the Mass, there is no obligation for the faithful to recite the same; all that God or his Church expect from them is to assist at that sacrifice with attention and devotion; and this they fully comply with, when they endeavor to follow the directions given above and use such prayers as are best adapted to each part of the Mass, though they be not the selfsame as the priest uses.

198. Can you explain to me by some example how a person may devoutly and profitably assist at this sacrifice, though he be ignorant of the prayers which the priest is saying?

Yes. What do you think if you or any good Christian had been present upon Mount Calvary, when Christ was offering himself upon the cross a sacrifice for the sins of the whole world; would not the very sight of what was occurring (provided that you had the same faith in Christ as you now have) have sufficed to excite in your soul most lively acts of love of God, thanksgiving for so great a mercy, detestation of your sins, etc., though you could neither hear any word from the mouth of Christ your high priest, nor know in particular what passed in his soul? Just so in the Mass, which is the same sacrifice as that which Christ offered upon the cross, because both the priest and the victim are the same: it is abundantly sufficient for the people's devotion, to be well instructed in what is then occurring, and to excite in their souls suitable acts of adoration, thanksgiving, repentance, etc., though they understand not the particular prayers used by the priest at that time.

I must add, that for the devoutly and profitably concurring in sacrifice offered to God, it is not only not necessary that the people should hear or recite the same prayers with the priest, but that even the very seeing of him is more than God was pleased to require in his law. Hence we find that the whole multitude of the people were praying without, when Zacharias went into the Temple to burn incense;[218] and it was expressly ordered that there should be no man in the Tabernacle or Temple when the high priest went with the blood of the victims into the sanctuary to make atonement.[219]

199. But does not St. Paul condemn the use of unknown tongues in the liturgy of the Church?[220]

He has not one word in that whole chapter of the liturgy of the Church, but only reprehends the abuse of the gift of tongues, which some amongst the Corinthians were guilty of; who, out of ostentation, affected to make exhortations or extemporary prayers in their assemblies in languages utterly unknown, which, for want of an interpreter, could be of no edification to the rest of the faithful. But this is far from being the practice of the Catholic Church, where all exhortations, sermons, and such like instructions are made in the vulgar language; where no new unknown extemporary prayers are recited but the ancient public liturgy and office of the Church, which, by long use are well known, at least as to the substance, by all the faithful; where, in fine, there is no want of interpreters, since the people have the Church offices interpreted in their ordinary prayer books, and the pastors are commanded to explain to them the mysteries contained in the Mass.[221]

[218] Cf. Lk 1:10
[219] Cf. Lv 16:17
[220] Cf. 1 Cor 14
[221] Cf. Council of Trent, Session 22

200. But why does the Church celebrate the Mass in Latin, rather than in the vulgar language?

First, because it is her ancient language, used in all her sacred offices, even from the apostles' days, throughout all the western parts of the world: and therefore the Church, which hates novelty, desires to celebrate her liturgy in the same language as the saints have done for so many ages. Second, for a greater uniformity in the public worship, so that a Christian, in whatsoever country he chances to be, may still find the liturgy performed in the same manner and in the same language to which he is accustomed at home; and the Latin is certainly, of all languages, the most proper for this, as being the most universally studied and known. Third, to avoid the changes to which all vulgar languages, as we find by experience, are daily exposed. For the Church is unwilling to be chopping and changing her liturgy at every turn of language.

201. Have any other Christians besides Roman Catholics ever celebrated their liturgy in a language which the greater part of the people did not understand?

Yes. It is the practice of the Greeks, as we learn from Alexander Ross, in his view of the religions of Europe,[222] and Mr. Breerwood in his *Enquiries*.[223] It is the practice of all other sects of Christians in the east and south, viz. of the Armenians, of the Syrians, of the Nestorians, of the Copts or Egyptians, of the Abassins or Ethiopians, who all use in their liturgies their ancient languages, which have long since ceased to be understood by the people, as we learn from Monsieur Renaudot in his *Dissertation Upon the Oriental Liturgies*. And as for protestants, we learn from Dr. Heylin's history of the Reformation that in Queen Elizabeth's time,

[222] Cf. Alexander Ross, *Pansébeia* (London: Williams, 1672), 481.
[223] Cf. Edward Breerwood, *Enquiries Touching the Diversity of Languages and Religions* (London: Mearne, 1674), 14.

the Irish parliament passed an act for the uniformity of common prayer: with permission of saying the same in Latin, where the minister had not the knowledge of the English tongue. But for translating it into Irish there was no care taken. The people are required by that statute, under several penalties, to frequent their churches, and to be present at the reading the English liturgy, which they understood no more than they do the Mass. By which means, we have furnished the Papists with an excellent argument against ourselves, for having the divine service celebrated in such a language as the people do not understand.[224]

Thus Dr. Heylin.

Chapter 9

Of the Sacrament of Penance

202. What do you mean by the sacrament of penance?
An institution of Christ, by which our sins are forgiven, which we fall into after baptism.

203. In what does this institution consist?
On the part of the penitent, it consists in these three things, viz. contrition, confession, and satisfaction; and on the part of the minister, in the absolution pronounced by the authority of Jesus Christ. So that penance is a sacrament by which the faithful that have fallen into sins, confessing the same with a true repentance and a sincere purpose of making

---

[224] Peter Heylin, *Ecclesia Restaurata* (London: Twyford, 1660), 128.

satisfaction to God, are absolved from their sins by the ministers of God.

204. How do you prove that the ministers of God have any such power as to absolve sinners from their sins?

I prove it from John 20, where Christ said to his ministers, "Receive ye the Holy Ghost, whosesoever sins ye forgive, they are forgiven unto them: and whosesoever sins ye retain, they are retained";[225] and Matthew 18, "Verily I say unto you, whatsoever ye shall bind on earth shall be bound in heaven, and whatsoever ye shall loose on earth shall be loosed in heaven."[226]

205. But was this power given to any besides the apostles?

It was certainly given to them and to their successors till the end of the world, no less than the commission of preaching, baptizing, etc. which, though addressed to the apostles, was certainly designed to continue with their successors, the pastors of the Church, forever, according to that of Christ: "Lo, I am with you always, even till the end of the world."[227] And so the protestant church understands these texts, in the order for the visitation of the sick in the *Book of Common Prayer*, where she prescribes a form of absolution the same in substance as that used in the Catholic Church, viz. "Our Lord Jesus Christ, who hath left power to his Church to absolve all sinners who truly repent and believe in him, of his great mercy forgive thee thine offences: and by his authority committed to me, I absolve thee from all thy sins, in the name of the Father, and of the Son, and of the Holy Ghost. Amen."[228]

---

[225] Jn 20:22-23
[226] Mt 18:18
[227] Mt 28:20
[228] *Book of Common Prayer* (1662)

206. Is it then your doctrine that any man can forgive sins?

We do not believe that any man can forgive sins by his own power, as no man by his own power can raise the dead to life: because both the one and the other equally belong to the power of God. But as God has sometimes made men his instruments in raising the dead to life, so we believe that he has been pleased to appoint that his ministers should in virtue of his commission, as his instruments and by his power, absolve repenting sinners; and as this is evident from the texts above quoted, it must be a false zeal, under pretext of maintaining the honor of God, to contradict this commission which he has so evidently given to his Church.

207. But will not sinners thus be encouraged to go on in their evil ways, upon the confidence of being absolved by the pastors of the Church, whenever they please, from their sins?

The pastors of the Church have no power to absolve anyone without a sincere repentance and a firm purpose of a new life; and therefore, the Catholic doctrine of absolution can be no encouragement to any man to go on in his sins.

208. What then is required on the part of the sinner in order to obtain forgiveness of his sins in the sacrament of penance?

Three things, viz. contrition, confession, and satisfaction. By *contrition* we mean a hearty sorrow for having offended so good a God, with a firm purpose of amendment. By *confession* we mean a full and sincere accusation made to God's minister, of all mortal sins, which after a diligent examination of conscience, a person can call to his remembrance. By *satisfaction* we mean a faithful performance of the penance enjoined by the priest.

209. What preparation then do you recommend before confession, in order to discharge oneself well of this important duty?

A person that is preparing himself for confession has four things to do before he goes to confession: First, he must pray earnestly to God for his divine grace, that he may be enabled to make a true and good confession. Second, he must carefully examine his own conscience in order to find out what sins he has committed, and how often. Third, he must take due time and pains to beg God's pardon, and to procure a hearty sorrow for his sins. Fourth, he must make firm resolutions with God's grace to avoid the like sins for the future, and to fly the immediate occasions of them.

210. Why must he begin his preparation by praying earnestly to God for his divine grace?

Because a good confession is a work of the utmost importance, and withal a difficult task, by reason of the pride of our hearts, and that fear and shame which is natural to us, and which the devil, who is a mortal enemy to confession, seeks to improve with all his power. And therefore a Christian that desires to make a good confession ought in the first place to address himself to God by fervent prayer for his divine assistance. And the more he finds the enemy busy to instill into him an unhappy fear or shame, the more earnestly must he implore the mercy and grace of God upon this occasion.

211. In what manner must a person examine his conscience in order to make a good confession?

He must use a moral diligence to find out the sins he has committed; which requires more or less time and care according to the length of time from his last confession, and the greater or less care that he usually takes of the state of his conscience. The common method of examination is to consider what one has done against any of the commandments of God; what neglects there may have been of Church precepts; how one has discharged oneself of the common duties of a Christian and of the particular duties of one's respective station of life; how far one has been guilty of any of the seven sins which are commonly called capital, because they are the springs or fountains from whence all our sins flow, etc. And for the helping of a person's memory in this regard, the table of sins which is found in the manual or other prayer-books may be of no small service.

212. Is a person to examine himself as to the number of times that he has been guilty of this or that sin?

Yes: because he is obliged to confess as near as he can, the number of his sins. But in sins of habit, which have been of long standing and very numerous, it will be enough to examine and confess the length of time that he has been subject to such a sin, and how many times he has fallen into it in a day, week, or month, one time with another.

213. What method do you prescribe to a person, in order to procure that hearty sorrow for sin which is the most necessary part of the preparation for confession?

The best method to procure it is to beg it heartily of God; for it must be his gift. None but God can give that change of heart which is so essential to a good confession, and he has been pleased to promise, "Ask and it shall be given you: seek and ye shall find: knock and it shall be opened unto you."[229] To this end also, pious meditations and considerations, and devout acts of contrition, which are found in books of devotion, will much contribute, if read leisurely and attentively, so as to sink into the heart. But because many persons content themselves with running over in haste the prayers before confession which they meet with in their books, with little or no change in the

---

[229] Mt 7:7

heart, which perhaps is grown hard by sinful habits, it is to be feared their performances are too often worth nothing in the sight of God.

214. What then do you advise in the case of habitual sinners, in order to procure a true change of heart?

I advise them to a spiritual retreat for some days, in which being retired as much as possible from the noise of the world, they may think upon the great truths of religion, of the end for which they came into this world, of the benefits of God, of the enormity of sin, of the sudden passing away of all that this world admires, of the four last things, of the passion of Christ, etc.; that so the serious consideration of these great truths, joined to retirement and prayer, may make a due impression on their hearts and effectually convert them to God. Those whose circumstances will not permit them to make a regular retreat, may at least endeavor, during some days, to think as often and as seriously as they can upon the truths abovementioned; and by frequently and fervently calling upon the Father of mercies in the midst of all their employments, they may hope to procure to themselves the like grace.

215. What must be the chief motive of a sinner's sorrow and repentance, in order to qualify him for absolution?

Divines are not perfectly agreed in the resolution of this query: but all are perfectly agreed in advising everyone to aim at the best motive he can, and that the best and safest way is to renounce and detest our sins for the love of God above all things.

216. What do you mean by the resolution of amendment, which you suppose to be a necessary ingredient in the preparation for confession?

I mean a full determination of the soul to fly for the future all willful sin, and the immediate occasions of it.

217. What do you mean by the immediate occasions of sin?

All such company, places, employments, diversions, books, etc., which are apt to draw a person to mortal sin either in deed, or at least in thought.

218. And is a person indispensably obliged to avoid all such immediate occasions of sin?

He is obliged to avoid them to the very utmost of his power, according to that gospel rule of parting even with a hand or an eye that is an occasion of offence to the soul.[230]

219. What scripture do you bring to recommend the confession of our sins to God's ministers?

First, the precept of God in the old testament, "When a man or woman shall commit any sin that men commit, to do a trespass against the Lord, and that person be guilty, then they shall confess their sin which they have done,"[231] etc. Second, the example of the people that hearkened to the preaching of St. John the Baptist, who were baptized by him, "confessing their sins."[232] Third, the prescription of St. James, "Confess your sins one to another";[233] that is, to the priests or elders of the Church, whom the apostle had ordered to be called for. Fourth, the practice of the first Christians, "Many that believed came, and confessed and declared their deeds."[234]

220. How do you prove that there is any command of Christ for the confession of our sins to his ministers?

I prove it from the commission which Christ has given to his ministers: "Receive ye the Holy Ghost: whosoever sins ye

[230] Cf. Mt 18:8-9
[231] Nm 5:6-7
[232] Mt 3:6
[233] Jas 5:16
[234] Acts 19:18

remit they are remitted unto them, and whosesoever sins ye retain, they are retained,"[235] and, "Verily I say unto you, whatsoever ye shall bind on earth, shall be bound in heaven: and whatsoever ye shall loose on earth, shall be loosed in heaven."[236] For it is visible that this commission of binding or loosing, forgiving or retaining sins, according to the merits of the cause and the disposition of the penitent, cannot be rightly executed without taking cognizance of the state of the soul of him who desires to be absolved from his sins by virtue of this commission; and consequently cannot be rightly executed without confession. So that we conclude with St. Augustine,[237] that to pretend it is enough to confess to God alone is making void the power of the keys given to the Church,[238] that it is contradicting the gospel and making void the commission of Christ.

221. Are Christians then obliged to confess all their sins to the ministers of Christ?

They are obliged to confess all such sins as are mortal, or of which they have reason to doubt lest they may be mortal; but they are not obliged to confess venial sins, because as these do not exclude eternally from the kingdom of heaven, so there is not a strict obligation of having recourse for the remission of them to the keys of the Church.

222. But by what rule shall a person be able to make a judgment whether his sins be mortal or venial?

All those sins are to be esteemed mortal which the word of God represents to us as hateful to God, against which it pronounces a woe, or of which it declares that such as do those things shall not enter into the kingdom of heaven; of these we have many

[235] Jn 20:22-23
[236] Mt 18:18
[237] Cf. Augustine, *Sermo 92*, n. 3.
[238] Cf. Mt 16:19

instances.[239] But though it be very easy to know that some sins are mortal, and others but venial, yet to pretend to be able always perfectly to distinguish which are mortal and which are not is above the reach of the most able divines; and therefore a prudent Christian will not easily pass over sins in confession, under pretense of their being venial, unless he be certain of it. And this caution is more particularly necessary in certain cases, where persons being ashamed to confess their sins are willing to persuade themselves they are but venial; for in such cases it is much to be feared, lest their self-love should bias their judgment.

223. Is it a great crime to conceal through shame or fear, any mortal sin in confession?

Yes, it is a great crime; because it is telling a lie to the Holy Ghost; for which kind of sin Ananias and Saphira were struck dead, by a just judgment of God.[240] It is acting deceitfully with God, and that in a matter of the utmost consequence. It is a sacrilege, because it is an abuse of the sacrament of penance, and is generally followed by another greater sacrilege, in receiving unworthily the body and blood of Christ. And what is still more dreadful, such sinners seldom stop at the first bad confession and Communion, but usually go on for a long time in these sins, and very often die in them. But it is not only a great crime to conceal one's sins in confession, it is a great folly and madness too; because such offenders, if they have not renounced their faith, know very well that these sins must be confessed, or that they must burn for them; and they cannot be ignorant that these bad confessions do but increase their burthen, by adding to it the dreadful guilt of repeated sacrileges which they will have far more difficulty of confessing, than these very sins of which they are now so much ashamed.

---

[239] Cf. Rom 1:29-31; 1 Cor 6:9-10; Gal 5:19-21; Eph 5:5; Apoc 21:8; Is 5; Ez 18
[240] Cf. Acts 5:1-10

224. Have you any instances in Church history of remarkable judgments of God upon those that have presumed to approach to the Blessed Sacrament without making a sincere confession of their sins?

Yes, we have several recorded by St. Cyprian[241] and other grave authors; but the most common, and indeed the most dreadful punishment of these sins, is a blindness and hardness of heart, which God justly permits such sinners to fall into, and which is the broad road to final impenitence.

225. Have you anything to offer by way of encouragement to sinners to confess their sins sincerely?

Yes. First, the great benefit that their souls will reap in the remission of their sins, promised by Christ,[242] and the other advantages which an humble confession of sins brings along with it; such as a present comfort and ease of conscience, a remedy against future sins, directions and prescriptions from the minister of God for the curing the spiritual maladies of the soul, etc. Second, that by this short passing confusion, which will last but a moment, they will escape the dreadful shame of having their sins written on their foreheads at the last day, to their eternal confusion. Third, that the greater their sins have been, the greater will be the joy, as of the whole court of heaven, so of their confessor here upon earth, to see their sincere conversion to God testified by the humble confession of their most shameful sins: upon which account, so far from thinking worse of them he will conceive far greater hopes of their future progress, and a more tender affection for them. Fourth, that by the law of God and his Church, whatever is declared in confession can never be discovered directly or indirectly to anyone, upon any account whatsoever, but remains an eternal secret betwixt God

---

[241] Cf. Cyprian, *Treatise 3*
[242] Cf. Mt 18:18; Jn 20:22-23

and the penitent soul; of which the confessor cannot, even to save his own life, make any use at all to the penitent's discredit, disadvantage, or any other grievance whatsoever.[243]

226. But suppose it has been the sinner's misfortune to have made a bad confession, or perhaps a great many bad confessions; what must he do to repair this fault, and to reinstate himself in God's grace?

He must apply himself to God by hearty prayer for his grace and mercy; and so prepare himself to make a good general confession of all his sins, at least from the time of his going astray; because all the confessions that he has made since he began to conceal his sins were all sacrilegious, and consequently null and invalid, and therefore must be all repeated again.

227. But is he obliged in this case to confess again those sins which he has confessed before?

He is, because the concealing of any one mortal sin in confession makes the whole confession worth nothing; and all the following confessions, until this fault is repaired, are all null; and therefore they must all be made again. But if it be to the same confessor who has a confused remembrance of the sins before confessed, it may suffice for the penitent to accuse himself in general terms of all that has been confessed before, and then to specify in particular the sins that have been omitted, together with the number of the bad confessions and Communions that have been made.

228. Are there any other cases in which the confession is worth nothing and consequently must be made again, besides this case of concealing mortal sin?

Yes, if the penitent has taken no care to examine his conscience,

---

[243] Cf. Decree of the Holy Office, November 18, 1682

or to procure the necessary sorrow for his sins or a true purpose of amendment, his confession is good for nothing and must be repeated. As also, if the priest to whom he has made this confession has not had the necessary faculties and approbation.

229. What if the penitent, through forgetfulness, pass over some mortal sin in confession?

This omission, provided there was no considerable negligence which gave occasion to it, does not make the confession invalid. But then the sin that has been thus omitted must be confessed afterwards, when the penitent remembers it; and if he remembers it before Communion, it ought to be confessed before he goes to Communion; if he remembers it not till after Communion, he must confess it in his next confession.

230. Is a person obliged to confess the circumstances of his sins?

He is obliged to confess such circumstances as quite alter the kind or nature of the sin, as also, according to many divines, such as very notoriously aggravate the guilt. But as for other circumstances, they need not be declared; and particularly in sins of unchastity it may sometimes be dangerous to be too circumstantial in expressing the manner of the sin.

231. Would it be a crime to neglect the penance or satisfaction enjoined by the priest?

Yes, it would; the more because we ought to regard the penance enjoined as an exchange which God makes of the eternal punishments, which we have deserved by sin, into these small penitential works.

232. Has the Church of God always enjoined penances to sinners?

Yes, she has, and in the primitive times much more severe than nowadays; when three, seven, or ten years of penance used to be imposed for sins of impurity, perjury, etc.

233. Does the Church at present approve of giving ordinarily very slight penances for very great sins?

So far from it, that the Council of Trent gives us to understand that a confessor, by such excessive indulgence, is in danger of drawing upon his own head the guilt of his penitent's sins, and declares that a priest ought to enjoin a suitable penance according to the quality of the crime and the penitent's ability.[244]

234. Ought the penitent to content himself with performing the penance enjoined, so as to take no farther thought about making satisfaction to God for his sins?

No, by no means. For it is to be feared, that the penance enjoined is seldom sufficient to take off all the punishment due to God's justice upon account of our sins; and it is certain, that the more a penitent is touched with a hearty sorrow for his offences against God, the more he will be desirous of making satisfaction and revenging upon himself by penitential severities the injury done to God by his sins. Hence the life of a good Christian ought to be a perpetual penance.

235. What then do you recommend to a penitent, besides the performance of his penance, in order to cancel the punishment due to his sins and to make satisfaction to the divine justice?

I recommend to him, first, ever to maintain in himself a penitential spirit, and in that spirit to perform all his prayers, daily offering up to God the sacrifice of a contrite and humble heart. Second, I recommend to him almsdeeds, both corporal and spiritual, according to his ability. Third, fasting and other mortifications; especially retrenching all superfluities in eating, drinking, and sleeping; all unnecessary diversions, and much more all such as are dangerous; all idle curiosity, vanity, etc. Fourth, I recommend to him to have recourse to indulgences,

---

[244] Cf. Council of Trent, Session 14

and to perform with religious exactitude the conditions thereunto required. Fifth, in fine, I recommend to him to take from the hands of God, in part of penance for his sins, all sicknesses, pains, labors, and all other crosses whatsoever, and daily to offer them up to God to be united to and sanctified by the sufferings and death of Jesus Christ.

236. What is the form and manner of confession?

The penitent, having duly prepared himself by prayer, by a serious examination of his conscience, and a hearty contrition for his sins, kneels down at the confession chair on one side of the priest, and making the sign of the cross upon himself, asks the priest's blessing, saying, "Pray, Father, give me your blessing." Then the priest blesses him in the following words: "The Lord be in thy heart, and in thy lips, that thou mayest truly and humbly confess all thy sins, in the name of the Father, and of the Son, and of the Holy Ghost, Amen." After which the penitent says the confiteor, in Latin or in English, as far as *Mea culpa*, etc., and then accuses himself of all his sins, as to the kind, number, and aggravating circumstances; and concludes with this or the like form: "Of these, and all other sins of my whole life, I humbly accuse myself; I am heartily sorry for them, I beg pardon of God, and penance and absolution of you my ghostly father." And so he finishes the confiteor, "Therefore, I beseech thee," etc. And then attends to the instructions given by the priest, and humbly accepts the penance enjoined.

237. What is the form of absolution?

First, the priest says, "May the Almighty God have mercy on thee, and forgive thee thy sins, and bring thee to life everlasting, Amen." Then stretching forth his right hand towards the penitent, he says:

May the almighty and merciful Lord give thee pardon, absolution, and remission of thy sins. Amen.

Our Lord Jesus Christ absolve thee, and I, by his authority, absolve thee; in the first place, from every bond of excommunication or interdict, as far as I have power and thou standest in need; in the next place, I absolve thee from all thy sins, in the name of the Father, + and of the Son, and of the Holy Ghost. Amen.

May the passion of our Lord Jesus Christ, the merits of the Blessed Virgin Mary, and of all the saints, and whatsoever good thou shalt do, or whatsoever evil thou shalt suffer, be to thee unto the remission of thy sins, the increase of grace, and the recompense of everlasting life. Amen.

238. In what case is a confessor to defer or deny absolution?

The rule of the Church is to defer absolution, excepting the case of necessity, to those of whose disposition the confessor has just cause to doubt, and to deny absolution to those who are certainly indisposed for it; which is the case of all such as refuse to forgive their enemies, or to restore ill-gotten goods, or to forsake the habits or immediate occasions of sin, or, in a word, to comply with any part of their duty, to which they are obliged under mortal sin.[245]

239. How do you prove, from all that has been said, that penance, i.e. the confession and absolution of sinners, is properly a sacrament?

Because it is an outward sigh of inward grace, ordained by Jesus Christ; which is the very notion and definition of a sacrament. The outward sign is found in the sinner's confession, and the form of absolution pronounced by the priest; the inward grace is the remission of sins promised by Jesus Christ,[246] and the

---

[245] Cf. *Rituale Romanum*
[246] Cf. Jn 20:22-23

ordinance of Christ is gathered from the same place and from Matthew 18.[247]

Chapter 10

Of Indulgences and Jubilees

240. What do you mean by indulgences?

There is not any part of the doctrine of the Catholic Church that is more grossly misrepresented by our adversaries than this of indulgences; for the generality of protestants imagine that an indulgence is a leave to commit sin, or at least, that it is a pardon for sins to come; whereas, indeed, it is no such thing. There is no power in heaven or earth that can give leave to commit sin; and consequently there is no giving pardon beforehand for sins to come. All this is far from the belief and practice of the Catholic Church. By an indulgence, therefore, we mean no more than a releasing to true penitents the debt of temporal punishment which remained due to their sins; after the sins themselves, as to the guilt and eternal punishment, had been already remitted by the sacrament of penance or by perfect contrition.

241. Be pleased to explain this a little farther?

That you may understand this the better, take notice that in sin there are two things: there is the guilt of the sin, and there is the debt of punishment due to God upon account of the sin. Now upon the sinner's repentance and confession, the sin is remitted as to the guilt, and likewise as to the eternal punishment in hell

---

[247] Cf. Mt 18:18

due to every mortal sin; but the repentance and conversion is seldom so perfect as to release the sinner from all debt of temporal punishment due to God's justice, which the penitent must either discharge by the way of satisfaction and penance; or if he be deficient therein, he must expect to suffer hereafter, in proportion to this debt which he owes to the divine justice. Now an indulgence, when duly obtained, is a release from this debt of temporal punishment.

242. **How do you prove, that after the guilt of sin and the eternal punishment has been remitted, there remains oftentimes a debt of temporal punishment due to the divine justice?**
I prove it, first, from scripture; where, to omit other instances, we find in the case of King David, that although upon his repentance the prophet Nathan assured him that the Lord hath put away his sin, yet he denounced unto him many temporal punishments which should be inflicted by reason of this sin, which accordingly after ensued.[248] Second, I prove it from the perpetual practice of the Church of God, of enjoining penances to repenting sinners in order to cancel this punishment due to their sins.

243. **How do you prove that the Church has received a power from Christ of discharging a penitent sinner from this debt of temporal punishment, which remains due upon account of his sins?**
I prove it by that promise of our Lord made to St. Peter: "I will give unto thee the keys of the kingdom of heaven: and whatsoever thou shalt bind on earth shall be bound in heaven: and whatsoever thou shalt loose on earth shall be loosed in heaven."[249] Which promise, made without any exception, reservation, or limitation, must needs imply a power of loosing or

---

[248] Cf. 2 Kgs 12
[249] Mt 16:19

releasing all such bonds as might otherwise hinder or retard a Christian soul from entering heaven.

244. Did the primitive Church ever practice anything of this nature?
Yes, very frequently; in discharging penitents, when there appeared just cause for it, from a great part of the penance due to their sins, as may be seen in Tertullian, St. Cyprian, and other ancient monuments. And of this nature was what St. Paul himself practiced in forgiving (as he says in the Person of Christ, that is, by the power and authority received from him) the incestuous Corinthian, without expecting his going through a longer course of penance.[250]

245. But were these primitive indulgences understood to release the punishment due to sin in the sight of God, or only that which was enjoined by the Church in her penitential canons?
Both one and the other, as often as they were granted upon a just cause; according to what our Lord had promised, "Verily I say unto you, whatsoever you shall bind on earth shall be bound in heaven, and whatsoever you shall loose on earth shall be loosed in heaven."[251]

246. What conditions are necessary for the validity of an indulgence?
First, on the part of him that grants the indulgence, besides sufficient authority, it is necessary that there be a just cause or motive for the grant; for, according to the common doctrine of the best divines, indulgences granted without cause will not be ratified by Almighty God. Second, on the part of him that is to obtain the indulgence, it is requisite that he duly perform the conditions prescribed, such as going to confession and Communion, fasting, alms, prayer, etc., and that he be in the state of

[250] Cf. 2 Cor 2:10
[251] Mt 18:18

grace; for it is in vain to expect the remission of the punishment due to sin, whilst a person continues in the guilt of mortal sin.

247. Does an indulgence so far remit all temporal punishment as to free a penitent from all obligation of doing penance for his sins?

No; for the obligation of doing penance for sin and leading a penitential life is an indispensable duty. Hence the Church usually enjoins penitential works, in order for the obtaining of indulgences. And the opinion of the learned Cardinal Cajetan and others is highly probable, that one condition for attaining to the benefit of an indulgence, in the release of the punishment of the next life, is a disposition to do penance in this life; for the treasure of the Church, out of which indulgences are granted, is intended by our great master for the relief of the indigent; yet not so as to encourage the lazy, who refuse to labor at all for themselves.

248. Are you then of opinion, that a Christian receives no farther benefit by an indulgence than he would do by the penitential works which he performs for the obtaining of that indulgence?

I am far from being of that opinion: for, according to that way of thinking, no benefit would be reaped from the indulgence, but only from the works performed for the obtaining of it. Whereas the Church of God has declared, in the Council of Trent, that "indulgences are very wholesome to Christian people."[252] But what many divines maintain is that regularly speaking, there is required though not an equality, yet some proportion at least between the works to be done for the obtaining of an indulgence, and the indulgence itself; and this I believe to be true.[253]

[252] Council of Trent, Session 25
[253] Cf. De Soto, *4tum. Dist.* 21. Q. 2. *Art.* 2, and Francis Sylvius in *Supplem.* 25, *Art.* 2. *Quæsito* 2. *Conclus.* 5.

249. What is meant by the treasure of the Church, out of which indulgences are said to be granted?

The treasure of the Church, according to divines, are the merits and satisfaction of Christ and his saints, out of which the Church, when she grants an indulgence to her children, offers to God an equivalent for the punishment which was due to the divine justice. For the merits and satisfaction of Christ are of infinite value, and never to be exhausted, and are the source of all our good; and the merits and satisfactions of the saints, as they have their value from Christ and through him are accepted by the Father, so by the communion which all the members of Christ's mystical body have one with another, are applicable to the faithful upon earth.

250. What is meant by a plenary indulgence?

That which, when duly obtained, releases the whole punishment that remained due upon account of past sins.

251. What is meant by an indulgence of seven years, or of forty days?

By an indulgence of so many years or days is meant the remission of the penance of so many years or days, and consequently of the punishment corresponding to the sins, which, by the canons of the Church, would have required so many years or days of penance.[254] And thus, if it be true that there ever were any grants of indulgences of a thousand years or more, they are to be understood with relation to the punishment corresponding to the sins, which according to the penitential canons would have required a thousand or more years of penance. For since, by these canons, seven or ten years of penance were usually assigned for one mortal sin of lust, perjury, etc., it follows, that habitual sinners, according to the rigor of the canons, must have been liable to great numbers of years of penance, and per-

---

[254] Cf. Bellarmine, *On Indulgences*, Bk. 1, Ch. 9

haps some thousands of years. And though they could not be expected to live so long as to fulfil this penance; yet, as by their sins they had incurred a debt of punishment proportionable to so long a time of penance, these indulgences, of so many years, if ever granted (which some call in question), were designed to release them from this debt.

252. What is the meaning of indulgences for the dead?
They are not granted by way of absolution, since the pastors of the Church have not that jurisdiction over the dead: but they are only available to the faithful departed by way of suffrage, or spiritual succor applied to their souls out of the treasure of the Church.

253. What is the meaning of a jubilee?
A jubilee, so called from the resemblance it bears with the jubilee year in the old law (which was a year of remission, in which bondsmen were restored to liberty and every one returned to his possessions[255]), is a plenary indulgence granted every twenty-fifth year, as also upon other extraordinary occasions, to such as being truly penitent, shall worthily receive the Blessed Sacrament and perform the other conditions of fasting, alms, and prayer, usually prescribed at such times.

254. What then is the difference betwixt a jubilee and any other plenary indulgence?
A jubilee is more solemn, and accompanied with certain privileges, not usually granted upon other occasions, with regard to the being absolved by any approved confessor from all excommunications and other reserved cases, and having vows exchanged into the performance of other works of piety. To which we may add, that as a jubilee is extended to the whole

[255] Cf. Lv 25, 27

Church, which at that time joins as it were in a body in offering a holy violence to heaven by prayers and penitential works; and as the cause for granting an indulgence at such times is usually more evident, and more or greater works of piety are prescribed for the obtaining it, the indulgence of consequence is likely to be much more certain and secure.

255. What are the fruits which usually are seen amongst Catholics at the time of a jubilee?
As at that time the Church most pressingly invites all sinners to return to God with their whole hearts, and encourages them by setting open her spiritual treasure in their favor, so the most usual effects of a jubilee are the conversions of great numbers of sinners, and the multiplying of all sorts of good works amongst the faithful. So far it is from being true that indulgences are an encouragement to sin, or an occasion of a neglect of good works, as our adversaries unjustly object.

Chapter 11

Of the Sacrament of Extreme Unction

256. What do you mean by extreme unction?
I mean the anointing of the sick, prescribed St. James: "Is any one sick among you, let him call for the priests of the church, and let them pray over him, anointing him with oil in the name of the Lord: and the prayer of faith shall save the sick man, and the Lord shall ease him; and if he be in sins, they shall be forgiven him."[256]

---

[256] Jas 5:14-15

257. How do you prove that this anointing of the sick is a sacrament?

Because it is an outward sign of an inward grace, or a divine ordinance to which is annexed a promise of grace in God's holy word. The anointing, together with the prayers that accompany it, are the outward sign; the ordinance of God is found in the words of St. James above quoted; the inward grace is promised in the same place, "The prayer of faith shall save the sick man . . . and if he be in sins, they shall be forgiven him."[257]

258. How do you prove that this ordinance was designed for all ages, and not only for the time of the apostles?

Because the words of the scripture in which this ordinance is contained are no way limited to the apostles' time, no more than the words of the ordinance of baptism,[258] and because the Church of God, the best interpreter of his word and ordinances, has practiced it in all ages.

259. To what kind of people is the sacrament of extreme unction to be administered?

To those who, after having come to the use of reason, are in danger of death by sickness; but not to children under the age of reason, nor persons sentenced to death, etc.

260. Can the same person receive the sacrament of extreme unction more than once?

Yes, but not in the same illness; except it should be of long continuance or that the state of the sick man should be changed so as to recover out of the danger, and then fall into the like case again.

---

[257] Cf. Jas 5:15
[258] Cf. Mt 28:19-20

261. What are the effects and fruits of the sacrament of extreme unction?

First, it remits sins, at least such as are venial; for mortal or deadly sins must be remitted before receiving extreme unction, by the sacrament of penance and confession. Second, it heals the soul of her infirmity and weakness, and a certain propension to sin contracted by former sins, which are apt to remain in the soul as the unhappy relics of sin; and it helps to remove something of the debt of punishment due to past sins. Third, it imparts strength to the soul, to bear more easily the illness of the body, and arms her against the attempts of her spiritual enemies. Fourth, if it be expedient for the good of the soul, it often restores the health of the body.

262. What kind of oil is that which is made use of in the sacrament of extreme unction?

Oil of olives, solemnly blessed by the bishop every year on Maundy-Thursday.

263. What is the form and manner of administering this sacrament?

First, the priest, having instructed and disposed the sick person for this sacrament, recites, if the time permits, certain prayers prescribed in the *Ritual*, to beg God's blessing upon the sick, and that his holy angels may defend them that dwell in that habitation from all evil. Second is said the confiteor, or general form of confession and absolution; and the priest exhorts all present to join in prayer for the person that is sick; and if opportunity permit, according to the quality or number of persons there present, to recite the seven penitential psalms with the litanies, or other prayers, upon this occasion. Third, the priest, making three times the sign of the cross upon the sick person, at the name of the Blessed Trinity, says, "In the name of the Father, and of the Son, and of the Holy Ghost, may all power of the devil be extinguished in thee, by the laying on of our hands,

and by the invocation of all the holy angels, archangels, patriarchs, prophets, apostles, martyrs, confessors, virgins, and all
the saints. Amen." Fourth, dipping his thumb in the holy oil, he
anoints the sick person in the form of the cross, upon the eyes,
ears, nose, mouth, hands, and feet; at each anointing making
use of this form of prayer: "Through this holy unction, and his
own most tender mercy, may the Lord pardon thee whatever
sins thou hast committed by the sight. Amen." And so of the
hearing, and the rest, adapting the form to the several senses.
Fifth, after this the priest goes on:

Lord have mercy on us. Christ have mercy on us. Lord have
mercy on us. Our Father, etc. And lead us not into temptation.

R: But deliver us from evil.
V: Save thy servant.
R: Trusting in thee, O my God.
V: Send him, O Lord, help from thy sanctuary.
R: And do thou defend him from Sion.
V: Be to him, O Lord, a tower of strength.
R: From the face of the enemy.
V: Let not the enemy have any power over him.
R: Nor the son of iniquity be able to hurt him.
V: Lord, hear my prayer.
R: And let my cry come unto thee.
V: The Lord be with you.
R: And with thy spirit.

Let us pray. O Lord God, who has said by thy apostle James:
Is any one sick among you? Let him call for the priests of
the Church, and let them pray over him, anointing him
with oil in the name of the Lord; and the prayer of faith
shall save the sick, and the Lord shall ease him; and if he
be in sins they shall be remitted to him: heal we beseech

thee, O our Redeemer, by the grace of the Holy Ghost, the maladies of this sick man, cure his wounds, and forgive him his sins; drive away from him all pains of mind and body, and mercifully restore unto him perfect health, both as to the interior and exterior, that being recovered by thy mercy, he may return to his former duties, who livest and reignest, etc. Amen.

Let us pray. Look down, we beseech thee, O Lord, on thy servant N. fainting under the infirmity of his body, and refresh a soul which thou hast created: that he, being improved by thy chastisements may be saved by thy medicine. Through Christ our Lord. Amen.

Let us pray. O holy Lord, Almighty Father, everlasting God, who, by imparting the grace of thy benediction to sick bodies, preserve, according to the multitude of thy mercies, the work of thy hands; favorably attend to the invocation of thy name, and deliver thy servant from his illness, and restoring him to health, raise him up by thy right hand, strengthen him by thy virtue, defend him by thy power, and restore him with all desired prosperity to thy holy Church. Through Christ our Lord. Amen.

As to what belongs to the order of the visitation of the sick, and the prayers and devotions proper upon that occasion, as also the manner of assisting those that are dying, consult the *Roman Ritual*; out of which I shall present you with the following form of the recommendation of a departing soul.

Chapter 12

The Order of Recommending a Departing Soul

264. **What is the form or order of the recommendation of a soul to God in its last passage?**
First, there is a short litany recited, adapted to that occasion; then the following prayers:

> Go forth, O Christian soul, from this world, in the name of God the Father Almighty, who created thee; in the name of Jesus Christ the Son of the living God, who suffered for thee; in the name of the Holy Ghost, who has been poured forth upon thee; in the name of the angels and the archangels; in the name of the thrones and dominations: in the name of the principalities and powers; in the name of the cherubim and seraphim; in the name of the patriarchs and prophets; in the name of the holy apostles and evangelists; in the name of the holy martyrs and confessors; in the name of the holy monks and hermits; in the name of the holy virgins, and of all the saints of God: Let thy place be this day in peace, and thy abode in the holy Sion. Through Christ our Lord. Amen.

> O God most merciful, O God most clement, O God, who, according to the multitude of thy tender mercies, blottest out the sins of the penitent, and graciously remittest the guilt of their past offences; mercifully regard this thy servant N. and vouchsafe to hear him, who with the whole confession of his heart begs for the remission of all his sins. Renew, O most merciful Father, whatever has been corrupted in him through human frailty, or violated through

the deceit of the enemy: and associate him as a member of redemption to the unity of the body of the Church. Have compassion, Lord, on his sighs; have compassion on his tears, and admit him, who has no hope but in thy mercy, to the sacrament of thy reconciliation. Through Christ our Lord. Amen.

I recommend thee, dear brother, to the Almighty God, and commit thee to his care, whose creature thou art; that when thou shalt have paid the debt of all mankind by death, thou mayest return to thy Maker, who formed thee of the dirt of the earth. When thy soul therefore shall depart from the body, let the resplendent multitude of the angels meet thee; let the court of apostles come unto thee; let the triumphant army of the martyrs, clad in their white robes, conduct thee; let the glorious company of illustrious confessors encompass thee; let the choir of joyful virgins receive thee; and mayest thou meet with a blessed repose in the bosom of the patriarchs: Let Christ Jesus appear to thee with a mild and cheerful countenance, and order thee a place amongst those that are to stand before him forever.

Mayest thou never know the horror of darkness, the crackling of flames or racking torments. May the most wicked enemy, with all his evil spirits, be forced to give way: may he tremble at thy approach in the company of angels, and fly away into the vast chaos of eternal night. Let God arise, and his enemies be dispersed: and let them that hate him fly before his face: let them, like smoke, come to nothing, and as wax that melts before the fire, so let sinners perish in the sight of God, but may the just feast and rejoice in his sight. Let then all the legions of hell be confounded and put to shame, and may none of the ministers of Satan dare to stop thee in thy way.

May Christ deliver thee from torments, who was crucified for thee. May Christ deliver thee from eternal death, who vouchsafed to die for thee. May Christ the Son of God place thee in the ever-pleasant greens of his paradise, and may he, the true shepherd, number thee amongst his sheep. May he absolve thee from all thy sins, and place thee at his right hand in the lot of his elect. Mayest thou see thy Redeemer face to face, and standing always in his presence, behold with happy eyes the most clear truth. Mayest thou be placed amongst the companies of the blessed, and enjoy the sweetness of the contemplation of thy God, forever. Amen.

Receive thy servant, O Lord, into the place of salvation, which he hopes for from thy mercy. **R:** Amen.

Deliver, O Lord, the soul of thy servant from all the perils of hell, from pains and all tribulations. **R:** Amen.

Deliver, O Lord, the soul of thy servant, as thou delivered Enoch and Elias from the common death of the world. **R:** Amen.

Deliver, O Lord, the soul of thy servant, as thou delivered Noah from the flood. **R:** Amen.

Deliver, O Lord, the soul of thy servant, as thou delivered Abraham from Ur of the Chaldeans. **R:** Amen.

Deliver, O Lord, the soul of thy servant, as thou delivered Job from his sufferings. **R:** Amen.

Deliver, O Lord, the soul of thy servant, as thou delivered Isaac from being sacrificed by the hand of his father Abraham. **R:** Amen.

Deliver, O Lord, the soul of thy servant, as thou delivered Lot from Sodom, and the flames of fire. **R:** Amen.

Deliver, O Lord, the soul of thy servant, as thou delivered Moses from the hands of Pharaoh, King of Egypt. **R:** Amen.

Deliver, O Lord, the soul of thy servant, as thou delivered Daniel from the lion's den. **R**: Amen.

Deliver, O Lord, the soul of thy servant, as thou delivered the three children from the fiery furnace, and from the hands of a wicked king. **R**: Amen.

Deliver, O Lord, the soul of thy servant, as thou delivered Susannah from her false accusers. **R**: Amen.

Deliver, O Lord, the soul of thy servant, as thou delivered David from the hands of King Saul and from the hands of Goliath. **R**: Amen.

Deliver, O Lord, the soul of thy servant, as thou delivered Peter and Paul out of prison. **R**: Amen.

And as thou delivered the most blessed virgin and martyr St. Thecla from three most dreadful torments, so vouchsafe to deliver the soul of this thy servant, and make it rejoice with thee in the happiness of heaven. **R**: Amen.

We commend to thee, O Lord, the soul of thy servant N. And we beseech thee, O Lord Jesus Christ, the Savior of the world, that thou wouldst not refuse to admit into the bosom of thy patriarchs, a soul for which, in thy mercy, thou wast pleased to come down upon earth. Own him for thy creature, not made by any strange gods, but by thee the only living and true God; for there is no other God but thee, and none that can equal thy works. Let his soul rejoice in thy presence, and remember not his former iniquities and excesses, the unhappy effects of passion or evil concupiscence; for although he has sinned he has not renounced the Father, Son, or Holy Ghost; but believed, and had a zeal for God, and faithfully worshipped him who made all things.

Remember not, O Lord, we beseech thee, the sins of his youth, and his ignorance; but according to thy great mercy, be mindful of him in thy heavenly glory. May the heavens be opened to him, and may the angels rejoice with him.

Receive, O Lord, thy servant into thy kingdom. Let St. Michael the archangel of God conduct him, who is the chief of the heavenly host. Let the holy angels of God come to meet him, and carry him to the city of the heavenly Jerusalem. May St. Peter the apostle receive him, to whom God has given the keys of the kingdom of heaven. May St. Paul the apostle assist him, who was a vessel of election. May St. John the chosen apostle of God intercede for him, to whom were revealed the secrets of heaven. May all the holy apostles pray for him, to whom our Lord gave the power of binding and loosing. May all the saints and elect of God intercede for him, who in this world had suffered torments for the name of Christ; that he, being delivered from the bonds of the flesh, may deserve to be admitted into the glory of the kingdom of heaven: by the bounty of our Lord Jesus Christ, who with the Father and the Holy Ghost liveth and reigneth forever and ever. Amen.

After which, if the sick person still continues to labor in his agony, it may be proper, as the *Ritual* prescribes, to continue reciting other psalms and prayers adapted to those circumstances.

265. What is the meaning of the lighting of a blessed candle and keeping it burning during a person's agony?

This light represents the light of faith in which a Christian dies, and the light of glory which he looks for. Besides, these candles are blessed by the Church, with a solemn prayer to God, to chase away the devils from those places where they shall be lighted.

266. What is the form of blessing candles?

The *Ritual* prescribes the following prayer:

V: Our help is in the name of the Lord.

R: Who made heaven and earth.

Let us pray. O Lord Jesus Christ, Son of the living God, bless + by our prayers these candles; pour forth upon them by the virtue of the holy + cross thy heavenly benediction, who hast given them to mankind to chase away darkness; and may they receive such a blessing, by the sign of the holy + cross, that in what place soever they shall be lighted or set up, the rulers of darkness, with all their ministers may depart, and trembling fly away from those dwellings; nor presume any more to disturb or molest those that serve thee, the Almighty God, who livest and reignest forever and ever. Amen.

267. What is the meaning of tolling the passing-bell, when a person is expiring?
To admonish the faithful to pray for him, that God may grant him a happy passage.

Chapter 13

Of the Office for the Burial of the Dead

268. What is the manner and order of burying the dead in the Catholic Church?
The pastor or parish priest, accompanied by his clerics, goes to the house of the deceased, and having sprinkled the body or coffin with holy water, recites the anthem, "If thou shalt observe iniquities, O Lord, O Lord who shall sustain it?" with Psalm 129, *De profundis*, "From the depths, I have cried," etc., in the end of which he says, "Eternal rest give to him, O Lord."

R: "And let perpetual light shine upon him." Then he repeats the anthem, "If thou shalt observe iniquities," etc.

After this, the body is carried to the church, the clergy going before, two and two, after the manner of a procession, and singing Psalm 50, *Miserere*, "Have mercy on me, O God, according to thy great mercy," etc., and the people following the corpse and praying in silence for the deceased. When they are come to the church, the corpse is set down in the middle of the church, with the feet towards the altar (except if the deceased was a priest, in which case the head is to be towards the altar), and wax tapers are lighted and set up around the coffin. Then, if time and opportunity permit, is recited the dirge, that is, the office of the matins and lauds for the dead, followed by a Solemn Mass for the soul of the deceased, according to the most ancient custom of the universal Church. The dirge and Mass being finished, the priest standing at the head of the deceased, begins the office of the burial as follows:

Enter not into judgment with thy servant, O Lord, for no man shall be justified in thy sight, except thou vouchsafe to grant him the remission of all his sins. Let not therefore, we beseech thee, the sentence of thy judgment fall upon him, whom the true supplication of Christian faith recommendeth to thee: but, by the assistance of thy grace, let him escape the judgment of thy vengeance, who, whilst he was living, was marked with the sign of the Holy Trinity: who livest and reignest forever and ever. Amen.

Then the choir sings the following responsory:

Deliver me, O Lord, from eternal death, at that dreadful day, when the heavens and earth shall be moved, when thou shalt come to judge the world by fire. V: I am struck with trembling, and I fear, against the day of account, and of the wrath to come; when the heavens and earth shall be moved. V: That day is a day of wrath, of calamity and misery, a great and most bitter day, when thou shalt come to judge the world by fire. V: Eternal rest give to him, O Lord, and let perpetual light shine upon him. Deliver me, O Lord, etc. as before till the verse, "I am struck," etc. Lord have mercy on us. Christ have mercy on us. Lord have mercy on us. Our Father, etc.

Here the priest puts incense in the thurible, and then going around the coffin, sprinkles it with holy water, and afterwards incenses the body, and then concludes the Lord's Prayer.

V: Lead us not into temptation.
R: But deliver us from evil.
V: From the gate of hell.
R: Deliver his soul, O Lord.
V: Let him rest in peace.
R: Amen.
V: O Lord hear my prayer.
R: And let my cry come to thee.
V: The Lord be with you.
R: And with thy spirit.

Let us pray. O God, whose property is always to show mercy and to spare, we humbly beseech thee for the soul of thy servant N. which thou hast this day commanded to depart out of this world, that thou wouldst not deliver it up into the hands of the enemy, nor put it out of thy memory forever, but that thou wouldst order it to be received by the holy angels, and conducted to paradise, its true country: that since it has believed and hoped in thee, it may not suffer the pains of hell, but take possession of everlasting joys, through Christ our Lord. Amen.

After this, whilst the body is carried towards the place of its interment, is sung or said the following anthem:

> May the angels conduct thee into paradise, may the martyrs receive thee at thy coming, and bring thee to the holy city of Jerusalem, may the choir of angels receive thee, and mayest thou have eternal rest with Lazarus, who was formerly poor.

When they are come to the grave, if it has not been blessed before, the priest blesses it by the following prayer, which is the same that we make use of in this kingdom in blessing the mould or earth which we put in the coffin with the corpse, in the private burial office:

> O God, by whose tender mercy the souls of the faithful find rest, vouchsafe to bless this tomb, and depute thy holy angel to guard it, and absolve from all the bonds of sin the souls of those whose bodies are here interred, that with thy saints they may ever rejoice without end in thee. Through Christ our Lord. Amen.

Then the priest sprinkles with holy water, and afterwards incenses both the corpse of the deceased and the grave. Then, whilst the body is put in the earth, is sung or said the following anthem, with the canticle *Benedictus*, or the song of Zacharias.[259]

> P: I am the resurrection and the life; he that believeth in me although he be dead, shall live; and everyone that liveth, and believeth in me, shall not die forever.[260]

Or else (as it is the custom in many places), when the body is

[259] Cf. Lk 1:68-79
[260] Jn 11:25

put in the earth, the priest, with the assistants, recites the penitential Psalm, *Miserere*. Then the priest says:

Lord have mercy on us. Christ have mercy on us. Lord have mercy on us. Our Father, etc. (Here he sprinkles the body with holy water.)

V: And lead us not into temptation.
R: But deliver us from evil.
V: From the gate of hell.
R: Deliver his soul, O Lord.
V: Let him rest in peace.
R: Amen.
V: O Lord hear my prayer.
R: And let my cry come unto thee.
V: The Lord be with you.
R: And with thy spirit.

Let us pray. Grant, O Lord, this mercy to thy servant deceased, that he (or she) may not receive a return of punishment for his (or her) deeds, who in his (or her) desires has held fast by thy will; that as here true faith has joined him (or her) to the company of thy faithful, so thy mercy there may associate him (or her) to the choirs of angels. Through Christ our Lord. Amen.

V: Eternal rest give to him, O Lord.
R: And let perpetual light shine upon him.
V: Let him rest in peace.
R: Amen.
May his soul, and the souls of all the faithful departed, through the mercy of God, rest in peace.

Then the priest, returning from the grave, recites the Psalm, *De profundis*, with the anthem, "If thou shalt observe iniquities, O Lord, O Lord who shall sustain it?"

Chapter 14

Of Prayers for the Dead, and of Purgatory

269. What is the meaning of prayers for the dead?
Praying for the dead is a practice as ancient as Christianity, received by tradition from the apostles, as appears by the most certain monuments of antiquity, and observed by the synagogue or church of God in the old testament, as appears from 2 Machabees 12, written long before Christ's time, and followed by the Jews to this day. A practice grounded upon Christian charity, which teaches us to pray for all that are in necessity, and to implore God's mercy for all that are capable of mercy; which we have reason to be convinced is the case of many of our deceased brethren, and therefore we pray for them.

270. How do you prove that the practice of praying for the dead is as ancient as Christianity?
From Tertullian, in his book of the *Soldier's Crown*,[261] written about a hundred years after the death of the apostles; where he reckons the oblations for the dead upon their anniversary days amongst the immemorial traditions observed by all Christians: and in his book *De Monogamia* where he affirms it to be the duty of a Christian widow to pray for the soul of her husband and to beg a refreshment for him, and to keep his

---

[261] Cf. Tertullian, *De Corona*, Ch. 3

anniversaries.[262] Hence, St. John Chrysostom tells us that it was
ordained by the apostles that the dead should be commemorated in the sacred mysteries,[263] and St. Augustine tells us that
it was a practice received from the fathers and observed by the
universal Church.[264] And it appears from St. Epiphanius that
Arius was ranked amongst the heretics by the Church in the
fourth century, for denying that the prayers of the living did
the dead any good.[265]

271. Is it any argument, in favor of prayers for the dead, that it was practiced by Judas Machabaeus and by the Jews before the coming of Christ?

Yes, a very great argument; First, because this practice is expressly approved in Chapter 12 of the second book of Machabees; which books, by many councils and fathers, are ranked
amongst the divine scriptures. Second, because the Jews in those
days were undoubtedly the people of God. Third, because as
Dr. Taylor writes:

We find by the history of the Machabees that the Jews did pray
and make offerings for the dead (which also appears by other
testimonies, and by their form of prayers still extant which
they used in the captivity). Now it is very considerable, that
since our blessed Savior did reprove all the evil doctrines and
traditions of the Scribes and Pharisees, and did argue concerning the dead and the resurrection against the Sadducees, yet
he spake no word against this public practice, but left it as he
found it; which he who came to declare to us the will of his

[262] Cf. Tertullian, *On Monogamy*, Ch. 10. See also Cyprian, *Epistle* 66; Arnobius, *Against the Heathen*, Bk. 4; Eusebius, *Life of Constantine*, Bk. 4, Ch. 71; Cyril of Jerusalem, *Catechetical Lecture 23*; Gregory Nazianzen, *Oration 10*.
[263] Cf. Chrysostom, *Homily 3 on Philippians*
[264] Cf. Augustine, *Sermon 32 de Verbis Apostoli*, Sec. 2
[265] Cf. Epiphanius, *Haeresi 75*

Father, would not have done, if it had not been innocent, pious and full of charity.[266]

272. But what reason is there to believe that our prayers can be of any service to the dead?

The same reason as there is to believe that our prayers are of service to the living; for whether we consult the scripture or primitive tradition, with relation to the promises or encouragements given in favor of our prayers, we shall nowhere find the dead excepted from the benefit of them; and the perpetual practice of the Church of God, which is the best interpreter of the scripture, has from the very beginning ever authorized prayers for the dead, as believing such prayers beneficial to them.

273. But are not they that have passed this mortal life arrived to an unchangeable state of happiness or misery, so that they either want not our prayers, or cannot he bettered by them?

Some there are, though I fear but few, that have before their death so fully cleared up all accounts with the Divine Majesty, and washed away all their stains in the blood of the Lamb, as to go straight to heaven after death; and such as those stand not in need of our prayers. Others there are, and their number is very great, who die in the guilt of deadly sin, and such as these go straight to hell, like the rich glutton in the gospel,[267] and therefore cannot be bettered by our prayers. But, besides these two kinds, there are many Christians, who, when they die, are neither so perfectly pure and clean as to be exempt from the least spot or stain, nor yet so unhappy as to die under the guilt of unrepented deadly sin. Now such as these the Church believes to be, for a time, in a middle state, which we call purgatory; and these are they who are capable of receiving benefit by our

[266] Jeremy Taylor, *A Discourse of the Liberty of Prophesying* (London: Royston, 1647), 256.
[267] Cf. Lk 16:19-31

prayers. For, though we pray for all that die in the communion of the Church, because we don't certainly know the particular state in which each one dies, yet we are sensible that our prayers are available for those only that are in this middle state.

274. But what grounds have you to believe that there is any such thing as a purgatory, or middle state of souls?

We have the strongest grounds imaginable from all kind of arguments; from scripture, from perpetual tradition, from the authority and declaration of the Church of God, and from reason.

275. What grounds have you for purgatory from scripture?

First, because the scripture teaches us in many places that it is the fixed rule of God's justice "to render to every man according to his works";[268] so that according to the works which each man has done in the time of his mortal life, and according to the state in which he is found at the moment of his departure out of this life, he shall certainly receive reward or punishment from God. Hence it evidently follows, that as by this rule of God's justice, they that die in great and deadly sins, not cancelled by repentance, will be eternally punished in hell; so by the same rule, they that die in lesser or venial sins (which is certainly the case of a great many), will be punished somewhere for a time, till God's justice be satisfied, and this is what we call purgatory.

Second, because the scripture assures us that there shall in no wise enter into the heavenly Jerusalem anything that defileth, or that is defiled.[269] So that if the soul is found to have the least spot or stain at the time of her departure out of this life, she cannot in that condition go straight to heaven. Now how few are there that depart this life perfectly pure from the

---

[268] Ps 61:13; Mt 16:27; Rom 2:6; Apoc 22:12
[269] Cf. Apoc 21:27

dregs and stains to which we are ever subject in this state of mortality? And yet God forbid that every little spot or stain should condemn the soul to the everlasting torments of hell. Therefore, there must be a middle place for such souls as die under these lesser stains.

Third, because the scripture assures us that we are to render an account hereafter to the great Judge, even for every idle word that we have spoken;[270] and, consequently, every idle word, not cancelled here by repentance, is liable to be punished by God's justice hereafter. Now no one can think that God will condemn a soul to hell for every idle word; therefore there must be another place of punishment for those that die guilty of these little transgressions.

Fourth, because St. Paul informs us that every man's work shall be made manifest by a fiery trial; and that they who have built upon the foundation (which is Christ) wood, hay, and stubble (that is, whose works have been very imperfect and defective, though not to the degree of losing Christ), shall suffer loss; but themselves shall be saved, "yet so as by fire";[271] which place cannot be well explained any otherwise than of the fire of purgatory.

Fifth, because our Lord tells us that whosoever speaketh against the Holy Ghost, it shall not be forgiven him, "neither in this world, neither in the world to come."[272] Where our Lord (who could not speak anything absurd or out of the way) would never have mentioned forgiveness in the world to come, if sins not forgiven in this world could never be forgiven in the world to come. Now if there may be forgiveness of any sin whatsoever in the world to come, there must be a middle place or purgatory; for no sin can enter heaven to be forgiven there, and in hell there is no forgiveness.

[270] Cf. Mt 12:36
[271] Cf. 1 Cor 3:13-15
[272] Mt 12:32

Add to these texts of scripture the prison mentioned, out of which a man shall not come till he has paid the uttermost farthing;[273] and the spirits in prison, to which our Savior is said to have gone to preach.[274]

276. What grounds have you for purgatory from perpetual tradition?

Because, as we have seen already, the Jewish church, long before our Savior's coming, and the Christian Church, from the very beginning, have offered prayers and sacrifice for the repose and relief of the faithful departed; as appears from innumerable testimonies of the fathers, and from the most ancient liturgies of all Christian Churches and nations, Romans, Greeks, Syrians, Armenians, Nestorians, Egyptians, Ethiopians, Indians, Mosarabes, etc. Which consent, so ancient and so universal, of all ages and of all nations before the pretended Reformation, is a most convincing argument that this practice came by tradition from the apostles; and consequently that the belief of a purgatory is an apostolic tradition; for what sense could there be in praying for the repose and relief of the souls of the faithful departed, if there were no middle place, but all went straight to heaven or hell?

277. What grounds have you for the belief of a purgatory from the authority of the Church?

Because the Church of Christ has declared that there is a purgatory, as well by condemning of old Arius for a heretic, for denying that the prayers of the living did the dead any service, as also by the express definitions of her general councils. Now the scripture most evidently teaches us in many places, that we are to hear and to obey the Church, and that Christ and the Holy Ghost will be always with the Church to guide her into

[273] Cf. Mt 5:26
[274] Cf. 1 Pt 3:18-20

all truth, and that the gates of hell shall not prevail against her. So that what the Church has thus declared can be no error; but must needs be a most certain truth.

278. What grounds have you for the belief of a purgatory from reason?

Because reason teaches these two things; First, that every sin, be it never so small, is an offence of God and consequently deserves punishment from the justice of God: and therefore that every person that dies under the guilt of any such offence unrepented, must expect to be punished by the justice of God. Second, that there are some sins in which a person may chance to die, that are so small, either through the levity of the matter or for want of a full deliberation in the act, as not to deserve everlasting punishments. From whence it plainly follows, that besides the place of everlasting punishments, which we call hell, there must be also a place of temporal punishment for such as die in those lesser offences, and this we call purgatory.

279. But does not the blood of Christ sufficiently purge us from all our sins, without any other purgatory?

The blood of Christ purges none that are come to the use of reason from any sin without repentance; and therefore such sins as have not been here recalled by repentance, must be punished hereafter, according to the established rule of divine justice; either in hell, if the sins be mortal, or if venial, in purgatory.

280. Do you then think that any repentance can be available after death?

No; but God's justice must take place after death, which will render to every man according to his works. So that we don't believe that the repentance of the souls that are in purgatory, or anything else that they can then do, can cancel their sins; but they must suffer for them till God's justice be satisfied.

281. Are they not then capable of relief in that state?

Yes they are, but not from anything that they can then do for themselves, but from the prayers, alms, and other suffrages offered to God for them by the faithful upon earth, which God in his mercy is pleased to accept by reason of that communion which we have with them, by being fellow members of the same body of the Church, under the same head, which is Christ Jesus.

282. But what do you say to that text of scripture, "If the tree fall toward the south, or toward the north, in the place where the tree falleth, there it shall lie"?[275]

I say that it is no way evident that this text has relation to the state of the soul after death; but if it be so understood as to have relation to the soul, it makes nothing against purgatory, because it only proves what no Catholic denies: viz. that when once a soul is come to the south or to the north, that is to heaven or to hell, its state is unchangeable.

283. But does not the scripture promise rest after death to such "as die in the Lord"?[276]

Yes it does, but then we are to understand that those are said to die in the Lord, who die for the Lord by martyrdom; or at least those who, at the time of their death, are so happy as to have no debts nor stains to interpose between them and the Lord. As for others who die but imperfectly in the Lord, they shall rest indeed from the labors of this world; but as their works that follow them are imperfect, they must expect to receive from the Lord according to their works.

---

[275] Eccles 11:3
[276] Apoc 14:13

284. Christ said to the thief upon the cross, "this day thou shalt be with me in paradise";[277] what appearance then is there that anyone dying in God's grace should go to purgatory?

The case of this penitent thief, to whom Christ was pleased to give a full discharge at once of all his sins, was extraordinary, as his faith and confession was extraordinary; and therefore to make a general rule from this particular instance is a bad way of arguing. The more, because we have reason to be convinced that not one in a thousand dies so perfectly penitent as to be perfectly purged before death from all the dregs of sin, which was the particular grace granted to this good thief.

If you ask me what is meant by paradise in that text, and how the good thief could be with Christ that day in paradise, before our Lord had taken possession of heaven for himself and us by his resurrection and ascension; I answer that our Lord descending after death into limbo, to the holy fathers, made that place a paradise, by manifesting his glory to those happy souls; and this was the paradise into which he introduced the good thief immediately after his death.

Chapter 15

Of the Sacrament of Holy Orders

285. What do you mean by the sacrament of holy orders?

A sacrament by which the ministers of Christ are consecrated to their sacred functions, and receive grace to discharge them well.

---

[277] Lk 23:43

286. How do you prove that holy orders are a sacrament?

Because they are a visible sign of invisible grace, and that by divine institution, or by the ordinance of Christ, which alone can annex the gift of grace to any outward rite or ceremony. The outward and visible sign is found in the imposition or laying on of the bishop's hands and prayer: after which sort we find the seven deacons ordained,[278] and St. Paul and St. Barnabas.[279] The invisible grace conferred by this imposition of hands is attested, "Stir up the grace of God, which is in thee by the imposition of my hands";[280] and the divine institution of holy orders is gathered as well from the use of the apostles, and the perpetual tradition of the Church, as from those texts in which Christ bequeathed the whole power of the priesthood to his disciples and to their successors: "Do this in remembrance of me";[281] and, "Receive ye the Holy Ghost: whosesoever sins ye remit, they are remitted unto them; and whosesoever sins ye retain, they are retained."[282]

287. By what steps do persons ascend in the Catholic Church to the order of priesthood?

First, they must be initiated by the clerical tonsure, which is not properly an order, but only a preparation for orders. The bishop cuts off the extremities of their hair, to signify their renouncing the world and its vanities; and he revests them with a surplice, and so receives them into the clergy; they making at the same time a solemn profession of taking the Lord for their inheritance and portion forever.

Second, they must pass through the minor or lesser orders, which have been received from the primitive Church: viz. the

---

[278] Cf. Acts 6:6
[279] Cf. Acts 13:3
[280] 2 Tm 1:6
[281] Lk 22:19
[282] Jn 20:22-23

orders of porter or doorkeeper of the Church; lector, or reader of the lessons in the divine office; exorcist, whose function is to read the exorcisms and prayers of the Church over those who are possessed or obsessed by the devil; and acolyte, whose function is to serve at Mass, light the candles in the church, etc. All these are ordained by receiving from the bishop the instruments or books belonging to their respective offices, and by solemn prayers prescribed in the *Pontifical*. Third, from the minor orders they are promoted to the order of subdeacon, which is the first of those that are called holy. In the conferring this order, the bishop puts the candidates in mind, that hitherto they have had their liberty to quit the ecclesiastical calling and engage themselves by marriage in the world; but if they will be ordained subdeacons, which he leaves to their choice, they are thereby tied forever to the service of God and his Church in the state of perpetual continence. Subdeacons also are obliged to the canonical hours of the Church office; and in the high Mass assist the deacon in his ministry.

Fourth, from the order of subdeacon they are advanced to the order of deacon, which is conferred upon them by the imposition of the bishop's hand, and by delivering to them the book of the gospels. The deacon's office is to assist the bishop or priest in the Sacrifice of the Mass, to sing and to preach the gospels, to baptize, etc.

Fifth, from the order of deacon the next assent is to the order of priest, or presbyter, above which is the order of bishops, amongst whom the chief is called the pope.

288. In what manner is the order of priesthood administered?

The person that is to be ordained is presented to the bishop by the archdeacon, desiring, in the name of the Church, that he may be promoted to priesthood, and bearing testimony of his being worthy of that office. Then the bishop publishes to the clergy and people there present the designed promotion, that if anyone has anything to allege against the person that is to be ordained, he may freely declare it. If no one appears to allege anything against him, the bishop proceeds to admonish him of the duties and functions of the priesthood, and to exhort him to a diligent discharge thereof. After which, both the bishop and the person that is to be ordained prostrate themselves in prayer, whilst the litanies are sung or said by the choir or clergy there present; which being ended, the bishop stands up, and the person that is to be ordained kneels. The bishop first, and then all the priests there present, one after another, lay both their hands on his head, which imposition of hands is immediately followed by the solemn prayers of consecration, and by revesting him with the priestly ornaments; then the Holy Ghost is invoked by the hymn, *Veni Creator*.

After which the bishop anoints the hands of the person ordained, and then delivers into his hands the chalice with the wine and water, and the paten with the bread, saying, "Receive the power to offer sacrifice to God, and celebrate Mass, as well for the living as for the dead, in the name of the Lord." Then the person ordained says Mass with the bishop, and receives the Holy Communion at his hands. At the end of the Mass the bishop again imposes his hands upon him, saying those words of Christ: "Receive the Holy Ghost: whose sins thou shalt forgive, they are forgiven them; and whose sins thou shalt retain, they are retained." After which he receives from him the promise of obedience, and gives him the kiss of peace.

Chapter 16

Of the Superiority of Bishops, and of
the Supremacy of the Pope

289. How do you prove that besides priests or presbyters, there has been always in the Church the order of bishops, superior to that of priests?

I prove it both from scripture and perpetual tradition. The new testament in several places mentions bishops,[283] and it is visible that the angels of the seven churches of Asia, mentioned in the first, second, and third chapters of Apocalypse, were the bishops of those sees, and accordingly had a jurisdiction over them. It is no less visible, from the epistles of St. Paul to Timothy and Titus, that both one and the other were bishops, with power of ordaining inferior priests; and Timothy in particular is instructed by the apostle in what manner he is to comport himself to the priests under him.[284] And as for perpetual tradition, it is evident from all kind of monuments, and from the most ancient Church history, that the Church has always been governed by bishops, and that the apostles everywhere established bishops. Thus St. Irenaeus,[285] Tertullian,[286] and other ancients assure us that Linus and Clement were ordained bishops by St. Peter and St. Paul for the See of Rome. Thus Eusebius and other ancient monuments inform us that St. Mark was the first bishop of Alexandria, and was succeeded by Anianus; that Evodius and Ignatius, disciples of the apostles, were, after St. Peter, the first bishops of Antioch; that St. James was constituted by the

[283] Cf. Phil 1:1; 1 Tm 3:2; Ti 1:7; Acts 20:28
[284] Cf. 1 Tm 5:17-19
[285] Cf. Irenaeus, *Against Heresies*, Bk. 3, Ch. 3
[286] Cf. Tertullian, *Prescription Against Heretics*

apostles the first bishop of Jerusalem, and had for successor Simeon the son of Cleophas; that St. Polycarp was made bishop of Smyrna by St. John, etc.

290. How do you prove that amongst bishops, one should be head, and have a jurisdiction over the rest?

Because Christ has so appointed, who gave that preeminence to St. Peter with respect to the rest of the apostles; as appears from Matthew 16 when, in reward of his faith and confession, he confirmed to him the name of Peter or Rock; and promised to him that upon this rock he would build his Church, and the gates of hell should not prevail against it, and that he would give him the keys of the kingdom of heaven, etc.[287] And from John 21 when our Lord, after having asked St. Peter, "Dost thou love me more than these?" three times, committed to him the charge of all his lambs and sheep without exception; that is, of his whole Church.[288] Hence, St. Matthew, reckoning the names of the twelve apostles, says, "The first, Simon, who is called Peter."[289] Now it does not appear that he could be said the first, upon any other account but by reason of his supremacy; for that he was first in age is more than appears, and that he was first in calling is not true, for St. Andrew came to Christ before Peter, and was probably the elder brother. And certain it is, that the evangelists, in reckoning up the names of the apostles upon several occasions, neither follow the order of their age nor of their calling; yet they always reckon Peter in the first place, and sometimes more clearly to intimate his preeminence, name him alone as chief or prince, as St. Mark: "Simon, and they that were with him,"[290] St. Luke: "Peter, and they that were with

[287] Cf. Mt 16:16-19
[288] Cf. Jn 21:15-17
[289] Mt 10:2
[290] Mk 1:36

him,"[291] Acts 2: "Peter standing up with the eleven,"[292] Acts 5: "Peter and the apostles answered and said,"[293] etc., where the protestant translation has foisted in the word "*other* apostles," as clearly seeing that the former expression (which is that of the original) too clearly expressed St. Peter's being something more than the rest.

It is also worth observing that our Lord was pleased to teach the people out of Peter's ship,[294] that he ordered the same tribute to be paid for himself and Peter,[295] that he particularly prayed for Peter, that his faith should not fail, and ordered him to confirm or strengthen his brethren,[296] etc. Hence St. Peter's supremacy is acknowledged by the perpetual tradition of the holy fathers.[297]

291. How do you prove that St. Peter was to have a successor in this office of chief bishop of the Church?

Because as Christ established his Church to remain till the end of the world,[298] so most certainly he designed that the form of government which he established in his Church should remain forever. Hence, supposing the supremacy of St. Peter, which we have proved above from scripture, it cannot be questioned but that our Lord designed that this supremacy, which he appointed

---

[291] Lk 9:32
[292] Acts 2:14
[293] Acts 5:29
[294] Cf. Lk 5:3
[295] Cf. Mt 17:26
[296] Cf. Lk 22:32
[297] Cf. Origen, *Commentary on Romans* 6, *Homily 5 on Exodus*; Basil, *Preface On the Judgment of God*; Cyril of Jerusalem, *Second Catechesis*; Epiphanius, *Haeresi 51, Haeresi 54, Anchoratus,* Sect. 6; Chrysostom, *Homily 2 on Psalm 50, Homily 54 on Matthew*; Cyril of Alexandria, *Commentary on John*, Bk. 12; Asterius, bishop of Amasæa, *Sermon on Saint Peter and Saint Paul.* Among the Latins, see Cyprian, *Epistle 69*; Optatus of Milevis, *Against the Donatists,* Bk. 2, 7; Ambrose, *Commentary on Luke,* Bk. 10; Jerome, *Against Jovinianus,* Bk. 1; Augustine, *De Baptismo,* Bk. 2, Ch. 1; Leo the Great, *Letter 14*; Gregory the Great, *L. 4, Epist. 32.*
[298] Cf. Mt 28:20

for the better government of his Church and the preserving of unity, should not die with Peter, no more than the Church (with which he promised to remain forever), but should descend, after Peter's decease, to his successors. For it is not to be imagined that Christ should appoint a chief bishop for the government of his Church and maintaining unity in the apostles' time, and design another kind of government for succeeding ages, when there was like to be so much greater danger of schism, and consequently so much greater need of one head, to preserve all in one faith and one communion.

292. But how do you prove that the pope or bishop of Rome is this successor of St. Peter?

I prove it, first, because the Church never acknowledged any other for her chief pastor: and no other does, or ever did, put in a claim to the spiritual supremacy in quality of St. Peter's successor; so that, supposing what has been proved, that Christ appointed a chief pastor for his Church, the bishop of Rome must be the man.

Second, I prove it from the continuous sense of the holy fathers and councils that have acknowledged this supremacy in the see of Rome and her bishops. See St. Ignatius, disciple of the apostles, in the beginning of his *Epistle to the Romans*, where he calls the Church of Rome the presiding Church; who calls the same the greatest and most ancient Church, founded by the two most glorious apostles Peter and Paul. And Irenaeus adds, that all sectaries are confounded by the Roman tradition: for "to this Church, by reason of its more powerful principality," says he, "it is necessary that every Church resort," or have recourse; "in which [Church] the apostolical tradition has always been preserved by those that are in every place."[299] And see St. Cyprian, in his *Epistle 54* to Pope Cornelius, where he calls the

[299] Irenaeus, *Against Heresies*, Bk. 3, Ch. 3

see of Rome the chair of Peter, and the principal Church from which the priestly unity has its origin: *Ecclesiam principalem, unde unitas sacerdotalis exorta est.*[300]

See also St. Optatus, bishop of Milevis, in his second book *Against Parmenianus*, the Donatist bishop of Carthage, where he thus addresses himself to his adversary:

> You cannot pretend to be ignorant that Peter held first the bishop's chair in the city of Rome, in which Peter, head of all the apostles sat; in which one chair unity might be maintained by all, lest the rest of the apostles should each one claim his own separate chair. So that he is now a schismatic, and an offender, who against this single chair erects any other. In this one chair, which is the first of the properties of the Church, Peter first sat; to him succeeded Linus, to him Clement, etc. Give you now an account of the origin of your chair, you who claim to yourselves the holy Church.[301]

And St. Jerome, writing to Pope Damasus, tells him: "I am joined in communion with your holiness, that is, with the chair of Peter: upon that rock I know the Church is built: whoever eats the lamb out of this house is profane: whosoever is not in [this] ark shall perish in the deluge,"[302] etc.

And St. Augustine in his *Psalm Against the Donatists*, thus addresses himself to these schismatics: "Come brethren," says he, "if you have a mind to be ingrafted in the vine, it is a pity to see you lopped off in this manner from the stock. Reckon up the prelates in the very see of Peter; and in that order of fathers see which has succeeded which. This is the rock over which the proud gates of hell prevail not."[303] And in his *Letter 43*, he

---

[300] Cf. Cyprian, *Epistle 54*, n. 14
[301] Optatus of Milevis, *Against the Donatists*, Bk. 2., n. 2
[302] Jerome, *Letter 15*, n. 2
[303] Augustine, *Psalm Against the Donatists*

tells the Donatists that in the see of Rome the principality (or supremacy) of the apostolic Church was ever acknowledged: *Semper apostolicae cathedrae viguit principatus.*[304]

And St. Prosper in his dogmatic *Poem Against the Enemies of Grace*, calls Rome "the see of Peter, which being made to the world the head of pastoral dignity, rules by religion all that which she possesses not by her arms."[305] And to the same effect St. Leo the Great, in his first sermon upon St. Peter and St. Paul, thus addresses himself to Rome:

> These are they who have advanced thee to this glory, that being made the head of the world, by being St. Peter's see, thou hast a wider extent of religious empire than of earthly dominion. For though by thy many victories thou hast extended thy dominions far and near, by sea and land, yet that which has been subdued by the labor of thy arms is not so much as that which has been made subject to thee by Christian peace.[306]

All these fathers hitherto quoted flourished within four hundred years after the passion of Christ.

The supremacy of the bishops of Rome has also been acknowledged by many general councils: as by the General Council of Ephesus, in the sentence of deposition against Nestorius (AD 431), by the General Council of Chalcedon, in their epistle to St. Leo (AD 451), by the General Council of Constantinople, in their epistle to Pope Agatho (AD 680); not to mention the decrees of later general councils, especially Lateran IV (AD 1215), Lyons II (AD 1274), and that of Florence (AD 1439). Though as Pope Gelasius, long ago, in the Council of Rome, of seventy bishops (AD 494), has declared: "The Roman See hath not its preeminence over other Churches from any ordinances

[304] Augustine, *Letter 43*, Ch. 3
[305] Prosper, *De Ingratis, n. 40-41*
[306] Leo the Great, *Sermon 82, n.1*

of councils, but from the words of our Lord and Savior in the gospel, 'Thou art Peter, and upon this rock I will build my Church.'"[307]

293. But has the pope or bishop of Rome in every age since the days of the apostles, exercised this supremacy over other churches? Yes, most certainly. In the very age immediately after the apostles, that is, in the second century, Pope Victor threatened to excommunicate the bishops of Asia Minor for keeping Easter at an undue time;[308] and though it is probable he relented upon the remonstrances of St. Irenaeus and others, yet no one of them all charged him with usurping an authority which did not of right belong to him. In the third century, St. Cyprian wrote to Pope Stephen, desiring him to dispatch his letters into the province and to the people of Arles, by which they might be authorized to depose Marcianus the bishop of Arles, and substitute another in his place: *Dirigantur in provinciam . . . a te literae, quibus, absento Marciano alius in locum ejus substituatur.*[309]

In the fourth century, Pope Julius cited St. Athanasius, bishop of Alexandria (that is to say, the second patriarch of that Church), to his council at Rome, to answer the accusations of his adversaries; who accordingly did appear, and was there cleared.[310] The same Pope, as we learn from the historian Socrates[311] and Sozomenus,[312] about the same time restored by his authority to their respective sees (from whence they had been deposed by the Eusebians), St. Paul, bishop of Constantinople, St. Lucius, bishop of Adrianople, Marcellus, bishop of Ancyra in Galatia, and Asclepas, bishop of Gaza in Palestine.

---

[307] Gelasius, *Epistle 42*

[308] Cf. Eusebius, *Ecclesiastical History*, Bk. 5, Ch. 24

[309] Cf. Cyprian, *Epistle 66, n. 3*

[310] Cf. Athanasius, *Apologia Contra Arianos*; Theodoret, *Ecclesiastical History*, Bk. 2, Ch. 3

[311] Cf. Socrates, *Historia Ecclesiastica*, Bk. 2, Ch. 15

[312] Cf. Sozomen, *Church History*, Bk. 3, Ch. 8

And this, as Sozomenus expressly words it, because, by reason of the dignity of his see, the care of all belonged to him. In the fifth century, Pope Celestine deputed St. Cyril, Patriarch of Alexandria, to proceed as his delegate to the excommunication of Nestorius, patriarch of Constantinople.[313]

And in the same century, St. John Chrysostom and St. Flavian, both patriarchs of Constantinople, unjustly deposed by numerous councils in the East, appealed from their judgment: the one to Pope Innocent I, the other to Pope Leo the Great.[314] In the sixth century, Pope Agapetus deposed Anthymus patriarch of Constantinople; not to mention many other instances in all these centuries of the exercise of the pope's jurisdiction over other churches; and as for the following ages there is no dispute.

From all which it follows, that the protestant pretense of the pope's having received his supremacy from Phocas, the Emperor of Constantinople, who began to reign in the year 602, is a groundless fiction, like the idle tale of Pope Joan.

294. But does not our Lord intimate that amongst his disciples none should be the chief or head?[315]

No; But only that "he that is the greatest should be as the younger, and he that is chief as he that doth serve."[316] Which words, so far from denying, evidently suppose a chief; which is farther confirmed by our Lord's alleging himself for an example in the following verse, who was most certainly chief. So that what is here recommended, is not equality of jurisdiction, but humility in superiors.

[313] Cf. Council of Ephesus, Session 1
[314] Cf. Chrysostom, *Epistle to Pope Innocent*; Leo the Great, *Epistle 23*
[315] Cf. Lk 22:24-26
[316] Lk 22:26

295. But does not St. Paul say, "In nothing am I behind the very chiefest apostles, though I be nothing"?[317] Where was then St. Peter's supremacy?

It is visible that St. Paul speaks with regard to his labors, miracles, and doctrine, in which he was inferior to none; but whether St. Peter or he had a superior jurisdiction was foreign to the matter he had then in hand, and therefore no wonder that he takes no notice of it.

296. If St. Peter was head, how came St. Paul to withstand him to his face at Antioch?[318]

Because, as the apostle tells us in the same place, he was to blame, viz. in withdrawing himself from the table of the gentiles, for fear of giving offence to the Jews; and this it was that St. Paul reprehended, because of the danger of the gentiles taking scandal thereby. But this no way disproves St. Peter's superiority, since no one doubts but that a superior, when in fault, may sometimes lawfully be reprehended by an inferior. And, after all, do our adversaries imagine that the enhancing the dignity and authority of St. Paul makes anything against the bishop of Rome, who indeed inherits the succession both of St. Peter and St. Paul, who both honored Rome with their preaching and with their death?

297. But some protestants doubt whether St. Peter ever was at Rome; what say you to this?

Grotius, a learned protestant, writes that "no Christian ever doubted but St. Peter was at Rome."[319] And Chamierus, another learned protestant, tells us, that "all the fathers with great accord have asserted that Peter went to Rome and governed that Church." *Omnes patres magno consensu asseruerunt Petrum*

---

[317] 2 Cor 12:11
[318] Cf. Gal 2:11
[319] Cf. *Synopsi Criticorum*, p. 1540. H.

Romam esse pro-fectum, eamque ecclesiam administrasse.[320] And Dr. Pearson, the protestant bishop of Chester, one of the most eminent men that the Reformation has ever produced, has demonstrated by innumerable arguments that Peter was at Rome, and that the bishops of Rome are his successors.[321]

298. Does the scripture anywhere affirm that St. Peter was at Rome?

Saint Peter's first epistle seems to affirm it,[322] where by Babylon, the best interpreters understand Rome, so called by the apostle (as afterwards by St. John in the Apocalypse[323]) because of its being then the chief seat both of the empire and of heathenish idolatry, as formerly Babylon had been. And so this place is understood by St. Papias, disciple of the apostles, and Clement of Alexandria, as alleged by Eusebius[324] and by St. Jerome,[325] by venerable Bede, Oecumenius, and others. Nor is there any probability that the Babylon here mentioned could be that in Chaldea, which, at this time, was nothing but a heap of ruins; nor that in Egypt, which was but a very inconsiderable place in those days, and in which no monuments of antiquity give us the least hint that St. Peter ever preached.

But if the scripture had been entirely silent in this matter, we have it proved by universal tradition, which is the means by which we come to the knowledge of the scripture itself. And indeed there is a more universal tradition for St. Peter's being at Rome, than there is for many parts of the scripture which protestants receive: for whereas many of the ancient fathers have called in question some books of scripture, for instance, the Apocalypse, the Epistle to the Hebrews, etc., and there is

---

[320] Chamierus, L. 13, c. 4, Sec. 2
[321] Cf. Johannis Pearsonii, *Opera Posthuma* (London: Roycroft, 1688), 27ff.
[322] Cf. 1 Pet 5:13
[323] Cf. Apoc 17:5, 18
[324] Cf. Eusebius, *Ecclesiastical History*, Bk. 2, Ch. 15
[325] Cf. Jerome, *De Scriptoribus in Marco*

scarce any part of the Bible or new testament but what has been rejected by some heretics of old; yet we cannot find that St. Peter's being at Rome was ever called in question by any single man, infidel or Christian, Catholic or heretic, for thirteen or fourteen hundred years after Christ. Though all heretics and schismatics, as being always enemies of the Church of Rome, would have been most glad to have called in question this succession of St. Peter (which the bishops of Rome ever gloried in), had not the matter of fact been out of dispute. The ancient fathers that have attested St. Peter's being at Rome, besides many others, are St. Irenaeus,[326] St. Denys, bishop of Corinth, Caius and Origen,[327] Tertullian,[328] St. Cyprian,[329] Arnobius,[330] Lactantius,[331] Eusebius,[332] St. Athanasius,[333] St. Cyril of Jerusalem,[334] St. Ambrose,[335] St. Jerome,[336] Sulpitius Severus,[337] St. Augustine,[338] St. John Chrysostom,[339] Orosius,[340] St. Peter Chrysologus,[341] St. Optatus,[342] and Theodoret.[343]

---

[326] Cf. Irenaeus, *Against Heresies*, Bk. 3. Ch. 3

[327] As alleged by Eusebius, *Ecclesiastical History*, Bk. 3

[328] Cf. Tertullian, *Prescription Against Heretics*, Ch. 36; *Scorpiace*, Ch. 15

[329] Cf. Cyprian, *Epistle 51, Epistle 54*

[330] Cf. Arnobius, *Against the Heathen*, Bk. 2

[331] Cf. Lactantius, *De Mortibus Persecutorum*, Ch. 2

[332] Cf. Eusebius, *Ecclesiastical History*, Bk. 2, Ch. 14, Bk. 3, Ch. 4

[333] Cf. Athanasius, *Apologia de Fuga*, n. 18

[334] Cf. Cyril of Jerusalem, *Catechetical Lecture 6*

[335] Cf. Ambrose, *Hexameron*, Bk. 4, Ch. 8

[336] Cf. Jerome, *de Scriptoribus Eccles. in Petro et in Marco, Chronicon*, Annum 43 and 69

[337] Cf. Sulpitius Severus, *Sacred History*, Bk. 2

[338] Cf. Augustine, *De Haeresibus*, Ch. 1, *Letter 53, Answer to Petilian the Donatist*, Bk. 2, Ch. 51

[339] Cf. Chrysostom, *Tom. 5. Hom. 12*

[340] Cf. Paulus Orosius, *Seven Books of History Against the Pagans*, Bk. 7, Ch. 6

[341] Cf. Peter Chrysologus, *Letter to Eutyches*

[342] Cf. Optatus of Milevis, *Against the Donatists*, Bk. 2

[343] Cf. Theodoret, *Commentary on Romans, Hæreticarum Fabularum Compendium*, Bk. 1, Ch. 1

Chapter 17

Of the Celibacy of the Clergy

299. What is the reason why the Catholic clergy are not allowed to marry?
Because at their entering into holy orders, they make a solemn promise to God and the Church to live continently. Now the breach of such a promise as this would be a great sin; witness St. Paul, where speaking of widows that are for marrying, after having thus engaged themselves to God, he says they have damnation, "because they have cast off their first faith,"[344] that is, their solemn engagement made to God.

300. But why does the Church receive none to holy orders, but such as are willing to make this solemn engagement?
Because she does not think it proper that they who, by their office and functions, ought to be wholly devoted to the service of God and the care of souls, should be diverted from these duties by the distractions of a married life. "He that is unmarried, careth for the things that belong to the Lord, how he may please the Lord. But he that is married, careth for the things that are of the world, how he may please his wife."[345]

301. But was it always a law in the Church that the clergy should abstain from marriage?
It always was a law in the Church that bishops, priests, and deacons should not marry after having received holy orders; and we have not one example in all antiquity, either in the

[344] Cf. 1 Tm 5:11-12
[345] 1 Cor 7:32-33

Greek or Latin Church, of any such marriage: but it has been at some times and in some places, as at present among the Greeks, permitted for priests and deacons to continue with their wives which they had married before their ordination, though even this was disallowed by many ancient canons.

The Apostolic Canons allows none of the clergy to marry, but those that are in the minor orders, that is, lectors and cantors.[346] The Council of Neo-Caesarea, which was more ancient than that of Nicea, in its first canon, orders that if a priest marries, he should be deposed.[347] The Council of Ancyra, which was held about the same time, orders the same thing with regard to deacons, except they protested at the time of their ordination that they could not live unmarried, and were therefore presumed to be dispensed with by the bishop.[348] The great Council of Nicea, in the third canon, forbids clergymen to have any woman in their house, except it be mother, sister, or aunt, etc.; a caution which would never have been thought on, if they had been allowed to have wives.[349]

In the West, the Council of Illiberis, which was held about the close of the third century, Canon 33, commands bishops, priests, deacons, and subdeacons to abstain from their wives, under pain of degradation. The Second Council of Arles, Canon 2, ordains that no married man be made priest, unless he promise conversion, that is, to live continently. The Second Council of Carthage, Canon 2, ordains that bishops, priests, and deacons should live continently and abstain from their wives; "and this because the apostle so taught, and all antiquity observed." *Ut quod apostoli docuerunt, et ipsa servavit antiquitas, nos quoque custodiamus.* And the Fifth Council of Carthage (AD 398), Canon 2, ordains in like manner, that all bishops, priests,

---

[346] Cf. *Apostolic Canons*, Can. 27
[347] Cf. Council of Neocaesarea, Can. 1
[348] Cf. Council of Ancyra, Can. 10
[349] Cf. Council of Nicea, Can. 3

and deacons should abstain from their wives, or be deposed. There are many other ancient canons to the like effect, as well as decrees of the ancient popes, as of Siricius,[350] of Innocent I,[351] and St. Leo the Great.[352]

Hence St. Epiphanius, who flourished in the East in the fourth century, in his great work, *Against All Heresies*, writes thus: "The Church does not admit him to be a deacon, priest, bishop or subdeacon, though he be a man of one wife, who makes use of conjugal embraces."[353] He adds that this "is observed in those places chiefly in which the canons of the Church are exactly kept, which being directed by the Holy Ghost; aims always at that which is most perfect; that those who are employed in divine functions may have as little as can be of worldly distractions."[354] And St. Jerome: "Bishops," says he, "priests, and deacons, are chosen either virgins or widowers, or from the time of their priesthood perpetually chaste."[355] He affirms the same in his book against Vigilantius, by name of the churches of the East, and of Egypt, and of the see Apostolic;[356] and of all bishops, in his book against Jovinianus.[357] See also Origen's *Homily 13 on Numbers*, Eusebius' *Demonstratio Evangelica*, Bk. 1 Ch. 9; and St. John Chrysostom's *Sermon on the Patience of Job*.

If you ask the reason why the Church has insisted so much in all ages upon this point of discipline; besides the reason alleged above out of St. Paul,[358] "The reason of single life for the clergy," says Mr. Thorndyke, an eminent protestant divine, in his letters at the end of *Just Weights and Measures*,

---

[350] Cf. Siricius' *Epistle* to Himerius, bishop of Tarragona, Ch. 7
[351] Cf. Innocent I's *Epistle* to Victricius, bishop of Roan, Ch. 9
[352] Cf. Leo the Great's *Letter 14* to Anastasius, Ch. 3 and 4
[353] Epiphanius, *Haeresi 59*
[354] Ibid.
[355] Jerome, *Letter 48*, n. 21
[356] Cf. Jerome, *Against Vigilantius*, n. 2
[357] Cf. Jerome, *Against Jovinianus*, Bk. 1
[358] Cf. 1 Cor 7:32-33

is firmly grounded by the fathers and canons of the Church upon the precept of St. Paul, forbidding man and wife to part, unless for a time to attend unto prayer (1 Cor 7:5). For priests and deacons being continually to attend upon occasions of celebrating the Eucharist, which ought continually to be frequented; if others be to abstain from the use of marriage for a time, then they always.[359]

Thus far Mr. Thorndyke.

302. But were not the apostles married?

Some of them were, before they were called to the apostleship; but we don't find that they had any commerce with their wives after they were called by Christ. St. Jerome expressly affirms that they had not,[360] and this seems to be clear from Matthew 19, where St. Peter says to our Lord, "Behold we have forsaken all things and followed thee."[361] For that amongst the *all* which they had forsaken, wives also were comprehended, is gathered from the enumeration made by our Savior in verse 29, where he expressly nameth wives.

303. But does not St. Paul say, "Have we not power to lead about a sister, a wife, as well as other apostles,"[362] etc.?

The protestant translation has willfully corrupted the text in this place. It should have been translated a *woman*, a *sister*. The apostle speaks not of his wife, for it is visible he had none;[363] but he speaks of such pious women, as, according to the custom of the Hebrew nation, waited upon the apostles and other

---

[359] Herbert Thorndike, *Just Weights and Measures*, 2nd ed. (London: Roycroft, 1680), 239.

[360] Cf. Jerome, *Letter 48*

[361] Mt 19:27

[362] 1 Cor 9:5

[363] Cf. 1 Cor 7:7-8

teachers serving them in necessaries; as they had done also upon our Lord in the time of his mortal life.[364] Though St. Paul, that he might be less burthensome to the faithful, chose rather to serve himself, and live by the work of his own hands.

304. Does not the apostle require that bishops and deacons should be the husbands of one wife?[365]

The meaning of the apostle is not that every bishop, priest, or deacon should have a wife; for he himself had none, and he declares: "I say to the unmarried and widows, it is good for them if they abide even as I."[366] But his meaning is that none should be admitted to be a bishop, priest, or deacon that had been married more than once; which law has ever since been observed in the Catholic Church: for since it was not possible in those days of the first preaching of the gospel (when there were few or no converts, either among the Jews or gentiles, but such as were married) to have found a sufficient number of proper ministers if they had not admitted married men, they were consequently obliged to admit such to the ministry; but still with this limitation, provided they had not been twice married. But now the Church has a sufficient number of such as are trained up to a single life, and are willing to embrace perpetual continence; and therefore prefers such to the ministry, and is authorized so to do by the apostle.[367] And if, after having consecrated themselves to God in this kind of life, they should be for looking back and engaging in a married life, they are expressly condemned by the same apostle.[368]

---

[364] Cf. Lk 8:2-3
[365] Cf. 1 Tm 3:2, 12
[366] 1 Cor 7:8
[367] Cf. 1 Cor 7:32, 33, 38
[368] Cf. 1 Tm 5:12

305. Is it not said, "Marriage is honorable in all"?[369]

The protestant translation has strained the text to make it say more than the original, which may full as well be rendered in the imperative mood, thus: "Let marriage be honorable in all, and the bed undefiled; for whoremongers and adulterers God will judge," etc. In the same manner, as in the following verse, which is rendered in the protestant translation by the imperative, "Let your conversation be without covetousness," etc. So that the true meaning of this text is that married persons should not dishonor their holy state by any liberties contrary to the sanctity of it; but not to allow marriage to those who have chosen the better part, and consecrated themselves by vow to God.

306. But is not forbidding marriage called a "doctrine of devils"?[370]

It certainly was so in those of whom the apostle there speaks, viz. the Gnostics, the Marcionites, the Encratites, the Manicheans, and many other heretics who absolutely condemned marriage as the work of the devil. For our part, nobody reverences marriage more than we do; for we hold it to be a sacrament, and forbid it to none but those that have voluntarily renounced it to consecrate themselves more wholly to the divine service: and in such as these, St. Paul condemns it as much as we.[371] These same heretics also condemned absolutely the use of all kinds of meat, not on fasting-days only (as was also practiced by the Church), but at any time whatsoever; because they looked upon all flesh to be from an evil principle. It is evident these were the men of whom the apostle intended to speak.[372]

---

[369] Heb 13:4
[370] Cf. 1 Tm 4:1, 3
[371] Cf. 1 Tm 5:12
[372] Cf. 1 Tm 4

307. But do you think that a vow of continency so strictly obliges any person, that it would be a sin in such a person to marry?
Yes most certainly; because the law of God and nature requires that we should keep our vows to God. "When thou shalt vow a vow unto the Lord thy God, thou shalt not slack to pay it: for the Lord thy God will surely require it of thee; and it would be sin in thee. But if thou shalt forbear to vow, it shall be no sin in thee. That which is gone out of thy lips thou shalt keep and perform."[373] "Vow and pay unto the Lord your God."[374] "Pay that which thou hast vowed. Better it is that thou shouldst not vow, than that thou shouldst vow and not pay."[375] For if it be a crime to break our faith with man, how much more with God? If you say that the state of continency is not more acceptable to God than that of marriage, and therefore cannot be the proper matter of a vow, you contradict the doctrine of the apostle: "He that giveth his virgin in marriage, doth well; but he that giveth her not, doth better."[376]

Hence St. Augustine affirms that the breach of such a vow of chastity "is worse than adultery";[377] and St. John Chrysostom, "Though you call it marriage a thousand times, yet I maintain it is much worse than adultery, as God is better and greater than mortals."[378] Hence the Council of Illiberis, Canon 13; the Fourth Council of Carthage, Canon 104, and the great Council of Chalcedon, Canon 15, excommunicate those who presume to marry after such a vow. What would the Church of those ages have thought of a religion introduced into the world by men that had notoriously broke through these most solemn

[373] Dt 23:21-23
[374] Ps 75:12
[375] Eccles 5:3-4
[376] 1 Cor 7:38
[377] Augustine, *De Bono Viduitatis*, n. 14
[378] Chrysostom, *Ad Theodorum Lapsum*, Letter 2, n. 3

engagements, and who raised the fabric of their pretended Reformation upon thousands of broken vows?

308. But all have not the gift of continency; why then should the first reformers be blamed if, finding they had not this gift, they ventured upon marrying with nuns?

Continency is not required of all, but of such as have by vow engaged to keep it: and therefore, before a person engages himself by vow, he ought certainly to examine whether he has a call from God, and whether he can go through with what he thinks of undertaking. But after he has once engaged himself by vow, he is not now at liberty to go back, but may assure himself that the gift of continency will not be denied him that uses proper means to obtain and preserve it, particularly prayer and mortification; which because Luther laid aside, by quitting his canonical hours of prayer and other religious exercises, to which he had been accustomed in his convent, no wonder if he lost the gift of continency, which he owns he enjoyed whilst he was a popish friar. "Whilst I was a religious," says he, "I observed chastity, obedience and poverty: and in short, being wholly disengaged from the cares of this present life, I wholly gave myself up to fasting, watching and prayer."[379] But as soon as he commenced reformer, to demonstrate that he was changed for the worse, he declares, he had so far lost this gift, that he could not possibly live without a woman.[380]

309. But does not Christ say, concerning continency, "All men cannot receive this saying,"[381] and St. Paul, "If they cannot contain, let them marry: for it is better to marry than to burn"?[382]

No, both these texts are willfully corrupted in the protestant

---

[379] *In Gal.* 1. 15, T.5, *Witemb. Fol.* 291.2
[380] Cf. *Sermon. de Matrim. T.* 5. *Fol.* 119.1
[381] Mt 19:11
[382] Cf. 1 Cor 7:9

testament. In the original, Christ does not say, "All men *cannot* receive this saying"; but he says: "All men receive not this saying." And St. Paul does not say, "If they *cannot* contain, let them marry"; but he says, "If they do not contain, let them marry." Where he speaks not of such as have vowed chastity, but of other Christians, whom he advises rather to marry than to burn with unlawful lust here and for unlawful lust hereafter. And the same advice is most frequently inculcated by Catholic divines.

But as for those that have vowed chastity, they must make use of other means to prevent this burning, particularly prayer and fasting. But what a wretched case must that of the adversaries of the celibacy of the clergy be, when to maintain it they have in so many places willfully corrupted the scripture? And what a melancholy case it must be, that so many thousands of well-meaning souls should be wretchedly deluded with the pretense of God's pure word, when instead of this, they have nothing put into their hands but corrupted translations, which present them with a mortal poison instead of the food of life?

Chapter 18

Of Religious Orders and Confraternities

310. **What is the meaning of so many religious orders in the Catholic Church under different denominations; are not all Catholics of the same religion?**
Yes certainly, all Catholics; and consequently all these religious, though called by different denominations, are all of one religion, professing one and the same faith, acknowledging one and the same Church authority, and all the decisions of the

Church; subject to one and the same head, and closely united together in one communion.

311. In what then do these religious orders differ one from another, if they are all of one religion?
They differ in having different rules and constitutions prescribed by their respective founders; different habits; different exercises of devotion and penance; different institutes; some wholly sequestered from the world and devoted to prayer and contemplation; others employed in preaching, teaching, and converting souls; others tending the sick, redeeming captives, etc., so as to make a beautiful variety in the Church of God of different companions, all tending towards Christian perfection, though by different exercises, according to the spirit of their respective institutes.

312. Are not all these religious consecrated to God by certain vows?
Yes: there are three vows which are common to them all, viz. of poverty, chastity, and obedience. By the vow of poverty, they renounce all propriety to the things of this world, so as to have nothing at their own disposal; by the vow of chastity, they renounce all carnal pleasures; and by the vow of obedience, they give up their own will to follow that of God in the person of their superior.

313. How do we know that this voluntary poverty, perpetual chastity, and entire obedience, are agreeable to God?
That voluntary poverty, or renouncing the goods and possessions of this world, is agreeable to God, is evident from Matthew 19: "If thou wilt be perfect, go and sell all thou hast, and give to the poor, and thou shalt have a treasure in heaven, and come and follow me."[383] That perpetual chastity is agreeable to

[383] Mt 19:21

God, is no less evident from Matthew 19: "There be eunuchs which have made themselves eunuchs for the kingdom of heaven's sake: He that is able to receive it, let him receive it."[384] And that an entire obedience to lawful superiors must needs be agreeable to the Divine Majesty, is evident because obedience is better than sacrifice; since by obedience we give up to God and for God, that which is naturally most dear to us, viz. our liberty, and that which stands most in the way of our soul's welfare, viz. our own will and self-love.

314. Ought any Christians to embrace this state of life without a call from God?

No, certainly; it would be rashness to attempt it.

315. How shall any person know if he has a call from God to this state of life?

By consulting God, his director, and his own heart. In choosing a state of life, everyone ought to consult God, in the first place, by fervent prayer, begging daily of him like the convert St. Paul: "Lord, what wilt thou have me to do?"[385] He ought also to consult with a virtuous and prudent director, and to lay open to him the inclinations of his heart and the motives upon which he is inclined to embrace this kind of life; for there is no better proof of a call from God than when a person, after having consulted God by prayer, finds in himself a strong inclination to a religious life, and that for a long time, and upon motives which have nothing in them of self-love, but are such as could not be suggested but by the grace of God.

---

[384] Mt 19:12
[385] Acts 9:6

316. What are the motives upon which a Christian should embrace a religious life?

To do penance for his sins; to fly from the dangers and corruptions of this wicked world; to consecrate himself wholly to the service of God, and sanctify himself by the exact observance of his vows and all the exercises of a religious life; and to tend without ceasing to Christian perfection.

317. But may it not be feared, that young persons may too rashly engage themselves by vows in a religious state for which they are not fit?

To prevent this inconvenience, the Catholic Church suffers none to be professed in any order of men or women without a year's novitiate, by way of probation or trial.

318. Is a religious state of life very ancient in the Church of God?

Yes, very ancient; for not to mention St. John Baptist's life in the wilderness[386] and the lives of the first Christians of Jerusalem, who "had all things common," and "sold their possessions and goods," "continuing daily with one accord in the temple,"[387] etc., in which they exhibit a specimen of a religious life; we learn from the most certain monuments of antiquity that even in the three first centuries there were religious men, whom Eusebius calls *ascetae*, and great numbers of nuns or virgins consecrated to God; though neither the one nor the other was as yet formed into the regular monasteries till the beginning of the fourth century.

About the middle of the third century, St. Paul the first hermit, flying from the fury of the persecution begun by Decius, in the year 249, retired into the desert of Thebais, and there passed ninety years and upwards in a lonesome

---

[386] Cf. Mt 3:1-4
[387] Cf. Acts 2:44-46

cave, in conversation with God. His wonderful life is extant, written by St. Jerome.

About the year 271, St. Antony, a young gentleman of Egypt, left his estate and the world to consecrate himself to a religious life. He found, at his first retirement, some others that had already undertaken that kind of life, though few in number, and those living near the towns or villages; but he, by his example, drew great numbers after him into the desert, and is generally looked upon as the author and father of a monastic life. His life is written by the great St. Athanasius, and is full of excellent lessons of spirituality.

About the year 313, St. Pachomius retired from the world, and, after having lived some time in solitude with St. Palaemon, became the father of many religious, and the first founder of the famous congregation of Tabenne, to which he prescribed a rule which he had received from an angel.

From these beginnings, the deserts of Egypt and of Thebais soon were peopled with innumerable solitaries, and all those parts were full of religious of both sexes of admirable virtue; insomuch, that when Rufinus visited those countries in the latter end of the fourth century, he found in the city of Oxyrincus alone, ten thousand religious men, and twenty thousand nuns.

From Egypt, this kind of life, so agreeable to the principles of the gospel and the spirit of Christianity, quickly spread itself through all parts of the world inhabited by Christians. St. Hilarion having learned St. Antony's way of living, began to practice the like in Palestine about the beginning of the fourth century; and that country also was quickly replenished with religious men and women. Whilst St. James, afterwards bishop of Nisibis, St. Julian Sabas, and other great servants of God whose lives and miracles are recorded by Theodoret in his *Philotheus*, propagated the same way of living in Syria and Mesopotamia. About the same time, or not long after, the deserts of Pontus and Cappadocia began also to be inhabited by religious men, whose manner of life was embraced by those two great lights of the Church, St. Gregory Nazianzen and St. Basil; the latter of which composed an excellent rule for his religious, professed to this day by the Greek and Russian monks, and by some in Poland and Italy.

As for the western part of the Church, we find that the monastic life had already gained a great footing there in the fourth century. Saint Augustine informs us of a monastery near the walls of Milan, full of good religious men under the care of St. Ambrose,[388] of several such religious societies at Rome,[389] and also of a religious house near Treves in Germany, where two courtiers, upon reading the *Life of St. Antony*, consecrated themselves to God.[390] And the same St. Augustine, upon his return into Africa, after his conversion, propagated the same kind of life in that part of the world also.

In France, the great St. Martin, bishop of Tours, in the fourth century, whose apostolic life and miracles are recorded by Sulpicius Severus, founded the monastery of Marmoutier, in which he united together in one the clerical and monastical life, as St. Eusebius had done before him at Vercelli in Piedmont. But the most famous monastery in all France was that of the isle of Lerines, founded towards the close of the fourth century by St. Honoratus, afterwards bishop of Arles; which was the fruitful parent of many great saints and illustrious prelates.

As for our British Islands, though we know not the particular time when the first monasteries began to be established, yet we are assured that we were not long behind our neighbors in embracing this kind of life. The monastery of Bangor, in Wales, in which there were above two thousand monks, was very ancient; and we are told of an ancient monastery at Winchester, before the English Saxons came over into this land. As for

---

[388] Cf. Augustine, *Confessions*, Bk. 8, Ch. 6
[389] Cf. Augustine, *Of the Morals of the Catholic Church*, Ch. 33
[390] Cf. Augustine, *Confessions*, Bk. 8, Ch. 6

Ireland, St. Patrick, who established Christianity there, settled also the monastic discipline amongst his converts; which from thence was propagated to the Picts in Scotland by St. Columba, also known as Columkil, the apostle of that nation, who having first founded in Ireland the famous abbey of Dearmach, afterwards passing into Scotland, founded that in the isle of Hy; from which two monasteries many others, as well in Ireland as in Scotland, had their origin as following the institute of the aforesaid St. Columba, of whom Ven. Bede, in his third book of the *Ecclesiastical History of the English Church*, Chapter 4, writes thus: "Of whose life and words [he speaks of St. Columba], some writings are said to be preserved by his disciples. But whatsoever he was himself, this we know of him for certain, that he left successors renowned for much continency, the love of God, and regular observance."

From this monastery of the isle of Hoy, St. Aidan, the first bishop of Lindisfarn, and many other apostolic preachers came, who preached and established Christianity among the Northern English, as St. Augustine and his companions did amongst those of the South, St. Felix amongst the East English, and St. Birinus amongst those of the West.

319. **I should be glad to know which are the chief religious orders that flourish at present in the Church of God; together with the names of their founders, the time of their first institution, etc.?**

I shall endeavor to satisfy you as briefly as I can. And first as to the East, the orders that flourish there are those of St. Antony and of St. Basil, of which we have spoken already.

In the West, St. Augustine, upon his return into Africa, about the year 390, with diverse others his companions, entered into a religious society, wherein he lived for three years before his coming to Hippo. And after his coming to that city where he was first made priest, and afterwards bishop, he erected a monastery within his own house, living there with his clergy in common; to which institute the Canon Regulars of St. Augustine owe their origin, who have flourished ever since in the Church of God, and have branched out into diverse congregations: as that of St. John Lateran, that of St. Victor, of St. Genovesa, etc. As the hermits of St. Augustine's order, commonly called Austin Friars, derive their institute from his first religious society, before his coming to Hippo. These hermits were translated from the deserts into towns, by Pope Innocent the fourth, to the end that their godly conversation might be more profitable to their neighbors. From this order Luther apostatized in the 16th century, and like the dragon, "drew with him the third part of the stars of heaven," that is, great numbers of religious of all denominations, "and cast them to the earth."[391]

Towards the end of the fifth century, St. Benedict, also known as Bennet, retired from the world; and after having practiced for many years a religious life in a most eminent degree of perfection, founded twelve monasteries in Latium, and the thirteenth at Mount Cassin, in the kingdom of Naples, from which he happily passed to the mountain of eternity, in the sixth century. He composed an excellent rule, which was afterwards embraced by almost all the religious of the West up until the twelfth century, and has furnished the Church of God with innumerable prelates and apostolic men, and heaven with innumerable saints. The wonderful life of St. Bennet was written by St. Gregory the Great in his *Dialogues*.

From the *Rule of St. Benedict* many other orders have sprung besides the Benedictines; as the Cluniacenses, so called from their first abbey of Cluny in France. These were instituted by St. Odo in the tenth century, and for a long time flourished in great sanctity. The Camaldulenses, instituted by St. Romuald amongst the Apennine mountains, about the year 1000, and to

[391] Apoc 12:4

this day edifying the Church, yielding a sweet odor of sanctity to all that come near them. The monks of Valombrosa, instituted by St. John Gualbert in the ninth century, and called from the place of their first institution. The Cistercians, so called from their first abbey, were founded about the end of the eleventh century by St. Robert, abbot of Molesme in France.

St. Robert being obliged to return to his abbey of Molesme, left for his successor, St. Albericus who was succeeded by St. Stephen Harding, an Englishman, who had the happiness to receive St. Bernard into his society, by whose preaching and miracles this order was wonderfully propagated, and the religious of it, from him are commonly called Bernardines. Of this order is the famous abbey of La Trappe in France, which in these our days has renewed the austerities and abstracted lives of the primitive religious. I pass over several other religious professing the rule of St. Benedict, as the Silvestrines, the Grandimontenses, the Celestins, so called from St. Peter Celestine their founder, the Olivetans, etc.

Towards the end of the eleventh century, St. Bruno, a doctor of Paris, with six companions, retired from the world to the desert mountains of Carthusia, in the diocese of Grenoble in Dauphine, and there laid the foundation of the order of the Carthusians, formerly in England called the Charter-house monks; who to this day have happily preserved their primitive fervor, keeping perpetual silence (excepting only when they are singing the praises of God), perpetual abstinence, wearing always a rough hair shirt, and continually employed in prayer and contemplation.

About the year 1120, St. Norbert, who had exchanged the court life for the voluntary poverty recommended by the gospel, founded an order of Canon Regulars, from him called Norbertines, and Premonstratenses, from Prémontré, the place of their first abbey, in the diocese of Laon in France.

In the same age also was instituted in France the Order of

the Blessed Trinity, for the redemption of captives out of the hands of infidels, by St. John de Matha and St. Felix de Valois, two holy priests and solitaries invited to this charitable work by divine visions. As in the following age another order was instituted in Spain for the same end, by St. Peter Nolascus. This is commonly called the Order of our Lady de Mercede, of the Redemption.

About the year 1200, the Carmelites were first brought into Europe and were quickly spread through all parts of Christendom, where they have flourished exceedingly; nowhere more than heretofore in England, where from the color of their mantles they were called White Friars. These were originally hermits living upon Mount Carmel, who whilst the Christians were in possession of Syria and the Holy Land, were assembled together by Aimeric the patriarch of Antioch, and received a rule from Albert, patriarch of Jerusalem. This rule was afterwards mitigated by the pope; but embraced again in its full extent by St. Theresa in the sixteenth century, and by the friars and nuns that follow her reform, and are called Discalced, or Barefoot Carmelites.

Not long after the Carmelites' coming into Europe, God was pleased to raise two new orders, which have flourished from that time to this day, and furnished the Church with several popes, innumerable cardinals, bishops, ecclesiastical writers, and apostolic men; and have both been very fruitful in saints, viz. the Order of St. Dominic, and that of St. Francis. The Dominicans, or Friars Preachers, were instituted for preaching the gospel to infidels and sinners, which they have done with great success. These were formerly in our country called Black Friars, from the color of their cloak or outward habit, which is black, as the Franciscans were called Gray Friars. St. Francis would have his religious, for humility called Friars Minors, whom he trained up in great poverty and penance. And so great and speedy was the increase of this order, that in a chapter held by the saint himself at Assisi, there were assembled no less than five thousand religious. This order at present is the most numerous in the Church of God, and is divided into three chief branches under their respective generals, viz. the Conventuals, the Observants, and the Capuchins. The Observants are again subdivided into Cordeliers, Recollects, etc., besides which, there is the congregation of St. Peter of Alcantara, which is the strictest of all. The nuns which follow the rule of St. Francis are commonly called Poor Clares, from St. Clare, who first received the habit from St. Francis, and was their first abbess. Besides these there are Capuchinesses or Penitent nuns of the Third Order of St. Francis, etc.

Other orders that have been founded between the beginning of the thirteenth century and the sixteenth are the Servites, or Servants of the Blessed Virgin, instituted about 1232 by seven gentlemen of Florence, who retired themselves to a neighboring mountain to do penance; the Crucigeri, or Crutched Friars, though these, by some, are supposed to have been much more ancient; the Jesuati, instituted by St. John Colombin in 1356; the Brigittins, by St. Brigit in the year 1360; the Hieronimites, by Pedro Ferdinando in the year 1383; the Minims, by St. Francis of Paula in about the year 1450, etc.

The sixteenth century gave rise to several new orders; the Theatins, or Regular Clerks were instituted in the year 1528 by St. Cajetanus Thianæus, a man of apostolic life. This order flourishes very much in Italy; as well as the Barnabites, or Clerics Regular of St. Paul.

The Jesuits, or Society of Jesus, were instituted by St. Ignatius of Loyola in the year 1540 as a troop, or company of auxiliaries, to assist the pastoral clergy in that time of the Church's greatest necessity; to labor in the conversion and sanctification of souls; to train up youth in piety and learning; to defend the faith against heretics, and propagate it amongst infidels: in all which particulars this order has done signal services to the Church in these two last centuries. About the same time, St. John de Deo founded an order of religious brethren to take care of the sick, and to provide for them all necessary assistance both for soul and body.

In the beginning of the seventeenth century, St. Francis de Sales, bishop of Geneva, instituted the order of nuns of the Visitation of the Blessed Virgin. And thus have I given you a short account of the chief orders that at present flourish in the Church.

Besides these religious orders, there are certain regular congregations of clergy living in common, though not under the tie of religious vows: as the Oratorians instituted by St. Philip Nerius in the sixteenth century; the Fathers of the Christian Doctrine; the Lazarians, or Fathers of the Mission, etc.

320. **Are there not also many confraternities amongst the Catholics, in which many of the laity are enrolled; pray what is the meaning of these confraternities?**

These confraternities or brotherhoods are certain societies or associations instituted for the encouragement of devotion or for promoting of certain works of piety, religion, and charity; under some rules or regulations, though without being tied to them so far as that the breach or neglect of them would be sinful. The good of these confraternities is that thereby good works are promoted, the faithful are encouraged to frequent the sacrament, to hear the word of God, and mutually to assist one another by their prayers, etc.

Chapter 19

Of the Sacrament of Matrimony, and of the Nuptial Benediction

321. When was matrimony instituted?

It was first instituted by God Almighty between our first parents in the earthly paradise,[392] and this institution was confirmed by Christ in the new testament, where he concludes "What God hath joined together, let no man put asunder."[393] And our Lord, to show that this state is holy, and not to be condemned or despised, was pleased to honor it with his first miracle, wrought at the wedding of Cana.[394]

322. What are the ends for which matrimony is instituted?

For the procreation of children, which may serve God here, and people heaven hereafter; for a remedy against concupiscence; and for the benefit of conjugal society, that man and wife may mutually help one another, and contribute to one another's salvation.

323. How do you prove that matrimony is a sacrament?

Because it is a conjunction made and sanctified by God himself, and not to be dissolved by any power of man, as being a sacred sign or mysterious representation of the indissoluble union of Christ and his Church. Hence St. Paul expressly calls it a great sacrament or mystery, with regard to Christ and his Church;[395]

---

[392] Cf. Gn 2
[393] Mt 19:4-6
[394] Cf. Jn 2
[395] Cf. Eph 5:31-32

and as such it has been always acknowledged in the Catholic Church.[396]

324. Does matrimony give grace to those that receive it?

Yes; if they receive it in the dispositions that they ought, it gives a grace to the married couple to love one another according to God, to restrain the violence of concupiscence, to bear with one another's weaknesses, and to bring up their children in the fear of God.

325. How comes it then that so many marriages are unhappy, if matrimony be a sacrament which gives so great a grace?

Because the greatest part do not receive it in the dispositions they ought: they consult not God in their choice, but only their own lust or temporal interest; they prepare not themselves for it, by putting themselves in the state of grace; and too often are guilty of freedoms before marriage, which are not allowable by the law of God.

326. In what dispositions ought persons to receive the sacrament of matrimony?

They ought to be in a state of grace by confession; their intention ought to be pure, viz. to embrace this holy state for the ends for which God instituted it; and if they be under the care of parents, etc., they ought to consult them and do nothing in this kind without their consent.

327. In what manner does the Catholic Church proceed in the administration of matrimony?

First, she orders that the banns should be proclaimed on three Sundays, or festival-days, before the celebration of marriage;

---

[396] Cf. Ambrose, *On Abraham*, Bk. 1, Ch. 7; Augustine, *Of the Good of Marriage*, Ch. 18, 24, *De Fide et Operibus*, Ch. 17, *De Nuptiis Et Concupiscentia*, Bk. 1

to the end that if anyone knows any impediment why the parties may not by the law of God or his Church be joined in matrimony, he may declare it. Second, the parties are to be married by their own parish priest, in the presence of two or three witnesses. Third, the parties express, in the presence of the priest, their mutual consent; according to the usual form of the Church; after which the priest says: "I join you in matrimony, in the name of the Father, and of the Son, and of the Holy Ghost. Amen." Fourth, the priest blesses the ring according to this form:

V: Our help is in the name of the Lord.
R: Who made heaven and earth.
V: O Lord hear my prayer.
R: And let my cry come to thee.
V: The Lord be with you.
R: And with thy spirit.

Let us pray. Bless, + O Lord, this ring, which we bless + in thy name, that she that shall wear it, keeping inviolable fidelity to her spouse, may ever remain in peace and in thy will, and always live in mutual charity. Through Christ our Lord. Amen.

Then the priest sprinkles the ring with holy water; and the bridegroom taking it, puts it on the fourth finger of the left hand of the bride, saying, "In the name of the Father, and of the Son, and of the Holy Ghost. Amen." Here also according to the custom of England, the bridegroom puts some gold and silver into the hand of the bride, saying, "With this ring I thee wed, this gold and silver I thee give, and with my body I thee worship, and with all my worldly goods I thee endow."

After this the priest says:

V: Confirm, O God, this which thou hast wrought in us.

R: From thy holy temple which is in Jerusalem.

Lord have mercy on us. Christ have mercy on us. Lord have mercy on us. Our Father, etc. And lead us not into temptation.

R: But deliver us from evil.

V: Save thy servants.

R: Trusting in thee, O my God.

V: Send them help, O Lord, from thy sanctuary.

R: And defend them from Sion.

V: Be to them, O Lord, a tower of strength.

R: Against the face of the enemy.

V: O Lord hear my prayer.

R: And let my cry come to thee.

V: The Lord be with you.

R: And with thy spirit.

Let us pray. Look down, O Lord, we beseech thee, upon these thy servants, and afford thy favorable assistance to thy own institutions, by which thou hast ordained the propagation of mankind; that they who are joined together by thy authority, may be preserved by thy aid. Through Christ our Lord. Amen.

Fifthly, after this, if the nuptial benediction is to be given, the priest says the Mass appointed in the Missal, for the bridegroom and the bride; and having said the *Pater Noster*, turning about to the new married couple, he says over them the following prayers:

Let us pray. Mercifully give ear, O Lord, to our prayers, and let thy grace accompany this thy institution, by which thou hast ordained the propagation of mankind; that this tie, which is made by thy authority, may be preserved by thy grace. Through our Lord Jesus Christ, etc.

Let us pray. O God, who by thy omnipotent hand didst create all things of nothing; who at the first forming of the world having made man to the likeness of God, didst out of his flesh make the woman, and give her to him for his help, and by this didst inform us that what in its beginning was one ought never to be separated: O God, who by so excellent a mystery hast consecrated this union of both sexes, that thou wouldst have it to be a type of that great sacrament which is betwixt Christ and his Church: O God, by whom this contract and mutual commerce has been ordained, and privileged with a blessing, which alone has not been recalled, either in punishment of original sin, or by the sentence of the flood, mercifully look on this thy servant the bride, who being now to be given in marriage, earnestly desires to be received under thy protection.

May love and peace abound in her; may she marry in Christ faithful and chaste; may she ever imitate those holy women of former times; may she be as acceptable to her husband as Rachel, as discreet as Rebecca; may she in her years and fidelity be like Sarah, and may the author of evil at no time have any share in her actions; may she be steady in faith and the commandments; may she be true to her engagements, and flee all unlawful addresses; may she fortify her infirmity by thy discipline; may she be gravely bashful, venerably modest, and well-learned in the doctrine of heaven; may she be fruitful in her offspring; may she be approved and innocent; and may her happy lot be to arrive at length to the rest of the blessed in the kingdom of heaven, may they both see their children's children to the third and fourth generation, and live to a happy old age. Through the same Lord Jesus Christ, etc.

After the priest's Communion, they both receive the Blessed Sacrament, and in the end of the Mass, before the usual blessing of the people, the priest turns to the bridegroom and bride, and says:

The God of Abraham, the God of Isaac, and the God of Jacob be with you, and may he fulfil his blessing in you, that you may see your children's children to the third and fourth generation, and afterwards enter into the possession of everlasting life, by the help of our Lord Jesus Christ; who, with the Father and the Holy Ghost, liveth and reigneth God forever and ever. Amen.

Then the priest admonishes them to be faithful to one another, to love one another, and to live in the fear of God, and exhorts them to be continent, by mutual consent, at the times of devotion, and especially at the times of fasting, and of great solemnities, and so he finishes the Mass in the usual manner.

328. Is there any obligation of receiving this nuptial benediction when persons are married?
The Church wishes that it were never omitted in the first marriage, when it may be had, because of the blessing it draws down from heaven; and it would certainly be a fault for persons to marry without it, when and where it may be had.

329. Why does not the Church allow of this nuptial benediction, when the man or woman has been once married before?
Because the second marriage does not so perfectly represent the union of Christ and his Church, which is an eternal tie of one to one.

330. Why does the Church not allow of the solemnity of marriages from the first Sunday of Advent till after Twelfth-day, and from Ash-Wednesday till after Low-Sunday?
Because the times of Advent and Lent are times of penance, as

the times of Christmas and Easter are times of extraordinary devotion, and therefore are not proper for marriage feasts, or such like solemnities.

331. What are the duties of married people to one another?
You shall hear them from scripture.

> Let women be subject to their husbands, as to the Lord. Because the man is the head of the woman, as Christ is the head of the Church: he is the Savior of his body. Therefore, as the Church is subject to Christ, so also let women be to their husbands in all things. Husbands, love your wives, as Christ also loved the Church, and delivered himself for it. . . . So ought also husbands to love their wives as their own bodies: he that loveth his wife, loveth himself. For no one ever hated his own flesh, but nourisheth it, and cherisheth it, as Christ also doth the Church. Because we are members of his body, of his flesh, and of his bones. For this cause shall a man leave his father and his mother; and shall adhere to his wife, and they shall be two in one flesh. [Gen 2] This sacrament is great, but I say in Christ and in the Church. However, let every one of you in particular love his wife as himself; and let the wife reverence the husband.[397]

> Let women be subject to their husbands, to the end that if any believe not the word, they may be gained without the word by the conversation of the women. Beholding your chaste conversation in fear. Whose adorning let it not be in the outward plaiting of the hair, or laying on gold round about, or putting on apparel. But the hidden man of the heart, in the incorruptibility of a quiet and modest spirit, which is rich in the sight of God. For in this manner heretofore also holy women, hoping

[397] Eph 5:22-25, 28-33; Cf. Col 3:18-19

in God, adorned themselves, being subject to their husbands. As Sara obeyed Abraham, calling him lord, whose daughters you are. . . . Husbands in like manner dwelling with them according to knowledge, give honor to the woman as to the weaker vessel, and as to the joint-heirs of the grace of life, that your prayers may not be hindered.[398]

Let the husband render the [marriage] debt to his wife: and in like manner the wife to her husband. The wife hath not power of her own body, but the husband; and in like manner the husband hath not power of his own body, but the wife. Defraud not one another, unless perhaps by consent for a time, that you may give yourselves to prayer, and return again together to the same, lest Satan tempt you on account of your incontinency. Yet this I speak according to indulgence, not according to command. For I would have you all to be as myself. . . . But as to them who are joined in wedlock; it is not I but the Lord commands that the wife depart not from her husband. But if she shall depart that she remain unmarried, or be reconciled to her husband: and let not the husband put away his wife.[399]

They may teach the young women prudence, that they love their husbands, be tender of their children. Discreet, chaste, sober, having care of the house, gentle, submissive to their husbands, that the word of God be not blasphemed.[400]

There are also excellent documents for married people in the Book of Tobias, Chapter 6:

Then the angel Raphael said to him, hear me, and I will show thee who they are over whom the devil can prevail. For they

[398] 1 Pt 3:1-7
[399] 1 Cor 7:3-7, 10-11
[400] Ti 2:4-5

who in such manner receive matrimony, as to shut out God from themselves and from their mind, and to give themselves to their lust, as the horse and the mule, which have not understanding; over them the devil hath power. . . . Thou shalt take the virgin with the fear of the Lord, moved rather for love of children than for lust, that in the seed of Abraham thou mayst obtain blessing in children.[401]

And Chapter 3:

Thou knowest, Lord, that I never coveted a husband, and have kept my soul clean from all concupiscence. I never kept company with them that play, nor with them that walk in lightness did I make myself a partner. But a husband I consented to take, with thy fear, not with my lust.[402]

And Chapter 8:

Thou madest Adam of the slime of the earth, and gavest him Eve for his helpmate. And now, Lord, thou knowest that not for fleshly lust do I take my sister to wife, but only for the love of posterity, in which thy name may be blessed forever and ever.[403]

332. What are the duties of married people with regard to the education of their children?

They are obliged to train them up from their very infancy in the fear of God, and to give them early impressions of piety; to see that they be instructed in the Christian doctrine, and that they be kept to their prayers and other religious duties; in fine, to give

[401] Tb 6:16-17, 22
[402] Tb 3:16-18
[403] Tb 8:8-9

them good example, and to remove from them the occasions of sin, especially bad company and idleness.

333. Does the Catholic Church allow her children to marry with those that are not of her communion?

She has often prohibited such marriages, as may be seen in Canon 16 of the Council of Illiberis, Canon 10 of the Council of Laodicea, Canon 14 of the Council of Chalcedon, Canon 67 of the Council of Agde, etc. Though sometimes, and in some places, the pastors of the Church, for weighty reasons, have been forced to dispense with this law and to tolerate such marriages.

334. Why is the Church so averse to this kind of marriage?

First, because she would not have her children communicate in sacred things, such as matrimony is, with those that are out of her communion. Second, because such marriages are apt to give occasion to dissensions in families, whilst one of the parties draws one way, the other another. Third, because there is a danger of the Catholic party being perverted, or at least of not being allowed the free exercise of religion. Fourth, because there is a danger of the children being brought up in error, of which we have seen some sad instances. Where not, that those bargains are by no means to be allowed, by which the contracting parties agree to have the boys brought up in the religion of the father and the girls to follow the mother. God and his Church will have no such division, nor give up thus their right to anyone.

Chapter 20

Of the Churching of Women after Childbirth

335. What is the meaning of the churching of women after childbearing? Is it that you look upon them to be under any uncleanness, as formerly in the old law, or to be any ways out of the Church by childbearing?
No, by no means; but what we call the churching of women is nothing else but their coming to the Church to give thanks to God for their safe delivery, and to receive the blessing of the priest upon that occasion.

336. What is the form or manner of the churching of women?
The woman that desires to be churched, kneels down at the door or entry of the Church, holding a lighted candle in her hand; and the priest, vested with his surplice and stole, sprinkles her first with holy water, and then says:

V: Our help is in the name of the Lord.
R: Who made heaven and earth.

Anthem: This woman shall receive a blessing from the Lord.

Psalm 33 (34)
The earth is the Lord's, and the fulness thereof; the compass of the world and all that dwell therein. Because he hath founded it upon the seas, and prepared it upon the rivers. Who shall go up into the mountain of the Lord, or who shall stand in his holy place? The innocent of hands, and clean of heart, that hath not taken his soul in vain, nor sworn to his neighbor in guile. He shall receive blessing of the Lord,

and mercy of God his Savior. This is the generation of them that seek him, of them that seek the face of the God of Jacob. Lift up your gates ye princes, and be ye lifted up, O eternal gates, and the king of glory shall enter in. Who is this king of glory? The Lord, strong and mighty; the Lord, mighty in battle. Lift up your gates ye princes, and be ye lifted up, O eternal gates, and the king of glory shall enter in. Who is this king of glory? The Lord of powers, he is the king of glory.

V: Glory be to the Father, etc.
R: As it was in the beginning, etc.

Anthem: This woman shall receive a blessing from the Lord, and mercy from God her Savior; for this is the generation of them that seek the Lord.

After this the priest stretches out to her hand the end of his stole, and so introduces her into the Church, saying, "Come into the temple of God, adore the Son of the Blessed Virgin Mary, who has given to thee to be fruitful in thy offspring." Then she kneels before the altar, giving thanks to God for his benefits bestowed upon her, whilst the priest prays as follows:

Lord have mercy on us. Christ have mercy on us. Lord have mercy on us. Our Father, etc.

V: And lead us not into temptation.
R: But deliver us from evil.

V: Save thy handmaid, O Lord.
R: Trusting in thee, O my God.
V: Send her help, O Lord, from thy sanctuary.
R: And defend her from Sion.
V: Let not the enemy have any power over her.

R: Nor the son of iniquity presume to hurt her.

V: O Lord, hear my prayer.
R: And let my cry come to thee.
V: The Lord be with you.
R: And with thy spirit.

Let us pray. Almighty everlasting God, who, by the Blessed Virgin Mary's happy bringing forth, hast changed into joy the pains of the faithful in their child-bearing; mercifully look down upon this thy servant, who comes with joy to thy holy temple to return thee thanks; and grant that after this life she may, by the merits and intercession of the same Blessed Mary, deserve to be received with her child into the joys of everlasting happiness. Through Christ our Lord. Amen.

Then the priest sprinkles her again with holy water, in the form of the cross, saying, "May the peace and blessing of Almighty God, Father, + Son, and Holy Ghost come down upon thee, and remain with thee forever. Amen."

Chapter 21

Of the Fasts of the Catholic Church

337. Have you any reason to think that fasting and abstinence is agreeable to God?

Yes, certainly. John the Baptist's abstinence is commended,[404]

---

[404] Cf. Lk 1:15; Mt 3:4

and Anna the prophetess is praised for serving God with fastings and prayers night and day.[405] The Ninivites, by fasting obtained mercy.[406] Daniel joined fasting with prayer, and by fasting was disposed for heavenly visions.[407] The royal prophet humbled his soul in fasting.[408] Ezra and Nehemiah sought and found seasonable aid from God by fasting.[409] And God, by the prophet Joel, calls upon his people to turn to him with all their heart "in fasting, weeping and mourning."[410]

338. But did our Lord Jesus Christ design that his followers should fast?

Yes, he not only gave them an example by fasting forty days[411] and prescribed to them lessons concerning fasting,[412] but also expressly affirmed that after the bridegroom should be taken from them, that is, after his passion, resurrection, and ascension, all his children, that is, all good Christians, should fast.[413] Hence we find the first Christians at Antioch fasting,[414] and Paul and Barnabas ordained with prayer and fasting,[415] and priests ordained by them in every Church with prayer and fasting,[416] and the apostles "approving themselves as the ministers of God . . . in fasting."[417]

---

[405] Cf. Lk 2:37
[406] Cf. Jon 3:5
[407] Cf. Dn 9:3; 10:3, 7, 12
[408] Cf. Ps 34:13
[409] Cf. 1 Esd 8:23; 2 Esd 1:4
[410] Jl 2:12
[411] Cf. Mt 4:2
[412] Cf. Mt 6:16-18
[413] Cf. Mt 9:15; Mk 2:20; Lk 5:35
[414] Cf. Acts 13:2
[415] Cf. Acts 13:2-3
[416] Cf. Acts 14:22
[417] 2 Cor 6:4-5

339. Has fasting any particular efficacy against the devil?

Yes. "This kind [of devils] can come forth by nothing but by prayer and fasting," saith our Lord.[418]

340. What are the ends for which Christians are to fast, and for which the Church prescribes days of fasting and abstinence?

First, to chastise ourselves and to do penance for our sins, that so, like the Ninivites, we may obtain mercy of God. Second, to curb and restrain our passions and concupiscences, and to bring the flesh under subjection to the spirit. Third, to be enabled by fasting to raise our souls the easier to God, and to offer him purer prayer.

341. What are the rules prescribed by the Catholic Church with regard to eating on fasting days?

First, the Church prohibits all fleshmeat on fasting days, and in Lent eggs also and cheese. Formerly wine was prohibited; but this prohibition, by a contrary custom, has been long since laid aside. Secondly, the Church allows her children but one meal on fasting days; besides which, custom has introduced a small collation at night. Thirdly, the meal which the Church allows on fasting days must not be taken till towards noon: formerly, for the first twelve hundred years of the Church, the meal was not to be taken in Lent before the evening, and on the other fasting days not till three o'clock in the afternoon. These rules regard the days of fasting; but as to those that are only days of abstinence, such as the Sundays in Lent, the three Rogation days, and the Saturdays throughout the year, we are only obliged to abstain from flesh on those days, but no ways confined to one meal.

[418] Mk 9:28

342. But why does the Church prohibit flesh on days of fasting and abstinence?
Not that she looks upon any meats unclean by the new law, but she does it that her children may better comply with the ends of fasting, viz. mortification and penance, by abstaining on those days from that kind of food which is most nourishing and most agreeable.

343. But is not this condemned by the apostle, where he calls it "the doctrine of devils" to command to abstain from meats which God hath created to be received with thanksgiving?[419]
The apostle speaks of the doctrine of those, who, with the Marcionites, Manichaeans, and other heretics, forbid the use of meat not as the Church does, by way of mortification and penance on days of fasting and humiliation, but as a thing absolutely unclean, and unlawful to be used at any time, as coming from an evil principle. All that know anything of Church history, know that this was the system of many heretics, who also upon the same account absolutely condemned marriage, as tending to the propagation of flesh. Now they that know these things are guilty of the highest injustice in pretending that these words of the apostle were levelled at the Catholic Church, when their own conscience must tell them that they were designed for another set of people. The Catholic Church is far from condemning the use of God's creatures in proper times and seasons; but she neither does, nor ever did, think all kind of diet proper for days of fasting and penance. And in this particular, the modern Church is so far from going beyond the primitive Christians, that on the contrary, all kind of monuments of antiquity make it evident that our forefathers, in the first ages of the Church, were more severe in their abstinence than we now are.

[419] Cf. 1 Tm 4:1-3

344. But does not the apostle say, "Whatsoever is sold in the shambles, that eat, asking no question for conscience sake"?[420]

He speaks this not with relation to the days of fasting, as if any sorts of meat might be eaten on fasting days; but he speaks, as it is visible from the context, with regard to meats offered to idols; which some weak brethren were so much afraid of eating, that upon this account they dared not eat the meat sold in the shambles, lest it might have been offered to idols. Upon the same principle the apostle adds, "If any of them that believe not, invite you to a feast, and ye be disposed to go, whatsoever is set before you, eat, asking no question for conscience sake. But if any man say unto you, this is offered in sacrifice unto idols, eat not for his sake that showed it, and for conscience sake,"[421] etc.

345. Do you take it then to be a sin to eat meat on fasting days, or otherwise to break the Church fasts without necessity?

Yes, certainly; because it is a sin to disobey our lawful superiors, and more particularly to disobey the Church of God. "If he neglect to hear the church, let him be to thee as a heathen and a publican."[422]

346. Does not Christ say, "That which goeth into the mouth doth not defile a man"?[423]

True: it is not any uncleanness in the meat, as many heretics have imagined, or any dirt or dust which may stick to it by eating, without first washing the hands (of which case our Lord is speaking in the text you quote), which can defile the soul; for every creature of God is good, and whatsoever corporal filth enters in at the mouth is cast forth into the draught. But that

---

[420] 1 Cor 10:25
[421] 1 Cor 10:27-28
[422] Mt 18:17
[423] Mt 15:11

which defiles the soul when a person transgresses the Church fast is the disobedience of the heart, in breaking the precept of the Church, which God has commanded us to hear and to obey. And thus an Israelite would have been defiled in the time of the old law, by eating of blood or swine's flesh; and thus our first parents were defiled by eating the forbidden fruit—not by the uncleanness of the food, but by the disobedience of the heart to the law of God.

347. What are the conditions that ought to accompany a Christian fast, to make it such a fast as God has chosen?

The great and general fast of a Christian is to abstain from sin; and God would not accept of the fasts of the Jews,[424] because on the days of their fasting, they were found doing their own will and oppressing their neighbors. So that the first condition that ought to go along with our fasts is to renounce our sins; the second is to let our fasts be accompanied with almsdeeds and prayer;[425] the third is to endeavor to perform them in a penitential spirit.

348. What persons are excused from the strictness of the Church fast?

Children under age, sick people, women that are with child or that give suck; likewise those that upon fasting days are obliged to hard labor; and, in a word, all such who through weakness, infirmity, or other hindrance, cannot fast without great prejudice or danger. Where note, first, that if the cause be not evident, a person must have recourse to his pastor for dispensation. Second, that in some of the abovementioned cases, a person may be excused from one part of the fast, and not from another; or may be excused from fasting and yet not

---

[424] Cf. Is 58
[425] Cf. Tb 12:8

from abstinence. Third, that such as for some just cause are dispensed with from fasting, ought to endeavor, as far as their condition and circumstances will allow, to be so much the more diligent in their devotions, more liberal in their alms, more patient in their sufferings, and to make up by the interior spirit of penance what is wanting to the outward fast.

Of the Fast of Lent

349. When did the Church first begin to observe the fast of Lent?

We know no beginning of it; for it is a fast that has ever been observed by the Church from the time of the apostles, and stands upon the same foundation as the observation of the Lord's day, that is, upon apostolical tradition.

350. Have the ancient fathers often mentioned this solemn fast of forty days, which we call Lent?

Yes: it is mentioned by the holy fathers in innumerable places, who also inform us that they had received it by tradition from the apostles.[426] And the transgressors of this solemn fast are severely punished by Canon 69 of the Apostolic Canons.[427]

351. Have you anything else to offer to prove that the fast of Lent comes from an ordinance of the apostles?

Yes: it is proved by that rule of St. Augustine, viz. that what is found not to have had its institution from any Council, but to have been ever observed by the universal Church, that same must needs have come from the first fathers and founders of the

---

[426] Cf. Jerome, *Epistle 54 ad Marcellum*; Leo the Great, *Sermon 43*, *Sermon 46*

[427] "If any bishop, presbyter, or deacon, or reader, or singer, does not fast the holy Quadragesimal fast of Easter, or the fourth day, or the day of Preparation, let him be deposed, unless he be hindered by some bodily infirmity. If he be a layman, let him be excommunicated."

Church, that is, from the apostles.[428] But the fast of Lent is not found to have had its institution from any council, but to have been observed in all ages, from the very beginning, amongst all Christian people from East to West: therefore the fast of Lent is an apostolical ordinance and tradition.

352. For what ends was the fast of Lent instituted?

First, that by this yearly fast of forty days, we might imitate the fast of our Lord.[429] Second, that by this institution we might set aside the tithe, or tenth part of the year, to be more particularly consecrated to God by prayer and fasting; as it was commanded in the law to give God the tithes of all things. Third, that by this forty days fast, joined with prayers and almsdeeds, we might do penance for the sins of the whole year. Fourth, that we might at this time enter into a kind of spiritual exercise, and a retreat from the world; to look more narrowly into the state of our souls, to repair our decayed strength, and to provide effectual remedies against our usual failings for the time to come. Fifthly, that by this solemn fast we might celebrate in a more becoming manner the passion of Christ, which we particularly commemorate in the Lent. In fine, that this fast might be a preparation for the great solemnity of Easter, and for the paschal Communion.

353. In what spirit would the Church have her children undertake and go through the fast of Lent?

In a penitential spirit, that is, with a deep sense of repentance for having offended God, an earnest desire and resolution of a new life, and of mortifying and chastising themselves for their sins. These lessons she inculcates every day in her office and liturgy; witness the hymns prescribed for this holy time, the responsories, the collects, tracts, etc.

---

[428] Cf. Augustine, *Letter 54*
[429] Cf. Mt 4:2

I shall give you a specimen of the spirit of the Church in this regard, by setting down some passages of the scripture which she orders to be read in the canonical hours of prayer every day during this time: At lauds, Isaiah, 58: "Cry out, cease not, raise thy voice like a trumpet, and declare to my people their wickedness, and to the house of Jacob their sins."[430] At prime, or the first hour, Isaiah 55: "Seek the Lord, whilst he may be found; call upon him whilst he is near."[431] At terce, or the third hour, Joel 2: "Be converted to me with your whole heart, in fasting, and weeping, and mourning; and rend your hearts, and not your garments,"[432] saith the Lord Almighty. At sext, or the sixth hour, Isaiah 55: "Let the wicked man forsake his ways, and the unjust man his thoughts; and let him return to the Lord, and he will have mercy on him, and to our God, for his mercy is great."[433] At none, or the ninth hour, Isaiah 58: "Break thy bread to the hungry, and bring in the needy and the harborless into thy house: when thou shalt see the naked, clothe him, and despise not thy own flesh."[434] At vespers, or even-song, Joel 2: "Between the porch and the altar, the priests, the ministers of the Lord shall mourn, and they shall say, spare, O Lord, spare thy people, and let not thy inheritance fall into reproach, for the nations to domineer over them."[435]

To the same effect she often repeats in her office the following exhortation: "Let us repent and amend the sins which we have ignorantly committed, lest being suddenly overtaken by the day of our death, we seek for time of penance; and be not able to find it." And again: "Behold now is an acceptable time,

---

[430] Is 58:1
[431] Is 55:6
[432] Jl 2:12-13
[433] Is 55:7
[434] Is 58:7
[435] Jl 2:17

behold now are the days of salvation; let us recommend ourselves in much patience," etc.

354. Why do you call the first day of Lent, *Ash Wednesday?*

From the ceremony of blessing ashes upon that day, and putting
them upon the foreheads of the faithful, to remind them that
they must very quickly return to dust; and therefore must not
neglect to lay hold of this present time of mercy, and like the
Ninivites and other ancient penitents, do penance for their
sins in sackcloth and ashes. The prayers which are said by the
Church for the blessing of the ashes are directed for the obtaining of God the spirit of compunction and the remission of sins
for all those who receive those ashes; and the priest, in making
the sign of the cross with the ashes on the forehead of each one
of the faithful, says these words: "Remember man, that thou art
dust, and into dust thou shalt return."

**355. Was it ever the custom of the Catholic Church to meet on that
day to curse sinners?**

No; but to pray to God to obtain mercy for sinners.

**356. What benefit is it to the faithful to have regular times of fast-
ing set aside by the Church, rather than to be left to their own
discretion to fast when they please?**

First, it is to be feared that many would not fast at all, were they
not called upon by these regular fasts of the Church. Second,
it is not to be doubted but that sinners may more easily and
readily find mercy when they join thus all in a body with the
whole Church of God in suing for mercy.

**357. But is this mercy to be expected, if sinners only mortify them-
selves in point of eating, and in all other things indulge themselves in their accustomed liberties?**

It is certain that the true spirit of penance, which is the spirit of Lent, requires that they should be mortified not only in their eating, but also by retrenching all superfluities in other things, as in drinking, sleeping, idle visits, and unnecessary diversions, according to that of the Church hymn for Lent:

Utamur ergo parciùs
Verbis, cibis et potibus,
Somno, jocis, et arctiùs
Perstemus in custodia.[436]

358. What do you think of preparing for Lent by a carnival of debauchery and excess?

I think it is a relic of heathenism, infinitely opposite to the spirit of the Church. The very name of Shrove-tide, in the language of our forefathers, signifies the season or time of confession; because our ancestors were accustomed, according to the true spirit of the Church, to go to confession at that time, that so they might enter upon the solemn fast of Lent in a manner suitable to this penitential fast.

359. Why is the evening office, or vespers, said before dinner on all days in Lent, excepting Sundays?

It is a relic of the ancient custom of fasting in Lent till the evening.

360. Why is the alleluia laid aside during the time of Lent?

Because it is a canticle of joy, and therefore is omitted in this time of penance. But instead of it, the Church, at the beginning of all the canonical hours of her daily office, repeats those words, "Praise be to thee, O Lord, king of everlasting glory."

[436] From the ancient hymn *Ex More Docti Mystico*, attributed to Pope St. Gregory the Great (+604) and prayed throughout Lent in the *Roman Breviary*. One English rendering reads: "More sparing therefore let us make / our words and food and drink we take / our sleep and mirth—and closer barr'd / be every sense in holy guard."

361. Why is the fifth Sunday in Lent called Passion Sunday?
Because, from that day till Easter, the Church, in a particular manner, commemorates the passion of Christ.

362. Why are the crucifixes and altarpieces covered during this time, in which we celebrate Christ's passion?
Because the Church is then in mourning for her spouse, who in his passion was truly a hidden God, by concealing his divinity and becoming for us "as a worm, and no man, the reproach of men, and the outcast of the people."[437]

Of Other Days of Fasting and Abstinence in the Catholic Church

363. Does the Church observe any other days of fasting and abstinence besides the forty days of Lent?
Yes. She fasts upon the Wednesdays, Fridays, and Saturdays, in the four Ember-weeks; and upon the vigils or eves of some of her festivals; as also upon Fridays in this kingdom; and she abstains from flesh on the three Rogation days, on St. Mark's Day, and on the Saturdays throughout the year.

364. Which do you call the four Ember-weeks?
The four Ember-weeks are the weeks in which the Church gives holy orders, at the four seasons of the year, viz. the first week in Lent, Whitsun-week, the third week in September, and the third week in Advent; and they are called Ember-weeks, from the custom of our forefathers of fasting at that time in sackcloth and ashes, or from eating nothing but cakes baked under the embers, and from thence called ember-bread.

---

[437] Ps 21:7

365. Why has the Church appointed these fasts of the Ember-days at the four seasons of the year?

First, that no part of the year might pass without offering to God the tribute of a penitential fast. Second, that we might beg his blessing on the fruits of the earth, and give him thanks for those which we have already received. Third, that all the faithful might join at these times in prayer and fasting to obtain of God worthy pastors; these being the times of their ordination. Thus the primitive Christians fasted at the times of the ordination of their ministers.[438]

366. Why does the Church fast upon the eves or vigils of most holy days?

To prepare her children, by mortification and penance, for worthily celebrating those days.

367. Why do we abstain upon Fridays?

Because our Lord suffered for us upon a Friday. From this rule of fasting upon Fridays, we except the Fridays in Christmastime; as also those that occur betwixt Easter and Whitsuntide, by reason of the joy of those solemnities, and of our having Christ after his resurrection with us, according to that of our Lord, "Can the children of the bride-chamber fast while the bridegroom is with them? As long as they have the bridegroom with them they cannot fast."[439] However, though we don't fast on those days, yet we abstain from flesh; as we do also upon the Sundays of Lent, which are excepted from the rule of fasting. But if Christmas day occur upon a Friday or Saturday, we neither fast nor abstain.

[438] Cf. Acts 13:2-3, 14:22
[439] Mk 2:19

368. What is the meaning of the three Rogation days?

The Monday, Tuesday, and Wednesday before Ascension-day are called the three Rogation days, or days of solemn supplication and prayer. On these days we keep abstinence, and in every parish we go in procession, singing the litanies, to beg God's blessing upon the fruits of the earth and to be preserved from pestilences, famines, etc. Upon the same account we keep abstinence on the day of St. Mark, April 25, with the like solemn supplications and litanies.

369. And what is the meaning of keeping abstinence upon Saturdays?

Because Saturday was the day that our Lord lay dead in the tomb, and a day of mourning to his disciples. This abstinence is also a proper preparation for the solemnity of the Lord's day. In the East, instead of the Saturday, they fast upon the Wednesday, as being the day on which the Jews held their council against Christ, and on which he was sold by Judas.

Chapter 22

Of the Church Office, or the Canonical Hours of Prayer in the Catholic Church

370. What do you mean by the Church office?

It is a form of prayer, consisting of psalms, lessons, hymns, etc. used by all the clergy, and by the religious of both sexes in the Catholic Church. This office is divided into seven parts, commonly called the seven canonical hours, according to the different stages or stations of Christ's passion, viz. the matins or midnight office, to which are annexed the lauds, or morning praises of God; the first, third, sixth, and ninth hours of prayer, commonly called prime, terce, sext, and none; the vespers, or even-song; and the compline. All these are duly performed by the clergy and religious every day, according to that of the royal prophet, "Seven times in the day I gave praise to thee."[440]

371. Have you any warrant in scripture for these different hours of prayer?

Yes; as to the midnight office, King David tells us that he arose at midnight to confess to God;[441] and we find that St. Paul and Silas, even in prison, "prayed at midnight and sung praises to God."[442] As for the lauds, or praises of God at break of day, they are also recommended to us by the example of the psalmist: "O god, my God, to thee do I watch from the morning light";[443] and by the admonition of the wise man, that we ought to get up before the sun to bless God, and at the rising of light to adore him.[444]

Of prime, or the first hour of prayer at sunrising, we may understand that of the royal prophet, "In the morning thou shalt hear my voice,"[445] etc. At terce, or the third hour of prayer, it was that the apostles received the Holy Ghost.[446] At sext, or the sixth hour, St. Peter was praying when he was called by a vision to open the Church to the gentiles.[447] And we read of the same St. Peter with St. John going up to the Temple to the "ninth hour of prayer."[448]

For vespers, or even-song, and compline, which are evening prayer, we have the example of the royal prophet, "In the

---

[440] Ps 118:164
[441] Cf. Ps 118:62
[442] Acts 16:25
[443] Ps 62:2
[444] Ws 16:28
[445] Ps 5:4
[446] Cf. Acts 2:15
[447] Cf. Acts 10:9
[448] Acts 3:1

evening, and the morning, and at noonday, I will speak and declare, and he will hear my voice."[449] Hence we find, that the night office, the morning praises, the third, sixth, and ninth hours of prayer, and the even-song, were among the primitive Christians regularly observed, not only by the clergy but also by the rest of the faithful; to which the religious afterwards added the prime and compline.

372. Can you give me a short scheme of these canonical hours of prayer, according to the *Roman Breviary*?

Matins begin with the Lord's Prayer, the Hail Mary, and the Apostles' Creed: then after a versicle or two, to call for God's assistance, and the *Gloria Patri*, etc., follows Psalm 94 (95), by which we invite one another to praise and adore God. Then comes a hymn, which is followed by the psalms, with their proper anthems, and the lessons of the day, with their responsories. In the matins for Sunday, we read eighteen psalms and nine lessons: on festivals and saints' days, we read nine psalms and nine lessons, divided into three nocturns: on ferial, or common days, we read twelve psalms and three lessons. The psalms are so distributed, that in the week we go through the whole psalter: the lessons are partly taken out of the scriptures of the old and new testament, partly out of the acts of the saints, and the writings and homilies of the holy fathers. Upon festival days, during the whole paschal time, upon all Sundays from Easter to Advent, and from Christmas till Septuagesima, we close the matins with the *Te Deum*.

In the lauds we recite seven psalms, and one of the scripture canticles, with their respective anthems, and a hymn; then the canticle *Benedictus*, with the prayer or prayers of the day: and in the end an anthem and prayer of the Blessed Virgin Mary.

The prime begins with the *Pater*, *Ave*, and Creed, *Deus in*

[449] Ps 54:18

adjutorium, etc. *Gloria Patri*, etc. After which there follows a morning hymn, then Psalm 53 (54), with a part of Psalm 118 (119), to which on Sundays is prefixed Psalm 117, and subjoined the Athanasian Creed. Then follows an anthem, a capitulum, or short lesson with its responsory and diverse prayers to beg God's grace for the following day.

Terce, sext, and none begin with *Pater, Ave,* etc. and consist each of them of a proper hymn, and six divisions of Psalm 118: which excellent psalm the Church would have her clergy daily recite, because every verse of it contains the praises of God's holy law and commandments, or excites the soul to the love and esteem thereof, or in fine, prays for the grace to fulfil the same. After the psalm follows an anthem; then a short lesson, responsory and prayer: and each hour is concluded with a *Pater Noster.*

Vespers, or even-song, are begun also with *Pater, Ave,* etc., and consist of five psalms with their anthems, a short chapter or lesson, a hymn, and the *Magnificat,* or canticle of the Blessed Virgin Mary, with its proper anthem, and a collect or prayer, to which are usually joined three or four commemorations consisting of anthems, verses, and prayers.

Compline consists of the Lord's Prayer, the *confiteor*, etc., four psalms, an anthem, hymn, lesson, responsory, the canticle *Nunc dimittis* with its anthem, and some short prayers, which are closed with an anthem and prayer of the Blessed Virgin, and the *Pater, Ave,* and Creed.

Chapter 23

Of the Festivals of the Catholic Church

373. What are the days which the Church commands to be kept holy?

First, the Sunday, or the Lord's day, which we observe by apostolical tradition instead of the sabbath. Second, the feasts of our Lord's Nativity, or Christmas-day; his Circumcision, or New-Year's day; the Epiphany, or Twelfth-day, Candlemas-day, or the day of the Presentation of our Lord, and the Purification of his Blessed Mother; Easter day, or the day of our Lord's resurrection, with the Monday and Tuesday following; the day of our Lord's Ascension; Whitsunday, or the day of the coming of the Holy Ghost, with the Monday and Tuesday following; Trinity Sunday; Corpus Christi, or the feast of the Blessed Sacrament; and the feast of the Invention, or Finding of the Cross. Third, we keep the days of the Conception, Nativity, Annunciation, and Assumption of the Blessed Virgin Mary. Fourth, we observe the feast of All-Saints; of St. Michael, and of all the angels, commonly called Michaelmas-day; of St. John Baptist; of St. Joseph; of the twelve apostles, of the illustrious martyrs St. Stephen and St. Lawrence; of the Holy Innocents; and of St. Ann the mother of the Blessed Virgin. Fifth, in this nation we keep the days of St. Thomas of Canterbury, and of St. George, as our special patrons.

374. What warrant have you for keeping the Sunday, preferably to the ancient sabbath, which was the Saturday?

We have for it the authority of the Catholic Church, and apostolical tradition.

375. Does the scripture anywhere command the Sunday to be kept for the sabbath?

The scripture commands us to hear the Church[450] and to hold fast the traditions of the apostles;[451] but the scripture does not in particular mention this change of the sabbath. St. John speaks of the Lord's day,[452] but he does not tell us what day of the week this was, much less does he tell us that this day was to take place of the sabbath ordained in the commandments. St. Luke also speaks of the disciples meeting together to break bread on the first day of the week,[453] and St. Paul orders that on the first day of the week the Corinthians should lay by in store what they designed to bestow in charity on the faithful in Judea:[454] but neither one nor the other tells us that this first day of the week was to be henceforward the day of worship and the Christian sabbath; so that in very deed, the best authority we have for this is the testimony and ordinance of the Church. And therefore, those who pretend to be so religious observers of the Sunday, whilst they take no notice of other festivals ordained by the same Church authority, show that they act by humor, and not by reason and religion; since Sundays and holy days all stand upon the same foundation, viz. the ordinance of the Church.

[450] Cf. Mt 18:17; Lk 10:16
[451] Cf. 2 Thes 2:14
[452] Cf. Apoc 1:10
[453] Cf. Acts 20:7
[454] Cf. 1 Cor 16:2

376. But ought it not to be enough to keep one day in the week, according as it was prescribed in the commandments, without enjoining any other festivals or holy days; especially since it is expressly said in the commandment, "Six days shall thou labor and do all thy work"?[455]

God did not think it enough in the old testament to appoint the weekly sabbath, which was the Saturday, but moreover ordained several other festivals, commanding them to be kept holy, and forbidding all servile work on them: as the feast of the Pasch or Passover; the feast of Pentecost; the feast of the Sound of Trumpets, on the first day of the tenth month; the feast of Atonement, on the tenth day of the same month; the feast of Tabernacles, on the fifteenth day of the same month; etc.[456] So that when it is said in the law, "Six days shalt thou labor," etc., this must needs be understood, in case no holy day came in the week; otherwise the law would contradict itself.

377. But does not St. Paul reprehend the Galatians for observing days, and months, and times, and years?[457]

This is to be understood either of the superstitious observation of lucky or unlucky days, etc., or, as it is far more probable from the whole context, of the observation of the Jewish festivals; which with the old law were now abolished, but were taken up by the Galatians, together with circumcision, upon the recommendation of certain false teachers: but far was it from the design of the apostle to reprehend their observation of Christian solemnities, either of the Lord's day, or of other festivals observed by apostolical tradition, or recommended by the authority of the Church of Christ. For these come to us recommended by Christ himself, who says to the pastors

---

[455] Ex 20:9
[456] Cf. Lv 23
[457] Cf. Gal 4:10-11

of his Church, "he that heareth you, heareth me; and he that despiseth you, despiseth me."[458]

378. What was the reason why the weekly sabbath was changed from the Saturday to the Sunday?

Because our Lord fully accomplished the work of our redemption by rising from the dead on a Sunday, and by sending down the Holy Ghost on a Sunday. As therefore the work of our redemption was a greater work than that of our creation, so the primitive Church thought the day in which this work was completely finished was more worthy her religious observation than that in which God rested from the creation.

379. But has the Church a power to make any alterations in the commandments of God?

The commandments of God, as far as they contain his eternal law, are unalterable and indispensable; but as to whatever was only ceremonial, they cease to oblige, since the Mosaic law was abrogated by Christ's death. Hence, as far as the commandment obliges us to set aside some part of our time for the worship and service of our Creator, it is an unalterable and unchangeable precept of the eternal law, in which the Church cannot dispense: but for as much as it prescribes the seventh day in particular for this purpose, it is no more than a ceremonial precept of the old law, which obligeth not Christians. And therefore, instead of the seventh day, and other festivals appointed by the old law, the Church has prescribed the Sundays and holy days to be set apart for God's worship; and these we are now obliged to keep, in consequence of God's commandment, instead of the ancient sabbath.

[458] Lk 10:16

380. What was the reason of the institution of other festivals besides the Lord's day?

That we might celebrate the memory of the chief mysteries of our redemption; that we might give God thanks for all his mercies, and glorify him in his saints.

381. In what manner ought a Christian to spend the Sundays and holy days?

In religious duties; such as assisting at the great sacrifice of the Church and other public prayers, reading good books, and hearing the word of God, etc.

382. Why does the Church prohibit all servile works upon Sundays or holy days?

That the faithful may have nothing to take them off from attending to God's service and the sanctification of their souls upon these days. And certainly, a Christian that has any religious thoughts, can never think much of devoting now and then a day, to that great business, for which alone he came into this world.

383. What is the meaning of the institution of Christmas?

To celebrate the birth of Christ: to give God thanks for sending his Son into the world for our redemption; and that we may upon this occasion endeavor to study and to learn those great lessons of poverty of spirit, of humility, and of self-denial, which the Son of God teaches us from the crib of Bethlehem.

384. What is the reason that on Christmas day, Mass is said at midnight?

Because Christ was born at midnight.

385. Why are three Masses said by every priest upon Christmas day?

This ancient observance may be understood to denote three

different births of Christ: his eternal birth from his Father, his temporal birth from his mother, and his spiritual birth in the hearts of good Christians.

386. Are all the faithful obliged to hear three Masses on Christmas day?
No, they are not: though it would be very commendable so to do.

387. What is the meaning of the time of Advent before Christmas?
It is a time set aside by the Church for devotion and penance, and is called advent or *coming*, because in it we prepare ourselves for the worthy celebrating the mercies of our Lord's first coming, that so we may escape the rigor of his justice at his second coming.

388. What is the meaning of New-Year's day?
It is the octave of Christmas, and the day of our Lord's circumcision, when he first began to shed his innocent blood for us: and on this day we ought to study how we may imitate him by a spiritual circumcision of our hearts.

389. What is the meaning of the Epiphany, or Twelfth-day?
It is a day kept in memory of the coming of the wise men from the East, to adore our Savior in his infancy: and it is called epiphany, or *manifestation*, because our Lord then began to manifest himself to the gentiles. The devotion of this day is to give God thanks for our vocation to the true faith, and like the wise men to make our offerings of gold, frankincense and myrrh; that is, of charity, prayer, and mortification to our new-born Savior. On this day the Church also celebrates the memory of the baptism of Christ, and of his first miracle of changing water into wine in Cana of Galilee.

390. What is the meaning of Candlemas-day?

It is the day of the Purification of the Blessed Virgin after child-bearing, and of the Presentation of our Lord in the Temple; when the just man Simeon, who had a promise from the Holy Ghost of seeing the Savior of the world before his death, received him into his arms, and proclaimed him to be the light of the gentiles. Upon this account, the Church upon this day makes a solemn procession with lighted candles, which are blessed by the priest before Mass, and carried in the hands of the faithful as an emblem of Christ, who is the true light of the world. And from this ceremony this day is called Candlemas, or the Mass of candles.

391. What is the meaning of the Annunciation or Lady-day, the 25th of March?

It is the day of our Lord's incarnation, when he was first conceived by the Holy Ghost in the womb of the Blessed Virgin Mary; and it is called the Annunciation, from the message brought from heaven on this day to the Virgin by the angel Gabriel.

392. What is the meaning of the Holy Week before Easter?

It is a week of more than ordinary devotion in honor of the passion of Christ.

393. What is the meaning of Palm Sunday?

It is the day in which our Lord being about to suffer for us, entered into Jerusalem, sitting upon an ass, as had been foretold by the prophet Zachariah,[459] and was received with hosannas of joy, accompanied by a great multitude bearing branches of palms in their hands. In memory of which we go in procession round the Church on this day, bearing also branches of

[459] Cf. Zac 9:9

palms in our hands, to celebrate the triumphs of our victorious fathers.

394. What is the meaning of the tenebrae office in Holy Week?

The matins of Christ's passion, which formerly used to be said in the night, and are now said in the evening, on Wednesday, Thursday, and Friday in Holy Week, are called the tenebrae office, from the Latin word which signifies *darkness*; because towards the latter end of the office, all the lights are extinguished in memory of the darkness which covered all the earth whilst Christ was hanging upon the cross: and at the end of the office, a noise is made to represent the earthquake and splitting of the rocks, which happened at the time of our Lord's death.

395. What is the meaning of Maundy-Thursday?

It is the day on which Christ first instituted the Blessed Sacrament and began his passion by his bitter agony and bloody sweat. From the *Gloria in excelsis* of the Mass of this day until the Mass of Easter Eve, our bells are silent throughout the Catholic Church, because we are now mourning for the passion of Christ. Our altars are also uncovered and stripped of all their ornaments, because Christ our true altar hung naked upon the cross. On this day also, prelates and superiors wash in the Church the feet of their subjects, after the example of our Lord.[460]

396. What is the meaning of visiting the sepulchers upon Maundy-Thursday?

The place where the Blessed Sacrament is reserved in the Church, in order for the office of Good Friday (on which day there is no consecration), is by the people called the sepulcher, as representing by anticipation the burial of Christ. And where

[460] Cf. Jn 13

there are many churches, the faithful make their stations to visit our Lord in these sepulchers, and meditate on the different stages of his passion.

397. What is the meaning of Good Friday?
It is the day on which Christ died for us upon the cross. The devotion proper for this day, and for the whole time in which we celebrate Christ's passion, is to meditate upon the sufferings of our Redeemer, to study the excellent lessons of virtue which he teaches us by his example in the whole course of his passion; especially his humility, meekness, patience, obedience, resignation, etc., and above all, to learn his hatred of sin and his love for us; that we may also learn to hate sin, which nailed him to the cross; and to love him that has loved us even unto death.

398. What is the meaning of creeping to the cross and kissing it on Good Friday?
It is to express by this reverence outwardly exhibited to the cross, our veneration and love for him, who upon this day died for us on the cross.

399. What is the meaning of Holy Saturday?
It is Easter Eve, and therefore in the Mass of this day the Church resumes her alleluias of joy, which she had intermitted during the penitential time of Septuagesima and Lent. On this day is blessed the paschal candle, as an emblem of Christ and his light and glory, which burns during the Mass from Easter until Ascension, that is, during the whole time that Christ remained upon earth after his resurrection. This day and Whitsun-eve were anciently the days deputed by the Church for solemn baptism, and therefore on this day the fonts are solemnly blessed.

400. What is the meaning of Easter?
It is the chief feast of the whole year, as being the solemnity of

our Lord's resurrection. The devotion of this time is to rejoice in Christ's victory over death and hell, and to labor to imitate his resurrection by arising from the death of sin to the life of grace.

401. What is the meaning of Ascension day?

It is the yearly memory of Christ's ascending into heaven, forty days after his rising again from the dead. And therefore it is a festival of joy, as well by reason of the triumphs of our Savior on this day and the exaltation of our human nature by him now exalted above the angels, as likewise because our Savior has taken possession of that kingdom in our name, and is preparing a place for us; and in the meantime he there discharges the office of our high priest and our advocate, by constantly representing his death and passion to his Father in our behalf. It is also a part of the devotion of this day, to labor to disengage our hearts from this earth and earthly things, to remember that we are but strangers and pilgrims here, and to aspire after our heavenly country, where Christ our treasure is gone before us, in order to draw our hearts thither after him.

402. What is the most proper devotion for the time between Ascension and Whitsunday?

To prepare ourselves for the Holy Ghost, as the apostles did by retirement and prayer, and to purify our souls from sin, especially from all rancor and impurity.

403. What is the meaning of the solemnity of Whitsunday or Pentecost?

It was a festival observed in the old law, in memory of the law having been given on that day in thunder and lightning; and it is observed by us now in memory of the new law, having been promulgated on this day by the Holy Ghost's descent upon the apostles in the shape of tongues of fire. The proper devotion of this time is to invite the Holy Ghost into our souls by fervent prayer, and to give ourselves up to his divine influences.

404. What is the meaning of Trinity Sunday?

The first Sunday after Pentecost is called Trinity Sunday, because on that day we particularly commemorate that great mystery of three Persons in one God, and glorify the Blessed Trinity for the whole work of our redemption, which we have celebrated in the foregoing festivals.

405. What is the meaning of the solemnity of Corpus Christi?

It is a festival observed by the Church, to give God thanks for his goodness and mercy in the institution of the Blessed Sacrament; and to this end are ordained the processions and benedictions of this octave.

406. What is the meaning of the feast of the Invention (or Finding) of the Cross on May 3rd?

It is a day kept in memory of the miraculous finding of the cross of Christ by the Empress Helen, mother to Constantine the Great; and the chief devotion of the Church upon this day, as well as upon that of the Exaltation of the Cross (Sept. 14), is to celebrate the victorious death and passion of our Redeemer.

407. What are the days observed by the Church in honor of our Lady, the Blessed Virgin Mary?

Besides her Purification and Annunciation, of which we have already spoken, we keep the day of her Conception (December 8), the day of her birth, or Nativity (September 8), and the day of her happy passage to eternity (August 15), which we call her Assumption, it being a pious tradition that she was taken up to heaven both in body and soul, though not till after she had paid the common debt by death. We also keep the day of her Presentation or consecration to God in the Temple (November

21), and of her Visitation (August 2), but these are not holy days of obligation.

408. What is the meaning of keeping the festivals of the Blessed Virgin Mary, and of other saints?

First, to glorify God in his saints, and to give him thanks for the graces and glory bestowed upon them. Secondly, to communicate with these citizens of heaven, and to procure their prayers for us. Third, to encourage ourselves to imitate their examples.

409. Does not the Church also observe some days in honor of the angels?

We observe Michaelmas day in honor of St. Michael the archangel, and of all the heavenly legions. We also commemorate an illustrious apparition of St. Michael (May 8), and we keep the day of our angels guardians (October 2), to give God thanks for giving his angels a charge over us: though these two latter are not days of obligation.

410. How do you prove that we have angels for our guardians?

From Matthew 18: "Take heed that ye despise not one of these little ones; for I say unto you, that in heaven their angels do always behold the face of my Father that is in heaven."[461] Also, "Are they not all ministering spirits, sent forth to minister for them, who shall be heirs of salvation?"[462]

---

[461] Mt 18:10
[462] Heb 1:14

Chapter 24

Of the Invocation of Angels and Saints

411. What is the doctrine and practice of the Catholic Church, with regard to the invocation of angels and saints?

We hold it to be pious and profitable to apply ourselves to them, in the way of desiring them to pray to God for us; but not so as to address ourselves to them as if they were the authors or disposers of pardon, grace, or salvation; or as if they had any power to help us independently of God's good will and pleasure.

412. But in some of the addresses made to the saints or angels, I find petitions for mercy, aid, or defense; what say you to that?

The meaning of those addresses, as far as they are authorized by the Church, is no other than to beg mercy of the saints in this sense, that they would pity and compassionate our misery, and would pray for us. In like manner, when we beg their aid and defense, we mean to beg the aid and defense of their prayers; and that the angels, to whom God has given a charge over us, would assist us and defend us against the angels of darkness. And this is no more than what the protestant church asks in the collect for Michaelmas-day, praying that as the holy angels always serve God in heaven, so by his appointment they may succor and defend us upon earth.

413. Have you any reason to believe that it is pious and profitable to beg the prayers of the saints and angels?

We have the same reason to desire the saints and angels to pray for us, and to believe it profitable so to do, as we have to desire the prayers of God's servants here upon earth; or as St. Paul had to desire so often the prayers of the faithful, to whom he wrote his epistles.[463] For if it be pious and profitable to desire the prayers of sinners here upon earth (for all men here upon earth must acknowledge themselves sinners), how can it be otherwise than pious and profitable to desire the prayers of the saints and angels in heaven? Is it that the saints and angels in heaven have less charity for us than the faithful upon earth? This cannot be, since "charity never faileth,"[464] and instead of being diminished, is increased in heaven. Or is it that the saints and angels in heaven have less interest with God than the faithful upon earth? Neither can this be said, for as they are far more holy and pure, and more closely united to His Divine Majesty than the faithful upon earth, so must their interest in heaven be proportionally greater. Or is it, in fine, that the saints and angels have no knowledge of what passes upon earth, and therefore are not to be addressed to for their prayers? Neither is this true, since our Lord assures us that "there is joy in the presence of the angels of God over one sinner that repenteth,"[465] which could not be, if the citizens of heaven knew nothing of what passes here upon earth.

414. Have you any instances in scripture of the angels or saints praying for us, or offering up our prayers to God?

Yes: "The angel of the Lord answered and said, O Lord of hosts how long wilt thou not have mercy on Jerusalem, and on the cities of Judah, against which thou hast had indignation these threescore and ten years."[466] "The four and twenty elders fell down before the lamb, having every one of them harps and golden vials full of odors, which are the prayers of saints."[467] "And another angel came and stood at the altar, having a

---

[463] Cf. Rom 15:30; Eph 6:18-19; 1 Thes 5:25; Heb 13:18
[464] 1 Cor 13:8
[465] Lk 15:10
[466] Zac 1:12
[467] Apoc 5:8

golden censer; and there was given unto him much incense, that he should offer it with the prayers of all saints upon the golden altar which was before the throne. And the smoke of the incense, with the prayers of the saints, ascended up before God out of the angel's hand."[468]

415. Have you any instances in scripture of asking the blessing or prayers of angels or saints?

"God before whom my fathers Abraham and Isaac did walk, the God which fed me all my life long until this day, the angel which redeemed me from all evil, bless the lads."[469] "Grace be unto you, and peace from him which is, and which was, and which is to come, and from the seven spirits which are before his throne."[470] But if there had been no instances in scripture, both reason and religion must inform us that there cannot possibly be any harm in desiring the prayers of God's servants, whether they be in heaven or upon earth.

416. At least there is no command in scripture for desiring the prayers of the angels or saints; what say you to this?

The scripture did not command St. Paul to desire the prayers of the Romans, nor does it command a child to ask his father's blessing, nor the faithful to kneel at their prayers, or pull off their hats when they go to Church, yet these things are no less commendable, as being agreeable to the principles of piety and religion, and so it is with regard to the invocation of the saints and angels. In the meantime, we are sure that there is no law nor command in scripture against any of these things, and consequently that they are guilty of a crying injustice, who accuse

---

[468] Apoc 8:3-4
[469] Gn 48:15-16
[470] Apoc 1:4

us of a crime for begging the prayers of the saints, for "where there is no law there is no transgression."[471]

417. Does not God say, "I will not give my glory to another"?[472]

Yes, but that makes nothing against desiring the saints to pray to God for us; for this is no more robbing God of his honor, than when we desire the prayers of the faithful here below.

418. But does it not argue a want of confidence in God's mercy, to have recourse to the prayers of the saints?

No, by no means; no more than it argues a want of confidence in God's mercy, to have recourse to the prayers of our brethren upon earth. The truth is, though God be infinitely merciful and ready to hear our prayers, yet it is our duty, and his will, that we should neglect no means by which we may be forwarded in our progress to a happy eternity: and therefore it is agreeable to His Divine Majesty, that we should both pray ourselves without ceasing, and that we should also procure the prayers of our brethren, whether in heaven or on earth, that he may have the honor and we the profit of so many more prayers.

419. Have you any proof or instance in scripture that God will more readily hear his servants when they intercede for us, than if we alone were to address ourselves to him?

Yes. The Lord said to Eliphaz the Temanite, "My wrath is kindled against thee, and against thy two friends; for ye have not spoken of me the thing that is right, as my servant Job hath. Therefore take unto you now seven bullocks, and seven rams, and go to my servant Job, and offer up for yourselves a burnt offering, and my servant Job shall pray for you, for him will I

---

[471] Rom 4:15
[472] Is 42:8

accept; lest I deal with you after your folly, in that ye have not spoken of me the thing that is right, like my servant Job."[473]

420. But is it not an injury to the mediatorship of Christ to desire the intercession of the angels and saints?

No more than when we desire the intercession of God's servants here; because we desire no more of the saints than we do of our brethren upon earth, that is, we only desire of them to pray for us and with us, to him that is both our Lord and their Lord, by the merits of his Son, Jesus Christ, who is both our mediator and their mediator.

421. Does not St. Paul say, "There is one God, and one mediator between God and men, the man Jesus Christ";[474] and does not this exclude the intercession of the saints?

The words immediately following are, "Who gave himself a ransom for all"; so that the plain meaning of the text is, that Christ alone is our mediator of redemption. But as for intercession and prayer, as nothing hinders us from seeking the mediation of the faithful upon earth to pray for us, so nothing ought to hinder us from seeking the like from the saints and angels, though neither the one nor the other can obtain anything for us any other way than through Jesus Christ, who is the only mediator, who stands in need of no other to recommend his petitions.

422. Have you anything else to add in favor of the Catholic doctrine and practice of the invocation of saints?

Yes. First, that it is agreeable to the communion of saints, which we profess in the Creed, and of which the apostle speaks: "Ye are come unto Mount Sion, and unto the city of the living God, the heavenly Jerusalem, and to an innumerable company of

[473] Jb 42:7-8
[474] 1 Tm 2:5

angels; to the general assembly and Church of the first-born which are written in heaven, and to God the Judge of all, and to the spirits of just men made perfect, and to Jesus the mediator of the new covenant."[475] Second, that it is agreeable to the doctrine and practice of the ancient fathers, saints, and doctors of the Church; and this by the confession even of our adversaries: "I confess," says Mr. Fulk in his *Rejoinder to Bristow*, "that Ambrose, Augustine, and Jerome held invocation of saints to be lawful";[476] and that in Nazianzen, Basil, and Chrysostom is mention of invocation of saints, and that Theodoret also speaks of prayers to the martyrs.[477] And the Centuriators of Magdeburg, in their fourth century *Col. 295*, allege several examples of prayers to saints in St. Athanasius, St. Basil, St. Gregory Nazianzen, St. Ambrose, Prudentius, St. Epiphanius, and St. Ephrem. All which fathers, together with St. Augustine, St. Jerome, etc., are also charged by Mr. Brightman of establishing idolatry by invocation of saints, worshipping of relics, and such like wicked "superstitions."[478] And Mr. Thorndike writes thus:

> It is confessed, that the lights both of the Greek and Latin Church, St. Basil, St. Gregory Nazianzen, St. Gregory Nyssen, St. Ambrose, St. Jerome, St. Augustine, St. Chrysostom, St. Cyril of Jerusalem, St. Cyril of Alexandria, Theodoret, St. Fulgentius, St. Gregory the Great, St. Leo, and more, or rather all after that time, have spoken to the saints, and desired their assistance.[479]

[475] Heb 12:22-24

[476] William Fulke, *A Reioynder to Bristows Replie in Defence of Allens Scroll of Articles and Booke of Purgatorie* (London: Middleton, 1581), 5-6.

[477] Cf. Fulke, upon 2 *Pet.* i. §. 3. fol. 443

[478] Cf. Thomas Brightman, *A Revelation of the Apocalyps* (Amsterdam: Hondius, 1611), 391.

[479] Herbert Thorndike, *An Epilogue to the Tragedy of the Church of England* (London: J.M. and T.R., 1658), Bk. 3, 358. See also Melanchon, *Quartâ Parte Operum*, p. 218; Kemnitius, *Exam. Par.* 3. p. 200; Beza, *Praef. Nov. Test.*; Archbishop Whitgift's *Defense* against Cartwright, p. 473; and Daillè, *Advers. Lat. Tradit.* p. 53.

Third, that it stands upon the same foundation as all other Christian truths, viz. upon the authority of the Church of Christ, which the scripture commands us to hear, with which both Christ and his Holy Spirit will remain forever, and against which the gates of hell cannot prevail.[480] Fourth, that it has been authorized by God himself, by innumerable miracles in every age, wrought in favor of those that have desired the prayers and intercession of the saints.[481]

423. But what do you say to where St. Paul condemns the religion or worship of angels;[482] and to where the angel refused to be worshipped by St. John?[483]

I say, that neither one or the other makes anything against desiring the angels or saints to pray to God for us; for this is not giving them any adoration or divine worship, no more than when we desire the prayers of one another. Now it was adoration, or divine worship, which the angel refused to receive from St. John: "I fell at his feet to worship him,"[484] says the apostle. And it was a superstitious worship, and not the desiring of the prayers of the angels, which is condemned by St. Paul in Colossians 2. A *superstitious* worship, I say, either of bad angels, of whom the apostle speaks in verse 15, or if of good angels, in such a manner as to leave "Christ not holding the head," says the apostle in verse 19; such was the worship which many of the philosophers (against whom St. Paul warns the Colossians in verse 8) paid to angels or demons to whom they offered sacrifices, as to the necessary carriers of intelligence between the gods and men. Such also was the worship which Simon Magus

[480] Cf. Mt 16:18, 18:17, 28:20; Lk 10:16; Jn 14:16, 17, 26, 16:13
[481] Cf. Augustine, *City of God*, Bk. 22, Ch. 8
[482] Cf. Col 2:18
[483] Cf. Apoc 19:10
[484] Ibid.

and many of the Gnostics paid to the angels, whom they held to be the creators of the world.[485]

424. What do you think of making addresses to the angels or saints upon our knees? Is not this giving them divine worship?

No more than when we desire the blessing of our fathers or mothers upon our knees; which is indeed the very case, since what we ask of our parents, when we desire their blessing, is that they would pray to God for us; and this same we ask of the angels and saints.

425. But is it not giving to the angels and saints the attributes of God, viz. omniscience and omnipresence, that is, knowing all things, and being everywhere, if you suppose that they can hear or know all our addresses made to them?

No: we neither believe the angels and saints to be everywhere, nor yet to have the knowledge of all things, though we make no question but they know our prayers, since the scripture assures us that they offer them up to God.[486] If you ask me, "how they can know our prayers without being everywhere and knowing all things?" I answer, that there are many ways by which they may know them.

First, the angels may know them by being amongst us in quality of our guardians; and the saints may know them by the angels, whose conversation they enjoy.

Second, both angels and saints may see them and know them in God, whom they continually see and enjoy, or by revelation from God, as in God they see the repentance of sinners.[487] For they that see God face to face by the light of glory, discern all his divine attributes, and in them innumerable secrets

---

[485] Cf. Theodoret, *Ecclesiastical History*, Bk. 5, *Hæreticarum Fabularum Compendium*, Bk. 5, Ch. 9

[486] Cf. Apoc 5:8, 8:3-4

[487] Cf. Lk 15:10

impenetrable to nature. And therefore, though they themselves are not everywhere, yet, by contemplating him that sees and knows all things, they have a vast extent of knowledge of things that pass here below. "In thy light shall we see light,"[488] says the royal prophet, and "we shall be like to him," says St. John, "for we shall see him as he is."[489] For "now we see," says St. Paul, "through a glass darkly, but then face to face: now I know in part: but then shall I know, even as also I am known."[490]

Third, both angels and saints may know our petitions addressed to them, by the ordinary way by which spirits speak to one another and hear one another, and that is, by our directing our thoughts to them with a desire of opening our minds to them; for we can no otherwise understand or explain the speech and conversation of spirits, who having neither tongues nor ears, must converse together by the directing of their thoughts to one another. Now this kind of conversation by the thoughts may extend to ever so great a distance, as being independent on sound and all other corporal qualities, and consequently independent on distance.

Besides all this, the saints, whilst they were here upon earth, knew very well the miseries we labor under in this vale of tears; they also knew that good Christians earnestly desire to be helped by the prayers of God's saints; and as they knew this whilst they were here upon earth, so they know it still. Consequently, as their charity prompts them to pray for the faithful in general, so it is not to be doubted but they pray more particularly for those who stand most in necessity of their prayers, or most earnestly desire their prayers; it being the property of charity, which is perfect in heaven, to act in this manner. Hence it follows, that though we were even to suppose that the saints did not know in particular our addresses, yet it would still be

[488] Ps 35:10
[489] 1 Jn 3:2
[490] 1 Cor 13:12

profitable to desire their prayers, because they certainly pray for Christians in general, and for those more particularly who desire the help of their prayers.

In fine, the experience of seventeen hundred years, and the innumerable favors that have been granted in every age to those that have desired the prayers of the angels and saints, has convinced the Church of God that this devotion is both pleasing to God and profitable to us; and therefore we may dispense with ourselves from a curious inquiry into the manner of their knowing our request, since we find by experience so great benefit from them.

426. Does not the prophet Isaiah say that Abraham is ignorant of us?[491]

His meaning is plain, that the fatherly care and providence of God over his people was infinitely beyond that of Abraham and Israel, who were their parents according to the flesh. "Doubtless thou art our Father," says the prophet, "though Abraham be ignorant of us, and Israel acknowledge us not: thou, O Lord, art our Father, our Redeemer," etc. In the meantime, that Abraham was not ignorant of what passed amongst his children (though before Christ had opened heaven by his death, the patriarchs did not as yet enjoy the beatific vision) is clear from what we read in Luke 16:25-29.

And here I cannot but take notice how strangely unreasonable the notions of some people are, who make a scruple of allowing any knowledge to the saints and angels of God, whilst they are ready enough to grant that the devils both know our works and hear the addresses of their impious invokers; as if these wretched spirits of darkness, by nature alone, could know more than the saints, who, besides the light of nature, enjoy the light of grace and glory; or, as if those rebels had acquired any

---

[491] Cf. Is 63:16

greater degree of perfection and knowledge by their fall, than they would have had if they had remained angels.

427. But can you prove from scripture, that the saints enjoy God in heaven before the general resurrection?

Yes; this is visibly the doctrine of St. Paul, "For we know, that if our earthly house of this tabernacle were dissolved, we have a building of God, a house not made with hands, eternal in heaven. . . . Therefore we are always confident, knowing that whilst we are at home in the body, we are absent from the Lord (for we walk by faith, and not by sight); we are confident, I say, and willing rather to be absent from the body, and to be present with the Lord."[492] Where he visibly supposes that the souls of the saints, when let loose from their bodies by death, enter into the eternal tabernacles, are present with the Lord, and enjoy his sight. The same thing he supposes in Philippians 1: "I am in a strait betwixt two, having a desire to depart, and to be with Christ; which is far better. Nevertheless to abide in the flesh is more needful for you."[493]

Chapter 25

Of the Devotion of Catholics to the Blessed Virgin Mary

428. What is the meaning of the great respect and devotion of Catholics to the Blessed Virgin Mary?

It is grounded, first, upon her great dignity of Mother of God, and the close relation which she has thereby to Jesus Christ

[492] 2 Cor 5:1, 6-8
[493] Phil 1:23-24

her son; for how is it possible to love and honor Christ with our whole heart, and not value and love his Blessed Mother?

Second, it is grounded upon that super-eminent grace which was bestowed upon her to prepare her for that dignity; upon account of which she was saluted by the angel Gabriel, "full of grace"[494] (which the protestants, who are no great friends of this ever-blessed Virgin, have chosen rather to translate *highly favored*); and both by the angel and by St. Elizabeth she is styled, "Blessed among women."[495]

Third, it is grounded upon her extraordinary sanctity; for if she was full of grace before she conceived in her womb the fountain of all grace, to what a degree of sanctity and grace must she have arrived during so many years as she lived afterwards? Especially since she bore nine months in her womb the author of all sanctity, and had him thirty years under her roof, ever contemplating him and his heavenly mysteries,[496] and on her part never making any resistance to the affluence of his graces ever flowing in upon her happy soul.

Fourth, it is grounded upon that super-eminent degree of heavenly glory with which God has now honored her, in proportion to her grace and sanctity here upon earth, and the great interest she has with her blessed son, and through him with his heavenly Father.

429. Is there anything in scripture that insinuates this great devotion that should be in all ages to this Blessed Virgin?

Yes, it was foretold by herself in her Canticle: "Behold, from henceforth all generations shall call me blessed."[497]

[494] Lk 1:28
[495] Lk 1:42
[496] Cf. Lk 2:19, 51
[497] Lk 1:48

430. Do you then allow divine honor or worship to the Blessed Virgin Mary?

No, certainly. The Church in this, as in all other things, keeps the golden mean between the two extremes: she condemns those that refuse to honor this blessed Mother of God; but those much more that would give her divine worship. She thinks no honor that can be given to any pure creature too great for this Blessed Virgin; but as she knows that there is an infinite distance still between her and God, she is far from offering sacrifice to her, or paying her any worship that belongs to God alone. And whatever honor she gives the mother, she refers it to the glory of the son, as the chief motive and end of all her devotions.

431. But why do you call the Blessed Virgin the Mother of God?

Because she is truly the mother of Jesus Christ, who is true God and true man, and consequently she is truly the Mother of God; not by being mother of the divinity, but by being mother of him, who in one and the same Person, is both God and man. Hence she is called by St. Elizabeth, "the Mother of my Lord."[498]

432. Why does the Church in her hymns and anthems style the Blessed Virgin, Mother of Grace, and Mother of Mercy?

Because she is the mother of him who is the fountain of all grace and mercy; and is both most willing by reason of her super-eminent charity, and most able by her great interest with her son to obtain grace and mercy for us.

[498] Lk 1:43

433. **And why is she styled the Queen of Heaven, or the Queen of Angels and Saints?**
Because she is the mother of the King of Heaven, and the greatest of all the saints.

434. **What then do you think of those that presume to say she was no more than any other woman, nor ought to have any regard or honor paid to her?**
Such as these have very little regard to Jesus Christ, whose mother they treat with so much contempt.

435. **And what do you think of the opinion of those that say she had children by St. Joseph, after the birth of our Savior?**
This was a heresy condemned by the Church near fourteen hundred years ago as contrary to apostolical tradition, and to the very creed of the apostles, which styles her virgin. And that indeed she had determined by vow never to know man, the holy fathers gather from her words to the angel, "How shall this be, for I know not man?"[499]

436. **Who then were they that are called in the scripture the "brethren" of our Savior?**
They are named by St. Mark:[500] James and Joses or Joseph, and Jude, and Simon or Simeon. These were the sons of Mary, the wife of Cleophas, whom the gospel calls the sister, that is, the near kinswoman of the Blessed Virgin, and therefore her sons are called our Savior's brethren, according to the usual scripture phrase, by which those that are near akin are called brothers and sisters.

If you ask me how I prove that Mary the wife of Cleophas was mother to James and Joses, etc., I prove it evidently by

[499] Lk 1:34
[500] Cf. Mk 6:3

comparing the gospels together: Matthew 27:56 acquaints us, that amongst the women who had followed our Savior from Galilee ministering to him and who were present at his death, were Mary Magdalene, and Mary the mother of James and Joses, etc., which same thing is attested by Mark 15:40. Now John 19:25 expressly informs us that this Mary who stood by the cross was sister to the Blessed Virgin, and wife of Cleophas: so that James, Joses, etc., as it is manifest from the gospel, were not children of our Lady, but of her kinswoman, Mary, the wife of Cleophas.

437. But why then is our Savior called her "first-born"?[501]

It is a Hebrew phrase, not signifying that any were born after him, but that no one was born before him.

438. And why is it said of St. Joseph, that "he knew her not till she had brought forth,"[502] etc.?

This also was said according to a propriety of speech amongst the Hebrews, to signify what was not done before, without meddling with the question what was done after: this latter being foreign to the great point which the evangelist had then in view, which was to assure us that Christ was born of a virgin. We have examples of the like expressions in the old testament; as when, Psalm 109 (110), it is said, "The Lord said to my Lord, sit thou on my right hand, till I make my enemies thy footstool"[503]—will he therefore cease to sit at the right hand of his Father, after his enemies are made his footstool? No, certainly.

439. What is the common address which the Church makes to the Blessed Virgin Mary?

The Angelical Salutation or the Hail Mary: a great part of

[501] Cf. Mt 1:25; Lk 2:7
[502] Mt 1:25
[503] Ps 109:1

which is taken out of the gospel,[504] and the other part is added by the Church to beg the prayers of the Blessed Virgin for us sinners.

440. Why do Catholics so often repeat the Hail Mary?
To commemorate the incarnation of the Son of God, to honor his Blessed Mother, and to desire her prayers.

441. What is the meaning of the beads?
It is a devotion consisting of a certain number of Our Fathers and Hail Marys, directed for the obtaining of blessings from God, through the prayers and intercession of our Lady.

442. But is it not highly absurd that, according to the common way of saying the beads, there are repeated ten Hail Marys for one Our Father?
It would be absurd, indeed, and blasphemous too, if the meaning of this were to signify that the Blessed Virgin is either more powerful or more merciful than her son; or that we have a greater confidence in her than in him: but we are far from any such notions.

443. Why then is the Hail Mary repeated so much oftener in the beads than the Lord's Prayer?
Because the beads being a devotion particularly instituted to commemorate the incarnation of Christ, and to honor him in his Blessed Mother, it was thought proper to repeat so much the oftener that prayer which is particularly adapted to these ends. In the meantime it may be proper to take notice, first, that if in the beads there be ten Hail Marys said for one Our Father, in the Mass and office of the Church almost all the prayers are directed to God alone. Second, that every Hail Mary, both by

[504] Cf. Lk 1:28, 42

the nature of the prayer and the intention of the Church, is directed more to the honor of the Son than of the mother; as well because the Church, in honoring the mother, has principally in view the honor of the Son; as also because this prayer particularly relates to the incarnation of Christ; and if withal it begs the prayers of the Blessed Virgin, it is plain that he is more honored to whom we desire she should address her prayers, than she whom we only desire to pray for us. To which, if we add that her prayers are ten times better and more acceptable to God than ours, it will appear no ways absurd that we should frequently desire her prayers. For as to the repetition of the same prayer, it is what is recommended to us by the example of our Lord,[505] and has nothing of absurdity in it.

444. What is the meaning of the rosary?

The rosary is a method of saying the beads, so as to meditate upon the incarnation, passion, and resurrection of Christ. And it is divided into three parts, each part consisting of five mysteries, to be contemplated during the repeating of five decades or tens upon the beads. The first five are called the five joyful mysteries: viz. the annunciation, when our Lord was first conceived in his mother's womb; the visitation, when the Blessed Virgin visited her kinswoman St. Elizabeth, and by her was declared blessed among women, etc.; the nativity of our Lord; his presentation in the Temple, together with the purification of the Blessed Virgin; and his being found in the temple in the midst of the doctors, etc. The five next are called the dolorous or sorrowful mysteries, as having relation to the passion of Christ, and are: his prayer and agony in the garden; his being scourged at the pillar; his crowning with thorns; his carriage of the cross; and his crucifixion and death: the five last are called the five glorious mysteries, viz. the resurrection of our Lord;

---

[505] Cf. Mt 26:42-44

his ascension into heaven; the coming of the Holy Ghost; the assumption of the Blessed Virgin; and her coronation, together with the eternal glory of the saints in the kingdom of heaven.

445. What is the meaning of giving three tolls with the bells every morning, noon, and night, in all Catholic countries?

This is to remind the faithful of the great mystery of the incarnation of the Son of God; and it is the practice of all good Christians, when they hear these bells, to perform the devotion which we call the *Angelus Domini*.

446. What is this devotion, and in what manner is it performed?

The bell tolls three times, with a short space between each time. At the first toll we say, "The angel of the Lord declared to Mary, and she conceived of the Holy Ghost"; then we say the Hail Mary, etc. At the second toll we say, "Behold the hand-maid of the Lord; be it done to me according to thy word," Hail Mary, etc. At the third toll we say, "And the Word was made flesh, and dwelt amongst us"; Hail Mary, etc. Then we conclude with the following prayer:

Pour forth, we beseech thee, O Lord, thy grace into our hearts, that we, to whom the incarnation of Christ thy Son was made known by the message of an angel, may by his passion and cross be brought to the glory of resurrection. Through the same Christ Our Lord, Amen.

This devotion is used in all Catholic countries, and is called the *Angelus Domini*, from the first words, "The angel of the Lord," etc.

Chapter 26

Of the Use and Veneration of Relics in the Catholic Church

447. What do you mean by relics?

The dead bodies or bones of the saints we call relics; as also whatever other things have belonged to them in their mortal life.

448. And what is the doctrine and practice of the Church with regard to these things?

We keep such things as these with a religious respect and veneration for the sake of those to whom they have belonged, but principally for the sake of him to whom the saints themselves belonged; that is, for the greater glory of God, who is glorious in his saints, and to whom is referred all the honor that is given to his saints.

449. What reasons has the Church for showing this respect to the dead bodies or bones of the saints?

First, because they have been the victims and the living temples of God, in which His Divine Majesty has in a particular manner inhabited, and which he has sanctified by his presence and grace. And therefore, if God required of Moses[506] and of Joshua[507] to loose their shoes from off their feet, in respect to the ground on which they stood, as being rendered holy by his presence or that of his angels, we must conclude that it is agreeable to His Divine Majesty that we should testify the like honor to that venerable earth of the bodies of his saints, which

---

[506] Cf. Ex 3:5
[507] Cf. Jo 5:15-16

he in such an extraordinary manner has sanctified, by abiding in them as in his temples. Second, we know that the bodies of the saints are pre-ordained to a happy resurrection and eternal glory, and upon this account also deserve our respect. Third, the bodies and other relics of the saints have been, and are daily the instruments of the power of God, for the working of innumerable miracles which God, who is truth and sanctity itself, would never have effected, if it had not been agreeable to him that we should honor and respect these precious remnants of his servants. Fourth, the relics and shrines of the martyrs and other saints serve very much to encourage the faithful to an imitation of their virtues, and to help to raise their souls from the love of things present and temporal to the love of things eternal.

450. Did the primitive Christians show this respect to the relics of the saints?

Yes. Nothing is more evident from all kind of monuments of antiquity, than that the veneration of the relics of the saints is one of the most ancient things in Christianity. The learned Church historian, Eusebius, relates that St. James' chair was kept with great veneration by the Christians of Jerusalem, from the apostles' time till the days in which the historian wrote, that is, till the beginning of the fourth century.[508] The Acts of the Martyrdom of St. Ignatius, bishop of Antioch, disciple of the apostles, who suffered at Rome in the year 107, written by the Christians who accompanied him to Rome, bear record that his holy relics were carried to Antioch by the Christians, and left to that Church as an inestimable treasure. The Christians of Smyrna, in the account that they give of the martyrdom of their holy bishop St. Polycarp, disciple of the apostles, inform us that the faithful carried away his relics, which they valued

---

[508] Cf. Eusebius, *Ecclesiastical History*, Bk. 7, Ch. 19

more than gold and precious stones.[509] And that this veneration of relics was approved by all the most holy and most
learned bishops and doctors of the Church, and condemned
by none but infidels and heretics such as Julian the Apostate,
Einomius, and Vigilantius, may be seen in the writings of the
holy fathers.[510] This is to pass over many others, who all agree
in approving this practice; and all, or most of them, bear record
that God also has approved it by innumerable miracles.

**451. But have you any instance in scripture of miracles wrought by
the bones of God's saints, or other things belonging to them?**
Yes. We read of a dead man raised to life by the touch of the
bones of the prophet Elisha,[511] and that "from the body of Paul
were brought unto the sick handkerchiefs or aprons, and the
diseases departed from them, and the evil spirits went out of
them."[512]

**452. But does not Christ reprehend the Scribes and Pharisees for
building up and adorning the sepulchers of the prophets?[513]**
He does not reprehend them for the action, which in itself was
good, but for their wicked dispositions; inasmuch as, whilst
they would seem to honor the prophets and thereby obtain
the favor of the people, they sought all the while to fill up the
measure of their fathers, by persecuting unto death the Lord
of prophets.

---

[509] Cf. Eusebius, *Ecclesiastical History*, Bk.4, Ch. 15

[510] Cf. Basil, *Homily on Psalm 115, Homily 5 in Martyrem Julittam, Homily on the 40 Martyrs*; Gregory Nyssen, *Orat. de S. Theodoro Martyre*, T. 3; Gregory Nazianzen, *Oration 3 Against Julian*. Cyril of Jerusalem, *Catechetical Lecture 18*; John Chrysostom, *ad Pap. Ant. Hom*. 40, 47, 59, *L. Contra Gentiles, Hom*. 26 *in 2 Cor 2*; Ambrose, *Letter 22*; Jerome, *Against Vigilantius*; Augustine, *Confessions*, Bk. 9, Ch. 7, *Sermon 92 De Diversis Quaestionibus, City of God*, Bk. 22, Ch. 8, *Epist. 103*; Theodoret, *Contra Græcos*, Bk. 8.

[511] Cf. 4 Kgs 13:21

[512] Acts 19:12

[513] Cf. Mt 23:29-31

453. What kind of honor does the Catholic Church allow to relics?
An inferior and relative honor, as to things belonging to God's saints; but by no means divine honor.

454. But are not candles allowed to burn before them? And are they not sometimes fumed with incense?
These are honors indeed, but such as we may give to one another; as in effect we incense in the Church both clergy and people, and burn candles to our princes upon occasions of joy: for since these honors are no ways appropriated to God, either by the nature of the things in themselves, or by any divine ordinance, why may not the Church of God allow them to the relics of the saints? Not as divine honors, but as tokens of our love and respect to them; of our joy for the triumphs of Christ in his saints, and as emblems of their eternal life, light, and glory.

455. Does not this practice of the veneration of relics expose the faithful to the danger of idolatry and superstition, by honoring false relics?
No. First, because the Church of God, by her public canons and her zealous pastors, takes what care she can to prevent such impostures. Second, because, if by the wickedness of men it should sometimes happen that the faithful should be imposed upon in this regard, so far as to honor a false relic for a true one, there would be neither any idolatry nor superstition in the case, but a mistake on their part, innocent, as when a charitable Christian relieves an impostor or a hypocrite, innocently believing him to be a real object of charity.

456. But if the Church has so much zeal against false relics, how comes she to tolerate them in so many cases, as when divers churches pretend to possess the body of the same saint, for some or other of these must be false relics?
You are too hasty in concluding that these must needs be false

relics. First, because it often happens that some part of the body of a saint is in one place, and some part in another, in which case both places claim the body of such a saint, though they really possess only a part of it; and yet neither one nor the other is therefore to be charged with honoring false relics. Second, many of the saints and martyrs have borne the same name; and hence it easily happens that relics, which indeed belong to one saint, are attributed to another of the same name. Third, there have been many ancient martyrs whose names at present are not known, whose relics nevertheless have been all along honored by the Church: now it was easy that the ignorance of some, or the vanity of others, might attribute to them the names of other saints: so that all these may be true relics, notwithstanding they don't all belong to the saints to whom they are attributed.

457. **What is the meaning of making pilgrimages to the shrines or other memorials of the saints?**

To honor God in his saints, to excite devotion by the sight of those places sanctified by these heavenly pledges, and to obtain graces and blessings of God by the prayers of the saints. For though God be everywhere, and his bounty and mercy be not confined to any particular place, yet the experience of all past ages convinces us that it is his holy will and pleasure to bestow his favors more plentifully and to show more frequent and miraculous effects of his power and goodness in some places than in others.[514]

458. **Have not Catholics a more than ordinary veneration for the wood of the cross, the nails, thorns, and other instruments of Christ's passion?**

Yes they have; because these things have so close a relation to

---

[514] Cf. Augustine, *Epist.* 137

the passion of Christ, by which we were redeemed, and have been sanctified by the blood of our Redeemer.

Chapter 27

Of the Use of Pictures and Images in the Catholic Church

459. What is the doctrine of the Church with regard to pictures or images of Christ and his saints?
First, that it is good to keep them and retain them, and to have them in churches not only for ornament and for the instruction of the ignorant, but for the honor and remembrance of Christ and his saints, and for to help to raise our thoughts and our hearts to heavenly things. Second, that there is a relative honor due to them, by reason of the persons whom they represent.[515]

460. Does the Catholic Church give divine worship to the pictures or images of Christ or his saints?
No, by no means. The Second Council of Nicea, in Act or Session 7, has expressly declared that divine worship is not to be given them; to which the Council of Trent, in Session 25, has added that we "are not to believe that there is any divinity or power in them for which they are to be worshipped: and that we are not to pray to them, nor put our trust or confidence in them."[516]

[515] Cf. Second Council of Nicea, Act 7; Council of Trent, Session 25
[516] Council of Trent, Session 25

461. But does not the first (or second) commandment absolutely forbid the making of any image, or the likeness of anything in heaven, earth, or sea?

No, it only forbids the making of idols: that is, of such images as are made for gods and are worshipped as such, or in which a divinity or divine virtue and power is believed to reside. Hence the ancient version of the Septuagint (which is venerable by having been made use of by the apostles themselves) renders the words of the commandment thus, "thou shalt not make to thyself an idol,"[517] etc. And that God does not absolutely forbid the making of the likeness of anything, is not only the general belief of all Christians, who carry about with them without scruple the likeness of their kings in the current coin of their respective countries, but is visible from scripture, wherein God commanded the making of two cherubims of beaten gold, to be placed over the ark of the covenant in the very sanctuary;[518] and in like manner commanded the making of the brazen serpent, for the healing of those who were bit by the fiery serpents,[519] which serpent was an emblem of Christ.[520]

462. But at least does not God forbid by this commandment all honor or reverence to pictures or images?

He forbids all honor or reverence to idols or image gods, but not the relative honor which Catholics show to the pictures of Christ and his saints, for the sake of the persons represented by them; for it is visible, that the same images which by this commandment are forbid to be honored are also by the express words of the commandment forbid to be made. Now few or no Christians suppose that the pictures of Christ or his saints are forbid to be made; therefore they cannot infer from this

[517] Ex 20:4
[518] Cf. Ex 25:18-21
[519] Cf. Nm 21:8-9
[520] Cf. Jn 3:14-15

commandment that they are forbid to be honored, since this commandment does not speak of them at all, but only of idols or images set up to be worshipped for gods.

463. What then do you mean by this relative honor, which you allow to the pictures of Christ and his saints?

By a relative honor I mean an honor which is given to a thing, not for any intrinsic excellence or dignity in the thing itself, but only for the relation which it has to something else, which it represents or brings to our remembrance; as when Christians bow to the name of Jesus, which is an image or remembrance of our Savior to the ear as the crucifix is to the eye.

464. Have you any instances of this kind of relative honor allowed by protestants?

Yes: in the honor they give to the name of Jesus, to their churches, to the altar, to the bible, to the symbols of bread and wine in the sacrament, to the king's chair, etc. Such also was the honor which the Jews gave to the ark and cherubims, to the sanctuary, etc., and which Moses and Joshua gave to the land on which they stood, as being holy ground.[521]

465. How do you prove that there is a relative honor due to the images or pictures of Christ and his saints?

Because it is evidently agreeable, as well to nature and reason as to piety and religion, to express our esteem and affection for those whom we honor and love, by setting a value upon all things that belong to them, or have any relation to them. Thus good Christians, that love God with their whole hearts, honor all things that are dedicated to his service, or that are memorials of him, or have a relation to him; as his temples, his altars, his name, his word, his sacrament, the sacred vessels, etc. And thus

[521] Cf. Ex 3:5, Jo 5:15-16

it is that we honor the effigies of Christ, of his Blessed Mother, and of the saints, as memorials and representations of them, and as helps to raise our thoughts to them. And is it not thus that a loyal subject, a dutiful child, a loving friend, value the pictures of their king, father, or friend? And would not these very men that make no scruple of abusing the image of Christ, severely punish such as would abuse the image of the king?

466. Do you then allow of worshipping God by an image?

If you mean by worshipping God by an image, the raising up our hearts to God by or upon occasion of the sight of the picture or image; or the referring to Jesus Christ and to his worship whatever honor or respect we show to his picture or image; there can be no reason to disallow the worshipping of God by a picture or image. But if worshipping God by an image be so understood, as if the divinity in some particular manner resided in the image; or some virtue or power, for which it should be worshipped or trusted in; or as if our worship or prayers were believed to be more acceptable to God and to have more influence upon him, when offered or presented by or through any such image; such kind of worshipping God by an image is not only not allowed but condemned by the Catholic Church.[522]

467. What means then the blessing of crucifixes or other images, if no virtue or power be believed to reside in them after they are blessed?

The Church blesses all things that are used about the altar; not by way of imparting to them any intrinsic power or virtue, but by way of dedicating them to the divine service, and begging God's blessing for those that make use of them; so that whatever advantage may be supposed in the use of them after they

[522] Cf. Council of Trent, Session 25

are blessed more than before, is wholly to be attributed to the prayers of the Church.

468. **But are there not certain images to which great miracles are attributed; therefore Catholics must believe that in these at least there is some divinity, virtue, or power?**

There have been many instances of undoubted miracles wrought by God in the churches of the Blessed Virgin and other saints, in favor of those that have sought their prayers and intercession before their pictures or images. But these miracles are not to be attributed to any divinity or power in the image, but to the almighty power of God, moved to work these wonders by the prayers of his saints, and bearing testimony thereby to the faith of his Church, and showing his approbation of her religious practices.

469. **What do you think of the images or pictures of God the Father, or of the Blessed Trinity?**

I think that no corporal image can bear a resemblance with the divinity; and consequently that it would be unlawful to pretend to make any such likeness or resemblance. But where no such resemblance is pretended, I don't take it to be more unlawful to paint God the Father under the figure of a venerable man, because he was so represented in the vision of Daniel,[523] than it is to paint the Holy Ghost under the figure of a dove, because he appeared so when Christ was baptized.[524]

470. **What do you think of the charge of idolatry laid to the Church by some of her adversaries, upon account of the use and veneration of images?**

I think that nothing could be more visibly unjust than such a

---

[523] Cf. Dn 7:9
[524] Cf. Mt 3:16

charge, since idolatry is giving divine honor and service to an idol, or false god; which is far from being the case of the Catholic Church. We acknowledge one only true and living God in three Persons: Father, Son, and Holy Ghost. To him alone do we offer sacrifice or any other divine honors. Him alone do we adore in spirit and truth. Whatever else in heaven or on earth we religiously honor, we honor for his sake, and for the relation it has to him. And as for the worship of idols or false gods, it has been banished out of the world by the labors and preaching of our Church alone; so far are we from abetting idolatry.

471. What then do you think of the parallel which some would make between the heathen and Catholic worship?
I think that it is infinitely unjust and unreasonable, as must appear to any unprejudiced mind by the following remarks:

First, Catholics adore and offer sacrifice to one only true and living God; the heathens adored and offered sacrifice to many false gods.

Second, the supreme object of Catholic worship is the Sacred Trinity, blessed for evermore: the supreme object of the heathen worship was the sun, or some other part of God's creation; or else some wicked man, or more wicked devil. For heathen idolatry was, according to the apostle, "changing the truth of God into a lie, and worshipping and serving the creature more than the Creator, who is blessed forever."[525] The sun and his symbol, the fire, was of old the sovereign god of the Persians; as he was of late of the inhabitants of Peru; the same was worshipped as their chief god by the Phoenicians under the name of Baal; by the Ammonites under the name of Moloch; by the Moabites under the name of Chamos; by the Accaronites under the name of Belzebub; by those of Gaza, under the name of Mamas, etc., according to Vossius, Selden, and the

[525] Rom 1:25

whole nation of the Criticks, alleged by the protestant bishop Parker.[526] Him they called the king of heaven; as they called the moon or Astarte the queen of heaven. Of like nature was the sovereign object of the worship of the Egyptians, viz. Ammon the ram, and Osyris the bull, which are the two first signs of the Zodiac, and were worshipped as symbols of the sun, according to Bishop Parker.[527] The chief god of the Grecians and heathen Romans was Jupiter, who was originally a king that reigned in Crete, as the wiser heathens have acknowledged. He was not esteemed eternal by any of them, but the son of Saturn, that is, of time; and by much posterior to heaven and earth. As for his idols and oracles, he who gave answers thereby was no god, but an arch-devil, as Christians have ever believed.

Third, Catholics honor, though not with any part of divine worship, the angels and saints of God, as belonging to him, and as truly worthy of honor, upon account of the excellent gifts of grace and glory received from him: but they ask nothing of them but what they know must come from God's hands; and therefore their usual address to them is, *pray for us.* The heathens not only give the sovereign worship of adoration and sacrifice to their inferior deities, but looked upon them in many respects independent of their chief god (whilst they made him himself dependent upon fate), and accordingly they addressed themselves to them not as intercessors (for in the whole heathen theology we shall scarce once find an *Ora pro nobis*), but as distributers of blessings and gifts to men, according to their different offices and powers.

Fourth, those whom the Catholics honor with an inferior veneration for God's sake are indeed the ministers and servants of the one true God. The inferior deities of the heathens were

---

[526] Cf. Parker, *Test.* p. 97
[527] Cf. Ibid.

wicked wretches, such as Mars, Bacchus, Hercules, Venus, etc., or rather devils, as we learn from many texts of scripture.[528]

Fifth, as to images; not to speak of the immense distance between the objects represented by Catholics and by heathens, it is certain that the heathens (at the least the generality of them) believed the very idols to be gods.[529] And as for those who would seem to be more refined in their notion and worship, they believed at least that the idols by consecration became the bodies of their gods, the places of their peculiar residence, the symbols of their presence, and the seats of their power. And accordingly these as well as the others offered prayers and sacrifice to the idols, and gave them the names of the deities which they worshipped in them. Now we neither believe our images to be gods, nor to be the bodies of God, nor the peculiar places of his residence, nor symbols of his presence, nor to have any power or virtue in them; nor do we put our trust in them, or pray to them, or offer sacrifice or other divine honors to them. Therefore there is no similitude between the heathen worship and ours.

As for the Jewish worship of the golden calf in the wilderness, and afterwards of the calves of Jeroboam at Bethel and Dan, which some are willing to extenuate, as if they did not take these images to be gods, but thereby only meant to worship the God of Israel, the scripture gives us a quite different account. Witness these texts: "They have made them a molten calf, and have worshipped it, and have sacrificed thereunto, and said, these be thy gods, O Israel, which have brought thee up out of the land of Egypt. . . . They have made them gods of gold."[530] "They made a calf in Horeb, and worshipped the molten image: they changed their glory [their God] into the similitude of an

[528] Cf. Lv 17:7; Dt 32:17; Ps 105:37; 1 Cor 10:20
[529] Cf. Gn 31:30, 32; Ex 20:23; Lv 19:4; Jgs 18:24; 4 Kgs 17:29, 19:18; Is 44:17; Jer 2:26-27; Acts 19:26
[530] Ex 32:8, 31

ox that eateth grass: they forgot God their Savior, which had done great things in Egypt."[531] "To whom our fathers would not obey, but thrust him from them, and in their hearts turned back again into Egypt, saying to Aaron, make us gods to go before us. And they made a calf in those days, and offered sacrifice to the idol, and rejoiced in the works of their own hands. Then God turned and gave them up to worship the host of heaven."[532] And of the calves of Jeroboam, "He made two calves of gold and said unto them: Behold thy gods, O Israel, who brought thee up out of the land of Egypt. . . . He sacrificed to the calves that he had made."[533] And, he is accused by the prophet Abijah to have gone and made him other gods and molten images, and to have cast the Lord behind his back.[534] "He ordained him priest for the high places, and for the devils, and for the calves which he had made."[535] "There are with you golden calves, which Jeroboam made unto you for gods. . . . Have ye not cast out the priests . . . and made you priests after the manner of the nations; of them that be no gods . . . but as for us, the Lord is our God."[536]

But if anyone will be contentious and maintain that these idolatrous Israelites intended to worship in these calves, not the Egyptian Osiris, nor any other false divinity, but the God of Israel, because Aaron (who made the calf against his will by compulsion of the people) seems to give it the proper name of the God of Israel.[537] Supposing this to be true, their worship would still have been idolatrous, and these calves properly idols, because they believed (as is manifest from the texts above quoted) these very calves to be gods; or, if you will have it so,

[531] Ps 105:19-21
[532] Acts 7:39-42
[533] 3 Kgs 12:28, 32
[534] Cf. 3 Kgs 14:9
[535] 2 Par 11:15
[536] 2 Par 13:8-10
[537] Cf. Ex 32:5

to be the Lord of Israel; or, at least, that the divinity had upon their dedication insinuated itself into them, and accordingly they gave divine praises and offered sacrifice to them. Now to believe any image to be God, or to imagine any divinity, power, or virtue in it, for which it is to be worshipped, or to offer sacrifice to an image, is an idolatrous worship, and cannot be excused, however the image be pretended by its worshippers to represent the true God.

472. **Is there not in one of the Church hymns, and in one of the anthems of the *Roman Breviary*, a prayer to the cross? How then do you maintain that the Catholic Church does not attribute any power to images, nor prays to them?**
The prayer you speak of is not directed to the wood of the cross, but Christ crucified, by a figure of speech, as when St. Paul says that he glories "in the cross of Jesus Christ."[538]

Chapter 28

Of Exorcisms and Benedictions

473. **What do you mean by exorcisms?**
The rites and prayers instituted by the Church for the casting out devils, or restraining them from hurting persons, disquieting places, or abusing any of God's creatures to our harm.

474. **Has Christ given his Church any such power over the devils?**
Yes he has. This power was given to the apostles,[539] and to

---

[538] Gal 6:14
[539] Cf. Mt 10:1; Mk 3:15; Lk 9:1

the seventy-two disciples,[540] and to other believers.[541] And that this power was not to die with the apostles, nor to cease after the apostolic age, we learn from the perpetual practice of the Church and the experience of all ages.

475. What is the meaning of blessing so many things in the Catholic Church?

We bless churches and other places set aside for divine service, altars, chalices, vestments, etc., by way of devoting them to holy uses. We bless our meats and other inanimate things which God has given us for our use, that we may use them with moderation, in a manner agreeable to God's institution; that they may be serviceable to us, and that the devil may have no power to abuse them to our prejudice. We bless candles, salt, water, etc., by way of begging of God that such as religiously use them may obtain his blessing, etc.

476. But does it not favor of superstition to attribute any virtue to such inanimate things as blessed candles, holy water, agnus dei's, etc.?

It is no superstition to look for a good effect from the prayers of the Church of God; and it is in virtue of these prayers that we hope for benefit from these things, when used with faith; and daily experience shows that our hopes are not vain.

477. What do you mean by agnus dei's?

Wax stamped with the image of the Lamb of God, blessed by the pope with solemn prayers, and anointed with the holy chrism.

---

[540] Cf. Lk 10:19
[541] Cf. Mk 16:17

478. **What warrant have you in scripture for blessing inanimate things?**

"Every creature of God is good, and nothing to be refused, if it be received with thanksgiving: for it is sanctified by the word of God and prayer."[542]

479. **Why does the Church make use of the sign of the cross in all her blessings and consecrations?**

To signify that all our good must come through Christ crucified.

480. **What do you mean by holy water?**

Water sanctified by the word of God and prayer.

481. **What is the use of holy water?**

It is blessed by the Church with solemn prayers, to beg God's protection and blessing upon those that use it, and in particular that they may be defended from all the powers of darkness.

482. **Is the use of holy water very ancient in the Church of God?**

It is very ancient, since it is mentioned in the Apostolic Constitutions.[543] And as for our English nation in particular, it is visible from the epistles of St. Gregory the Great that we received it together with our Christianity.[544]

483. **Have the holy fathers and ancient Church writers left upon record any miracles done by holy water?**

Yes they have; more particularly upon those occasions when it has been used against magical enchantments and the power of the devil.[545]

---

[542] 1 Tm 4:4-5
[543] Cf. *Apostolic Constitutions*, Bk. 8, Ch. 29
[544] Cf. Gregory the Great, *Epistola ad Mellitum*
[545] Cf. Epiphanius, *Haeresi 30*; Jerome, *Life of St. Hilarion*; Theodoret, *Ecclesiastical History*, Bk. 5, Ch. 21; Palladius, *The Lausiac History*, Ch. 17.

484. What is the order and manner of making holy water?

First, the priest signs himself with the sign of the cross, saying: "Our help is in the name of the Lord." **R**: "Who made heaven and earth." Then he proceeds to the blessing of the salt which is to be mingled with the water, saying:

The Exorcism of the Salt

I exorcise thee, O creature of salt, by the living + God, by the true + God, by the holy + God; by that God, who by the prophet Elisha commanded thee to be cast into the water to cure its barrenness; that thou mayest by this exorcism be made beneficial to the faithful, and become to all them that make use of thee healthful both to soul and body, and that in what place soever thou shalt be sprinkled, all illusions and wickedness and crafty wiles of Satan may be chased away and depart from that place; and every unclean spirit commanded in his name, who is to come to judge the living and the dead, and the world by fire. Amen.

Let us pray. O almighty and everlasting God, we most humbly implore thy infinite mercy, that thou wouldst vouchsafe by thy piety to bless + and to sanctify + this thy creature of salt, which thou hast given for the use of mankind: that it may be to all that take it for the health of mind and body; and that whatever shall be touched or sprinkled with it, may be free from all uncleanness, and from all assaults of wicked spirits, through our Lord Jesus Christ, etc.

After this the priest proceeds to the blessing of the water, as follows:

The Exorcism of the Water

I exorcise thee, O creature of water, in the name of God + the Father Almighty, and in the name of Jesus Christ + his

Son our Lord, and in the virtue of the Holy + Ghost, that thou mayest by this exorcism have power to chase away all the power of the enemy; that thou mayest be enabled to cast him out and put him to flight with all his apostate angels, by the virtue of the same Jesus Christ our Lord, who is to come to judge the living and the dead, and the world by fire. Amen.

Let us pray. O God, who for the benefit of mankind hast made use of the element of water in the greatest sacrament, mercifully hear our prayers, and impart the virtue of thy blessing + to this element, prepared by many kinds of purifications; that this thy creature made use of in thy mysteries may receive the effect of thy divine grace for the chasing away devils and curing diseases; and that whatsoever shall be sprinkled with this water in the houses or the places of the faithful, may be free from all uncleanness, and delivered from evil; let no pestilential spirit reside there, no infectious air; let all the snares of the hidden enemy fly away; and may whatever envies the safety or repose of the inhabitants of that place be put to flight by the sprinkling of this water, that the welfare which we seek by the invocation of thy holy name may be defended from all sorts of assaults. Through our Lord Jesus Christ, etc.

Then the priest mingles the salt with the water, saying,

May this salt and water be mixed together in the name of the Father +, and of the Son +, and of the Holy + Ghost. Amen.

V: The Lord be with you.
R: And with thy spirit.

Let us pray. O God, author of invincible power, Father of an empire that cannot be overcome, and forever magnificently triumphant; who restrainest the forces of the adversary, who defeatest the fury of the roaring enemy, who mightily conquerest his malicious wiles; we pray and beseech thee, O Lord, with dread and humility, to regard with a favorable countenance this creature of salt and water, to enlighten it with thy bounty, and to sanctify it with the dew of thy fatherly goodness, that wheresoever it shall be sprinkled, all infestation of the unclean spirit may depart, and all fear of the venomous serpent may be chased away, through the invocation of thy holy name; and that the presence of the Holy Ghost may be everywhere with us, who seek thy mercy. Through our Lord Jesus Christ, etc.

The blessing being ended, the priest sprinkles himself and the people with this water, saying,

Thou shalt sprinkle me, O Lord, with hyssop, and I shall be cleansed; Thou shalt wash me, and I shall be made whiter than snow. Have mercy on me, O God, according to thy great mercy, etc. Glory be to the Father, etc.

After which he repeats the anthem, "Thou shalt sprinkle," etc. Then returning to the altar, he says:

V: O Lord show us thy mercy.
R: And give us thy salvation.
V: O Lord hear my prayer.
R: And let my cry come to thee.
V: The Lord be with you.
R: And with thy spirit.

Let us pray. Hear us, O holy Lord, Almighty Father, everlasting God, and vouchsafe to send thy holy angel from heaven to guard, cherish, protect, visit, and defend all that dwell in this habitation. Through Christ our Lord. Amen.

FINIS.

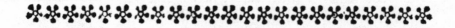

THE
GROUNDS
OF THE
Catholick Doctrine,

Contained in the

Profession of FAITH,

PUBLISH'D by

POPE *PIUS* the FOURTH,

BY WAY of

QUESTION and ANSWER.

The SEVENTH EDITION.

Be ready always to give an Answer to every one that asketh you a Reason of the Hope that is in you. 1 Peter iii. 15.

Printed in the YEAR M,DCC,LII.

Original Title Page
(English Secret Press, 1752)

The Grounds
of the Catholick Doctrine
Contained in the
Profession of Faith

PUBLISH'D by
POPE *PIUS* the FOURTH,
By WAY of
QUESTION and ANSWER.

The SEVENTH EDITION.

Be ready always to give an Answer to every one that
asketh you a Reason of the Hope that is in you.
1 Peter 3:15.

Printed in the YEAR 1752

A Profession of Catholic Faith

 N. N. with a firm faith believe and profess all and every one of those things which are contained in that Creed which the holy Roman Church maketh use of, viz. I believe in one God, the Father Almighty, Maker of heaven and earth, of all things, visible and invisible; and in one Lord Jesus Christ, the only begotten Son of God; born of the Father before all ages; God of God; light of light; true God of true God; begotten not made; consubstantial to the Father, by whom all things were made. Who, for us men and for our salvation, came down from heaven and was incarnate by the Holy Ghost of the Virgin Mary and was made man: Was crucified also for us under Pontius Pilate: He suffered and was buried: and the third day he rose again according to the scriptures: He ascended into heaven; sits at the right hand of the Father, and is to come again with glory to judge the living and the dead; of whose kingdom there shall be no end. And in the Holy Ghost, the Lord and Life-Giver, who proceeds from the Father and the Son, who, together with the Father and the Son, is adored and glorified, who spoke by the prophets. And (I believe), one, holy, Catholic, and apostolic Church: I confess one baptism for the remission of sins: and I look for the resurrection of the dead, and the life of the world to come. Amen.

I most steadfastly admit and embrace apostolical and ecclesiastical traditions, and all other observances and constitutions of the same Church. I also admit the holy scriptures according to that sense which our holy mother, the Church, has held, and does hold; to whom it belongs to judge of the true sense and interpretation of the scriptures: neither will I ever take and interpret them otherwise, than according to the unanimous consent of the fathers.

I also profess, that there are truly and properly seven sacraments of the new law, instituted by Jesus Christ our Lord, and necessary for the salvation of mankind, though not all for every one: to wit, baptism, confirmation, Eucharist, penance, extreme unction, orders, and matrimony; and that they confer grace; and that of these, baptism, confirmation, and orders cannot be reiterated without sacrilege. I also receive and admit the received and approved ceremonies of the Catholic Church, used in the solemn administration of all the aforesaid sacraments.

I embrace and receive all and every one of the things which have been defined and declared in the holy Council of Trent, concerning original sin and justification. I profess, likewise, that in the Mass there is offered to God, a true, proper, and propitiatory sacrifice for the living and the dead. And that in the most Holy Sacrament of the Eucharist, there is truly, really, and substantially, the body and blood, together with the soul and divinity, of our Lord Jesus Christ: and that there is made a conversion of the whole substance of the bread into the body, and of the whole substance of the wine into the blood; which conversion the Catholic Church calls transubstantiation. I also confess, that under either kind alone Christ is received whole and entire, and a true sacrament.

I constantly hold, that there is a purgatory, and that the souls therein detained are helped by the suffrages of the faithful. Likewise that the saints, reigning together with Christ, are to be honored and invoked, and that they offer prayers to God for us, and that their relics are to be had in veneration. I most firmly assert, that the images of Christ, of the Mother of God, Ever-Virgin, and also of the other saints, ought to be had and retained, and that due honor and veneration is to be given to them. I also affirm, that the power of indulgences was left by Christ in the Church, and that the use of them is most wholesome to Christian people. I acknowledge the holy, Catholic, apostolic Roman Church, for the mother and mistress of all churches; and I promise true obedience to the bishop of Rome, successor to St. Peter, prince of the apostles, and vicar of Jesus Christ.

I likewise undoubtedly receive and profess all other things, delivered, defined, and declared by the sacred canons and general councils, and particularly by the holy Council of Trent. And I condemn, reject, and anathematize all things contrary thereto, and all heresies which the Church has condemned, rejected, and anathematized.

I, N. N. do at this present, freely profess, and sincerely hold this true Catholic faith, without which no one can be saved; and I promise most constantly to retain and confess the same entire and unviolated, with God's assistance, to the end of my life.[1]

---

[1] This is Challoner's English rendering of the *Professio fidei Tridentina*, a creed promulgated in 1565 by Pope Pius IV under the auspices of the Council of Trent. Being one of the four major Catholic creeds, it was expanded slightly by Pope Pius IX in 1870 to reflect the dogmatic definitions of the First Vatican Council, and was long required to be formally sworn by those holding ecclesiastical office. It is also called the Tridentine Creed and the Creed of Pius IV.

Chapter 1

Of the Church

1. What is your profession as to the article of the Church?
It is contained in those words of the Nicene Creed: "I believe one, holy, Catholic, and apostolic Church."

2. What do you gather from these words?
1) That Jesus Christ has always a true Church upon earth. 2) That this Church is always one by the union of all her members in one faith and communion. 3) That she is always pure and holy in her doctrine and terms of communion, and consequently free from pernicious errors. 4) That she is Catholic, that is, universal, by being the Church of all ages, and more or less of all nations. 5) That this Church must have in her a succession from the apostles, and a lawful mission derived from them. 6) Which follows from all the rest, that this true Church of Christ cannot be any of the protestant sects, but must be the ancient Church communicating with the pope or bishop of Rome.

That Christ Has Always a True Church upon Earth

3. How do you prove that Christ has always a true Church upon earth?

From many plain texts of scripture, in which it is promised and foretold that the Church or kingdom established by Christ should stand till the end of the world. "Thou art Peter" (i.e. a rock), "and upon this rock will I build my church, and the gates of hell shall not prevail against it."[2] "Go ye, therefore, and teach all nations, baptizing . . . teaching them to observe all things whatsoever I have commanded you; and behold I am with you always, even to the end of the world."[3] They shall fear thee as long as "the sun and moon endure throughout all generations . . . in his days," that is, after the coming of Christ, "shall the righteous flourish, and abundance of peace, so long as the moon endureth."[4] "In the days of these kings shall the God of heaven set up a kingdom," the Church or kingdom of Christ, "which shall never be destroyed . . . and it shall stand forever."[5]

4. What other proof have you of the perpetual continuance of the Church of Christ?

The Creed, in which we profess to believe the holy Catholic Church. For the Creed, and every article thereof, must be always true: and therefore there must always be a holy Catholic Church.

5. Can you prove that Christ's Church upon earth is always visible?

Yes, from many texts of scripture, as Isaias 2 and Micheas 4, where the Church of Christ is described as a mountain upon the top of mountains, exposed to the view of all nations flowing

[2] Mt 16:18
[3] Mt 28:19-20
[4] Ps 71:5, 7
[5] Dn 2:44

unto it;[6] and Daniel 2, as a great mountain filling the whole earth;[7] Matthew 5, as a city set on a hill which cannot be hid;[8] Isaias 60, as a city whose gates shall be open continually, and shall not be shut day nor night, that men may bring thither the forces of the gentiles, and that their kings may be brought;[9] upon the walls of which God has set watchmen, which shall never hold their peace day nor night.[10]

That Christ's Church upon Earth Is Always One

6. How do you prove that Christ's Church upon earth can be but one?

From many texts of scripture: Canticle of Canticles 6, "My dove, my undefiled, is but one . . . fair as the moon, clear as the sun, terrible, as an army with banners."[11] John 10, "Other sheep I have which are not of this fold"; (viz. the gentiles, who were then divided from the Jews), "them also I must bring, and they shall hear my voice, and there shall be one fold, and one shepherd."[12] Ephesians 4, "there is one body and one spirit, as you are called in one hope of your calling, one Lord, one faith, one baptism."[13] In fine, as we have seen already, the Church of Christ is a kingdom which shall stand forever; and therefore must be always one. "For every kingdom divided against itself, is brought to desolation; and every city or house divided against itself, shall not stand."[14]

[6] Cf. Is 2:2-3; Mi 4:1-2
[7] Cf. Dn 2:35
[8] Cf. Mt 5:14
[9] Cf. Is 60:11
[10] Cf. Is 62:6
[11] Cant 6:8-9
[12] Jn 10:16
[13] Eph 4:4-5
[14] Mt 12:25

7. May not persons be saved in any religion?

No, certainly. St. Paul tells us that "without faith it is impossible to please God";[15] and St. Peter assures us that "there is no other name under heaven given to men, by which we may be saved," but the name of Jesus.[16] And Christ himself tells us, "He that believeth not shall be damned."[17] So that it is manifest from the holy scripture, that true faith is necessary to salvation. Now true faith, in order to please God and save our souls, must be entire; that is to say, we must believe without exception all such articles as by God and his Church are proposed to be believed; and he that voluntarily and obstinately disbelieveth any one of these articles is no less void of true saving faith than he that disbelieves them all, as St. James tells us, with regard to practical duties: "Whosoever shall keep the whole law, yet offend in one point, is guilty of all."[18] Hence St. Paul reckons heresies, that is, false religions, among those works of the flesh of which he pronounces, "that they who do such things shall not inherit the kingdom of God";[19] and God himself tells his Church, "the nation and kingdom that will not serve thee shall perish."[20]

8. Can anyone be out of the way of salvation without the guilt of mortal sin?

No; but all such as, through obstinacy, negligence, or indifference in matters of religion, will not hear the true Church and her pastors, are guilty of mortal sin. "If he neglect to hear the church, let him be to thee as a heathen man and a publican."[21] "He that heareth you" (the pastors of the Church), "heareth me;

[15] Heb 11:6
[16] Acts 4:12
[17] Mk 16:16
[18] Jas 2:10
[19] Gal 5:21
[20] Is 60:12
[21] Mt 18:17

and he that despiseth you, despiseth me, and he that despiseth me, despiseth him that sent me."[22]

9. But what do you think of those whose conscience persuades them that they are in the true Church?

If this error of theirs proceed from invincible ignorance, they may be excused from the sin of heresy; provided that in the sincere disposition of their hearts, they would gladly embrace the truth if they could find it out, in spite of all opposition of interest, passion, etc. But if this error of their conscience be not invincible, but such as they might discover if they were in earnest in a matter of so great consequence, their conscience will not excuse them; no more than St. Paul's, whilst out of blind zeal he persecuted the Church, or the mistaken conscience of the Jews, when putting the disciples of Christ to death, they thought they did a service to God.[23] "For there is a way that seemeth right unto a man; but the ends thereof are the ways of death."[24]

10. But does not the scripture somewhere say that "a remnant of all religions shall be saved"?

No; though I have often heard such words alleged by protestants, they are not anywhere to be found in scripture, from the beginning of Genesis to the end of Apocalypse. I suppose what has given occasion to their mistake must have been the words of St. Paul, where, quoting Isaias 10, he tells us, "Although the number of the children of Israel be as the sand of the sea, a remnant" (that is, a small part of them only) "shall be saved";[25] which remnant the apostle himself explains as such of the Jewish nation as at that time, by entering into the Church, were

[22] Lk 10:16
[23] Cf. Jn 16:2
[24] Prv 16:25
[25] Rom 9:27; Cf. Is 10:22

saved by God's grace.[26] But what is this relation to a salvation of a remnant of all religions? A doctrine so visibly contradicting the scripture that even the English protestant church herself, in the eighteenth of her Thirty-Nine Articles, has declared them to be accursed who presume to maintain it.[27]

That the Church of Christ Is Always Holy in Her Doctrine and Terms of Communion, and Always Free from Pernicious Errors

11. How do you prove this?

First, because, as we have seen above from Matthew 16, our Lord Jesus Christ, who cannot tell a lie, has promised that his Church should be built upon a rock, proof against all floods and storms, like the house of the wise builder,[28] and that the gates of hell, that is the powers of darkness, shall never prevail against it.[29] Therefore the Church of Christ could never cease to be holy in her doctrine; could never fall into idolatry, superstition, or any heretical errors whatsoever.

Secondly, because Christ, who is "the way, the truth, and the life,"[30] has promised to the pastors and teachers of the Church, to "be with them always, even to the end of the world."[31] Therefore they could never go astray by pernicious errors; for how could they go out of the right way of truth and life, who are

---

[26] Cf. Rom 11:5

[27] The full text of the 1571 version reads: "They also are to be had accursed that presume to say, That every man shall be saved by the law or sect which he professeth, so that he be diligent to frame his life according to that law, and the light of nature. For holy scripture doth set out unto us only the name of Jesus Christ, whereby men must be saved."

[28] Of whom he speaks in Mt 7:25.

[29] Cf. Mt 16:18

[30] Jn 14:6

[31] Mt 28:20

assured to have always in their company, for their guide, him who is the way, the truth, and the life?

Thirdly, because our Lord has promised to the same teachers, "I will pray the Father, and he shall give you another Comforter, that he may abide with you forever, even the Spirit of truth";[32] and he assures them that this Spirit of truth shall teach them all things;[33] and that he shall guide them "into all truth."[34] How then could it be possible that the whole body of these pastors and teachers of the Church, who, by virtue of these promises, were to be forever guided into all truth by the Spirit of truth, should at any time fall from the truth by errors in faith?

Fourthly, because God has made a solemn covenant, that after the coming of our Redeemer, his Spirit and his words, that is, the whole doctrine which this Redeemer was to teach, should be forever maintained by his Church through all generations. "The redeemer shall come to Zion. . . . This is my covenant with them, saith the Lord; my spirit which is upon thee, and my words which I have put into thy mouth, shall not depart out of thy mouth, nor out of the mouth of thy seed, nor out of the mouth of thy seed's seed, saith the Lord, from henceforth and forever."[35]

Fifthly, because the Church of Christ is represented as a "highway," a "way of holiness," a way so plain and so secure that even "fools should not err therein."[36] How then could it ever be possible that the Church herself should err?

Sixthly, because pernicious errors in faith and morals must needs be such as to provoke God's indignation: now God Almighty has promised to his Church, "As I have sworn that

[32] Jn 14:16-17
[33] Cf. Jn 14:26
[34] Jn 16:13
[35] Is 59:20-21
[36] Is 35:8

the waters of Noah shall no more go over the earth, so have I sworn, that I would not be wroth with thee, nor rebuke thee: for the mountains shall depart, and the hills be removed, but my kindness shall not depart from thee, neither shall the covenant of my peace be removed, saith the Lord, that hath mercy on thee."[37] So that, as we are assured that there shall not be a second flood; so we are that the Church of Christ shall never draw upon herself the wrath of God, by teaching errors contrary to faith.

In fine, the Church is called by St. Paul, "the pillar and ground of truth";[38] therefore she cannot uphold pernicious errors. From all which it is manifest, that the Church of Christ is infallible in all matters relating to faith; so that she can neither add to nor retrench from what Christ taught.

That the Church of Christ Is Catholic, or Universal

12. What do you understand by this?

Not only that the Church of Christ shall always be known by the name of Catholic, by which she is called in the Creed; but that she shall also be truly *catholic* or *universal* by being the Church of all ages, and of all nations.

13. How do you prove that the true Church of Christ must be the Church of all ages?

Because the true Church of Christ must be that which had its beginning from Christ; and, as he promised, was to continue to the end of the world.

[37] Is 54:9-10
[38] 1 Tm 3:15

14. How do you prove that the true Church of Christ must be the Church of all nations?

From many texts of scripture in which the true Church of Christ is always represented as a numerous congregation spread through the world. "In thy seed shall all the nations of the earth be blessed."[39] "Ask of me, and I will give thee the gentiles for thine inheritance; and the uttermost parts of the earth for thy possession."[40] "All the ends of the world shall remember and turn unto the Lord, and all the kindreds of the nations shall worship before thee."[41] "It is a light thing that thou shouldst be my servant, to raise up the tribes of Jacob. . . . I will also give thee for a light to the gentiles, that thou mayest be my salvation unto the end of the earth."[42] "Sing, O barren, that thou didst not bear, break forth into singing, and cry aloud, thou that didst not travail with child; for more are the children of the desolate, than the children of the married wife, saith the Lord. Enlarge the place of thy tent, and let them stretch forth the curtains of thine habitation: spare not, lengthen thy cords and strengthen thy stakes: for thou shalt break forth on the right hand and on the left: and thy seed shall inherit the gentiles."[43] "From the rising of the sun, even to the going down of the same, my name shall be great among the gentiles."[44]

[39] Gn 22:18
[40] Ps 2:8
[41] Ps 21:28
[42] Is 49:6
[43] Is 54:1-3
[44] Mal 1:11; Cf. Is 2:2-3; Mi 4:1-2; Dn 2:31

That the Church of Christ Must Be Apostolical, by a Succession of Her Pastors and a Lawful Mission Derived from the Apostles

15. How do you prove this?

First, because only those who can derive their lineage from the apostles are the heirs of the apostles; and consequently, they alone can claim a right to the scriptures, to the administration of the sacraments, or any share in the pastoral ministry; it is their proper inheritance, which they have received from the apostles, and the apostles from Christ. "As my Father hath sent me, even so I send you."[45]

Secondly, because Christ promised to the apostles and their successors, that he would be with them always even to the end of the world,[46] and that the Holy Ghost, the Spirit of truth, should abide with them forever.[47]

That Catholics, and Not Protestants, Are the True Church of Christ

16. How do you prove that the Catholic Church in communion with Rome is the true Church of Christ, rather than protestants or other sectaries?

From what has been already said in the foregoing sections: for first, the true Church of Christ can be no other than that which has always had a visible being in the world ever since Christ's time, as we have seen above. She was founded by Christ himself, with the express promise "that the gates of hell should not prevail against her."[48] She is the kingdom of

[45] Jn 20:21
[46] Cf. Mt 28:20
[47] Cf. Jn 14:16-17
[48] Mt 16:18

Christ, "which shall never be destroyed."[49] Therefore the true Church of Christ can be no other than the Catholic, which alone has had a visible being in the world ever since Christ's time; not the protestant, nor any other modern sect, which only came into the world since the year 1500: for those who came into the world 1500 years after Christ, came into the world 1500 years too late to be the religion or Church of Christ.

Secondly, the true Church of Christ, in virtue of the promises both of the old and new testament, was to continue pure and holy in her doctrine and terms of communion in all ages, even to the end of the world, as we have seen above, and consequently could never stand in need of a protestant Reformation. Therefore that which was of old the true Church of Christ must still be so, and it is in vain to seek for the true Church among any of the sects of pretenders to Reformation, because they all build upon a wrong foundation, that is, upon the supposition that the Church of Christ was for many ages gone astray.

Thirdly, the true Church of Christ must be *catholic* or *universal*; she must not only be the Church of all ages, but also more or less the Church of all nations, as we have seen above. She must be apostolical, by a succession and mission derived from the apostles, as we have also seen above. Now these characteristics cannot apply to any of our modern sects, but only to the old religion, which alone is the Church of all ages, and more or less of all nations; and which descends in an uninterrupted succession continued in the same communion from the apostles down to these our days. Therefore, the old religion alone is the true Church of Christ, which can be but one, and in one communion, as we have seen above.

[49] Dn 2:44

Chapter 2

Of Scripture and Tradition

17. What is your belief concerning the scripture?
That it is to be received by all Christians as the infallible word of God.

18. Do you look upon the scripture to be clear and plain in all points necessary; that is, in all such points wherein our salvation is so far concerned, that the misunderstanding and misinterpreting of it may endanger our eternal welfare?
No, because St. Peter assures us that in St. Paul's epistles "there are some things hard to be understood, which they that are unlearned and unstable wrest, as they do also the other scriptures, to their own destruction."[50]

19. How then is this danger to be avoided?
By taking the meaning and interpretation of the scripture from the same hand from which we received the book itself, that is, from the Church.

20. Why may not every particular Christian have liberty to interpret the scripture according to his own private judgment, without regard to the interpretation of the Church?
First, because "no prophecy of the scripture is of private interpretation."[51] Secondly, because, as men's judgments are as different as their faces, such liberty as this must needs produce as many religions almost as men. Thirdly, because Christ has

---

[50] 2 Pt 3:16
[51] 2 Pt 1:20

left his Church and her pastors and teachers to be our guides in all controversies relating to religion, and consequently in the understanding of holy writ. "He gave some apostles, and some prophets, and some evangelists, and some pastors and teachers, for the perfecting of the saints, for the work of the ministry, for the edifying of the body of Christ, till we all come in the unity of faith and of the knowledge of the Son of God unto a perfect man, unto the measure of the stature of the fulness of Christ. That we may henceforth be no more children tossed to and fro, and carried about with every wind of doctrine, by the sleight of men and cunning craftiness, whereby they lie in wait to deceive; but speaking the truth in love, may grow up into him in all things, which is the head, even Christ."[52] Hence St. John, in his first epistle, gives as this rule for the trying of spirits: "He that knoweth God heareth us" (the pastors of the Church), "he that is not of God, heareth not us: by this we know the spirit of truth, and the spirit of error."[53]

21. Why does the Church, in her profession of faith, oblige her children never to take or interpret the scripture otherwise than according to the unanimous consent of the holy fathers?
To arm them against the danger of novelty and error: "Remove not the ancient landmark which thy fathers have set."[54]

Of Apostolical and Ecclesiastical Traditions

22. What do you mean by apostolical traditions?
All such points of faith or Church discipline which were taught or established by the apostles and have carefully been preserved in the Church ever since.

[52] Eph 4:11-15
[53] 1 Jn 4:6
[54] Prv 22:28

23. What difference is there between apostolical and ecclesiastical traditions?

The difference is this, that apostolical traditions are those which had their origin or institution from the apostles; such as infant baptism, the Lord's day, receiving the sacrament fasting, etc. Ecclesiastical traditions are such as had their institution from the Church, as holy days and fasts ordained by the Church.

24. How are we to know what traditions are truly apostolical, and what not?

In the same manner and by the same authority by which we know what scriptures are apostolical, and what are not: that is, by the authority of the apostolic Church, guided by the unerring Spirit of God.

25. But why should not the scripture alone be the rule of our faith, without having recourse to apostolical tradition?

1) Because, without the help of apostolical tradition, we cannot so much as tell what is scripture and what is not. 2) Because infant baptism and several other necessary articles are either not at all contained in scripture, or at least not plain in the scripture without the help of tradition.

26. What scripture can you bring in favor of tradition?

"Therefore, brethren, stand fast, and hold the tradition, which ye have been taught, whether by word or our epistle."[55] "Ask thy father, and he will show thee, thy elders, and they will tell thee."[56]

---

[55] 2 Thes 2:14
[56] Dt 32:7; Cf. Ps 20:5-7; 1 Cor 11:2; 2 Thes 3:6; 2 Tm 1:13, 2:2, 3:14

Of the Ordinances and Constitutions of the Church

27. Why do you make profession of admitting and embracing all the ordinances and constitutions of the Church?

Because Christ has so commanded. "He that heareth you, heareth me: and he that despiseth you, despiseth me."[57] "As my Father hath sent me, even so I send you."[58] Hence St. Paul tells us, "Obey them that have the rule over you, and submit yourselves."[59]

28. Why does the Church command so many holy days to be kept? Is it not enough to keep the Sunday holy?

God, in the old law, did not think it enough to appoint the weekly sabbath, which was the Saturday; but also ordained other festivals, as that of the Passover, in memory of the delivery of his people from the Egyptian bondage, that of the Weeks or Pentecost, that of Tabernacles, etc., and the Church has done the same in the new law, to celebrate the memory of the chief mysteries of our Redemption, and to bless God in his saints. And in this protestants seem to agree with us, by appointing almost all the same holy days in their Common Prayer Book.

29. Is it not said in the law, "Six days shalt thou labor, and do all thy work"[60]? Why then should the Church derogate from this part of the commandment?

This was to be understood in case no holy days came in the week; otherwise the law would contradict itself, when in the twenty-third chapter of Leviticus it appoints so many other

---

[57] Lk 10:16
[58] Jn 20:21
[59] Heb 13:17
[60] Ex 20:9

holy days besides the sabbath, with command to abstain from all servile work on them.

30. **As to fasting days, do you look upon it as sinful to eat meat on those days without necessity?**
Yes; because it is a sin to disobey the Church: "If he neglect to hear the church, let him be to thee as a heathen and a publican."[61]

31. **Doth not Christ say, "That which goeth into the mouth doth not defile a man"?[62]**
True: it is not any uncleanness in the meat, as many ancient heretics imagined, or any dirt or dust which may stick to it by eating it without first washing the hands (of which case our Lord speaks in the text here quoted) which can defile the soul; for every creature of God is good, and whatsoever corporal filth enters in at the mouth, is cast forth into the draught. But that which defiles the soul, when a person eats meat on a fasting-day, is the disobedience of heart, in transgressing the precept of the Church of God. In like manner, when Adam ate of the forbidden fruit, it was not the apple which entered in by the mouth, but the disobedience to the law of God, which defiled him.

[61] Mt 18:17
[62] Mt 15:11

Chapter 3

Of the Sacraments

32. What do you mean by a sacrament?

An institution of Christ, consisting in some outward sign or ceremony, by which grace is given to the soul of the worthy receiver.

33. How many such sacraments do you find in scripture?

These seven: baptism, confirmation, Eucharist (which protestants call the Lord's Supper), penance, extreme unction (or the anointing of the sick), holy orders, and matrimony.

34. What scripture have you for baptism?

John 3: "Except a man be born of water and of the Spirit, he cannot enter into the kingdom of God."[63] "Go teach all nations, baptizing them in the name of the Father, and of the Son, and of the Holy Ghost."[64]

35. How do you prove that this commission given to the apostles of baptizing all nations, is to be understood of baptism administered in water?

From the belief and practice of the Church of Christ in all ages, and of the apostles themselves; who administered baptism in water: "See here is water," said the eunuch to St. Philip, "what does hinder me from being baptized? . . . and they went down into the water, both Philip and the eunuch; and he baptized him."[65] "Can any man forbid water," said St. Peter, "that these

[63] Jn 3:5
[64] Mt 28:19
[65] Acts 8:36, 38

should not be baptized who have received the Holy Ghost as well as we? And he commanded them to be baptized in the name of the Lord."[66]

36. What do you mean by confirmation?
Confirmation is a sacrament, wherein by the invocation of the Holy Ghost, and imposition of the bishop's hands with the unction of holy chrism, a person receives the grace of the Holy Ghost, and a strength in order to the professing of his faith.

37. What scripture have you for confirmation?
Acts 8, where Peter and John confirmed the Samaritans. "They prayed for them that they might receive the Holy Ghost. . . . Then laid they their hands on them, and they received the Holy Ghost."[67]

38. What scripture have you for the Eucharist, or the Supper of the Lord?
We have the history of its institution set down at large,[68] and that this sacrament was to be continued in the Church "till the Lord comes," that is, till the day of judgment, as we learn from St. Paul.[69]

39. What do you mean by the sacrament of penance?
The confession of sins, with a sincere repentance, and the priest's absolution.

[66] Acts 10:47-48
[67] Acts 8:15, 17
[68] Cf. Mt 26:20-29; Mk 14:17-25; Lk 22:14-20; 1 Cor 11:23-26
[69] Cf. 1 Cor 11:26

40. What scripture have you to prove that the bishops and priests of the Church have power to absolve the sinner that confesses his sins with a sincere repentance?

John 20: "Receive ye the Holy Ghost. Whosesoever sins ye remit, they are remitted unto them: And whosesoever sins ye retain, they are retained."[70] Matthew 18: "Verily I say unto you, Whatsoever ye shall bind on earth, shall be bound in heaven; and whatsoever ye shall loose on earth, shall be loosed in heaven."[71] Which texts protestants seem to understand in the same manner as we, since in their Common Prayer Book, in the order for the visitation of the sick, we find this rubric:

> Here shall the sick person be moved to make a special confession of his sins, if he feel his conscience troubled with any weighty matter. After which confession the priest shall absolve him (if he humbly and heartily desire it) after this sort: "Our Lord Jesus Christ, who hath left power to his Church to absolve all sinners who truly repent and believe in him, of his great mercy forgive thee thine offenses: and by his authority committed to me, I absolve thee from all thy sins, in the name of the Father, and of the Son, and of the Holy Ghost. Amen."[72]

41. How do you prove, from the text above quoted, the necessity of the faithful confessing their sins to the pastors of the Church in order to obtain the absolution and remission of them?

Because, in the text above quoted, Christ has made the pastors of the Church his judges in the court of conscience, with commission and authority to bind or to loose, to forgive or to retain sins, according to the merits of the cause and the disposition of the penitents. Now as no judge can pass sentence without having a full knowledge of the cause; which cannot be had in

---

[70] Jn 20:22-23
[71] Mt 18:18
[72] Rubric from the 1661 edition of the Anglican *Book of Common Prayer*.

this kind of causes, which regard men's consciences, but by their own confession; it clearly follows that he who has made the pastors of the Church the judges of men's consciences, has also laid an obligation upon the faithful to lay open the state of their consciences to them, if they hope to have their sins remitted. Nor would our Lord have given to his Church the power of retaining sins, much less the keys of the kingdom of heaven,[73] if such sins as exclude men from the kingdom of heaven might be remitted independently of the keys of the Church.

42. Have you any other texts of scripture which favor the Catholic doctrine and practice of confession?

Yes. We find in the old law, which was a figure of the law of Christ, that such as were infected with the leprosy, which was a figure of sin, were obliged to show themselves to the priests and subject themselves to their judgment.[74] Which, according to the holy fathers, was an emblem of the confession of sins in the sacrament of penance. And in the same law a special confession of sins was expressly prescribed: "When a man or woman shall commit any sin that men commit, to do a trespass against the Lord, and that person be guilty: Then they shall confess their sins which they have done."[75] The same is prescribed in the new testament, "Confess your faults one to another";[76] that is, to the priests or elders of the Church, whom the apostle had ordered to be called for.[77] And this was evidently the practice of the first Christians: "Many that believed came and confessed, and showed their deeds."[78]

[73] Cf. Mt 16:19
[74] Cf. Lv 13, 14; Mt 8:4
[75] Nm 5:6-7
[76] Jas 5:16
[77] Cf. Jas 5:14
[78] Acts 19:18

43. What do you mean by extreme unction?

You have both the full description and proof of it in James 5: "Is any sick among you, let him call for the elders (the priests) of the church, and let them pray over him, anointing him with oil in the name of the Lord: And the prayer of faith shall save the sick, and the Lord shall raise him up; and if he have committed sins, they shall be forgiven him."[79]

44. What is holy orders?

A sacrament instituted by Christ by which bishops, priests, etc., are consecrated to their respective functions, and receive grace to discharge them well.

45. When did Christ institute the sacrament of holy orders?

At his last supper, when he made his apostles priests, by giving them the power of consecrating the bread and wine into his body and blood: "Do this in remembrance of me."[80] To which he added, after his Resurrection, the power of forgiving the sins of the penitent.[81]

46. What scripture proof have you that holy orders give grace to those that receive them worthily?

The words of St. Paul to Timothy, whom he had ordained priest by imposition of hands: "Stir up the gift which is in thee, by the putting on of my hands";[82] and 1 Timothy 4: "Neglect not the gift that is in thee, which was given thee by prophecy, by the laying on of the hands of the presbytery."[83]

---

[79] Jas 5:14-15
[80] Lk 22:19
[81] Cf. Jn 20:22-23
[82] 2 Tm 1:6
[83] 1 Tm 4:14

47. When was matrimony instituted?

It was first instituted by God Almighty in paradise between our first parents; and this institution was confirmed by Christ in the new law, where he concludes, "What God hath joined together, let no man put asunder."[84]

48. How do you prove that matrimony is a sacrament?

Because it is a conjunction made and sanctified by God himself, and not to be dissolved by any power of man; as being a sacred sign, or mysterious representation of the indissoluble union of Christ and his Church, Ephesians 5: "For this cause shall a man leave his father and mother, and shall be joined to his wife, and they two shall be one flesh. This is a great mystery [a sacrament]; but I speak concerning Christ and the church," in Christ and in the Church.[85]

49. Why does not the Church allow for the marriage of the clergy?

Because, upon their entering into holy orders, they make a vow or solemn promise to God and the Church to live continently: now the breach of such a vow as this would be a great sin; witness St. Paul, when speaking of widows that are for marrying after having made such a vow as this, he says, they "have damnation, because they have cast off their first faith,"[86] that is, their solemn engagement made to God.

50. But why does the Church receive none to holy orders but those that make this vow?

Because she does not think it proper, that they, who by their office and functions ought to be wholly devoted to the service of God and the care of souls, should be diverted from these duties by the distractions of a married life. "He that is unmarried

[84] Mt 19:4-6
[85] Eph 5:31-32
[86] 1 Tm 5:11-12

careth for the things that belong to the Lord, how he may please the Lord. But he that is married, careth for the things that are of the world, how he may please his wife."[87]

51. Why does the Church make use of so many ceremonies in administering the sacraments?

To stir up devotion in the people, and reverence to the sacred mysteries; to instruct the faithful concerning the effects and graces given by the sacraments; and to perform things relating to God's honor and the salvation of souls with a becoming decency.

52. Have you any warrant from scripture for the use of such ceremonies?

Yes, we have the example of Christ, who frequently used the like ceremonies. For instance, in curing the man that was deaf and dumb;[88] in curing him that was born blind;[89] in breathing upon his apostles when he gave them the Holy Ghost.[90]

Chapter 4

Of the Real Presence and Transubstantiation

53. What is the doctrine of the Catholic Church in relation to this article?

We believe and profess, that in the most Holy Sacrament of the Eucharist, there is truly, really, and substantially the body and

---

[87] 1 Cor 7:32-33
[88] Cf. Mk 7:33-34
[89] Cf. Jn 9:6-7
[90] Cf. Jn 20:22-23

blood, together with the soul and divinity of our Lord Jesus Christ. And that there is a conversion (or change) of the whole substance of the bread into his body, and of the whole substance of the wine into his blood; which conversion (or change) the Catholic Church calls transubstantiation.

54. What proofs have you for this?

First, "As they were eating, Jesus took bread and blessed it, and broke it, and gave it to the disciples, and said, Take, eat; this is my body. And he took the cup and gave thanks, and gave it to them, saying, Drink ye all of it. For this is my blood of the new testament which is shed for many for the remission of sins."[91] "Take, eat: this is my body. . . . This is my blood of the new testament which is shed for many."[92] "This is my body which is given for you: this do in remembrance of me. . . . This cup is the new testament in my blood which is shed for you."[93] "Take, eat: this is my body which is broken for you. . . . This cup is the new testament in my blood."[94] Which words of Christ, repeated in so many places, cannot be verified, without offering violence to the text, any other way than by a real change of the bread and wine into his body and blood.

Secondly, "The cup of blessing which we bless, is it not the communion of the blood of Christ? The bread which we break, is it not the communion of the body of Christ?"[95] Which interrogation of the apostle is certainly equivalent to an affirmation; and evidently declares, that in the Blessed Sacrament we really receive the body and blood of Christ.

Thirdly, "Whosoever shall eat this bread or drink the cup of the Lord unworthily, shall be guilty of the body and blood

[91] Mt 26:26-27
[92] Mk 14:22, 24
[93] Lk 22:19-20
[94] 1 Cor 11:24-25
[95] 1 Cor 10:16

of the Lord. . . . He that eateth and drinketh unworthily, eateth and drinketh damnation to himself, not discerning the body of our Lord."[96] Now how should a person be "guilty of the body and blood of our Lord" by receiving unworthily, if what he received were only bread and wine, and not "the body and blood of our Lord"? Or where should be the crime of "not discerning the body of our Lord," if the "body of our Lord" were not there?

Fourthly:

> The bread that I will give is my flesh, which I will give for the life of the world. The Jews therefore strove amongst themselves, saying, How can this man give us his flesh to eat? Then Jesus said unto them, Verily, verily, I say unto you, except ye eat the flesh of the Son of man, and drink his blood, ye have no life in you. Whosoever eateth my flesh, and drinketh my blood, hath eternal life, and I will raise him up at the last day. For my flesh is meat indeed, and my blood is drink indeed. He that eateth my flesh, and drinketh my blood, dwelleth in me, and I in him. As the living Father hath sent me, and I live by the Father: so he that eateth me, even he shall live by me. This is that bread which came down from heaven, not as your fathers did eat manna and are dead; he that eateth of this bread shall live for ever.[97]

Hence the protestants, in their catechism in the Common Prayer Book, are forced to acknowledge that "the body and blood of Christ are verily and indeed taken and received by the faithful in the Lord's Supper." Now, how that can be *verily and indeed taken and received*, which is not *verily and indeed* there, is a greater mystery than transubstantiation.

---

[96] 1 Cor 11:27, 29
[97] Jn 6:52-59

> "The literal sense is hard to flesh and blood:
> But nonsense never can be understood."
> —Dryden's *Hind and Panther*

55. Are we not commanded to receive the sacrament in remembrance of Christ?[98]

Yes, we are: and St. Paul lets us know what it is that is to be the object of our remembrance when we receive, when he tells us, "Ye do show [or show forth] the Lord's death till he comes."[99] But this remembrance is no ways opposite to the real presence of Christ's body and blood: on the contrary, what better remembrance can there be of Christ's death and passion, than to receive under the sacramental veils the same body and blood in which he suffered for us?

56. Why then do you blame protestants for taking this sacrament in remembrance of Christ?

We do not blame them for taking it in remembrance of him: but we blame them for taking it as a bare remembrance, so as to exclude the reality of his body and blood. That is, we blame them for taking the remembrance and leaving out the substance; whereas the words of Christ require that they should acknowledge both.

57. But how is it possible that the sacrament should contain the real body and blood of Christ?

Because nothing is impossible to the Almighty; and it is the highest rashness, not to say blasphemy, for poor worms of the earth to dispute the power of God.

[98] Cf. Lk 22:19
[99] 1 Cor 11:26

Chapter 5

Of Communion in One Kind

58. What is the doctrine of the Church as to this point?

We profess "that under either kind alone Christ is received whole and entire, and a true sacrament."[100]

59. What proof have you for this?

Because, as we have seen in the foregoing chapter, the bread, by consecration, is truly and really changed into the body of Christ, and the wine into his blood: now both faith and reason tell us that the living body of the Son of God cannot be without his blood, nor his blood without his body; nor his body and blood without his soul and divinity. It is true, he shed his blood for us in his passion; and his soul at his death was parted from his body; but now he has risen from the dead immortal and impassible, and can shed his blood no more, nor die any more. "Christ being raised from the dead," says the apostle, "dieth no more, death has no more dominion over him."[101] Therefore whosoever receives the body of Christ, receives Christ himself whole and entire; there is no receiving him by parts.

60. But does not Christ say, "Except ye eat the flesh of the Son of man and drink his blood, ye have no life in you"?[102]

True. But according to the Catholic doctrine we do this, though we receive under one kind alone, because under either kind we receive both the body and blood of Christ; whereas our adversaries that make this objection receive neither one nor the

---

[100] Council of Trent, Session 21
[101] Rom 6:9
[102] Jn 6:54

other, but only a little bread and wine. Besides, this objection does not sound well in protestant mouths, because they say those words of Christ were not spoken of the sacrament, but only of faith.

61. Are all Christians commanded to drink of the cup, "Drink ye all of it"?[103]

No: that command was only addressed to the twelve apostles, who were all that were then present, "and they all drank of it."[104]

62. How do you prove that those words are not to be understood as a command directed to all Christians?

Because the Church of Christ, which is the best interpreter of his word, never understood them so; and therefore from the very beginning, on many occasions, she gave the Holy Communion in one kind, for instance, to children, to the sick, to the faithful in time of persecution, to be carried home with them, etc., as appears from the most certain monuments of antiquity.

63. But are not the faithful thus deprived of a great part of the grace of this sacrament?

No: because under one kind they receive the same as they would do under both, inasmuch as they receive Christ himself whole and entire, the Author and Fountain of all graces.

64. Why then should the priest in the Mass receive in both kinds any more than the rest of the faithful?

Because the Mass being a sacrifice, in which, by the institution of our Lord, the shedding of his blood and his death was to be in a lively manner represented; it is requisite that the priest,

[103] Mt 26:27
[104] Mk 14:23

who as the minister of Christ offers this sacrifice, should, for the more lively representing of the separation of Christ's blood from his body, consecrate and receive in both kinds as often as he says Mass. Whereas at other times, neither priest, nor bishop, nor the pope himself, even upon their death-bed, receives any otherwise than the rest of the faithful, viz. in one kind only.

65. Have you any texts of scripture that favor Communion in one kind?

Yes. First, all such texts as promise everlasting life to them that receive, though but in one kind; "The bread that I will give is my flesh, which I will give for the life of the world. . . . He that eateth me, even he shall live by me. . . . He that eateth of this bread shall live for ever."[105]

Secondly, all such texts as make mention of the faithful receiving the Holy Communion under the name of "breaking of bread," without any mention of the cup; "they continued steadfastly in the apostolic doctrine of fellowship, and in breaking of bread and in prayers. . . . Continuing daily with one accord in the temple, and breaking bread from house to house."[106] "Upon the first day of the week, when the disciples came together to break bread."[107] "He took bread and blessed it, and broke it, and gave it to them, and their eyes were opened and they knew him, and he vanished out of their sight."[108] "We being many, are one bread, and one body, for we are all partakers of that one bread."[109]

Thirdly, 1 Corinthians 11, where the apostle declares, that whosoever receives under either kind unworthily, is guilty both

[105] Jn 6:52, 58-59
[106] Acts 2:42, 46
[107] Acts 20:7
[108] Lk 24:30-31
[109] 1 Cor 10:17

of the body and blood of Christ. "Whosoever shall eat this bread, or drink this cup of the Lord unworthily, shall be guilty of the body and blood of our Lord."[110] Where the protestant translators have evidently corrupted the text, by putting in "and drink," instead of "or drink," as it is in the original.

66. What are the reasons why the Church does not give the Communion to all her children in both kinds?

First, because the danger of spilling the blood of Christ, which could hardly be avoided if all were to receive the cup. Secondly, because, considering how soon wine decays, the sacrament could not well be kept for the sick in both kinds. Thirdly, because some constitutions can neither endure the taste nor smell of wine. Fourthly, because true wine in some countries is very hard to be met with. Fifthly, in fine, in opposition to those heretics who deny that Christ is received whole and entire under either kind.

Chapter 6

Of the Mass

67. What is the Catholic doctrine as to the Mass?

That in the Mass there is offered to God a true, proper, and propitiatory sacrifice for the living and the dead.

68. What do you mean by the Mass?

The consecration and oblation of the body and blood of Christ under the sacramental veils or appearances of bread and wine;

---

[110] 1 Cor 11:27

so that the Mass was instituted by Christ himself at his last supper: Christ himself said the first Mass; and ordained that his apostles and their successors should do the like. "Do this in remembrance of me."[111]

69. What do you mean by a propitiatory sacrifice?

A sacrifice for obtaining mercy, or by which God is moved to mercy.

70. How do you prove that the Mass is such a sacrifice?

Because in the Mass Christ himself, as we have seen above, is really present, and by virtue of the consecration is there exhibited and presented to the eternal Father under the sacramental veils, which by their separate consecration represent his death. Now what can more move God to mercy, than the oblation of his only Son there really present, and under this figure of death, representing to his Father that death which he suffered for us?

71. What scripture do you bring for this?

The words of consecration as they are related by St. Luke: "This is my body which is given for you. . . . This cup is the new testament in my blood which [cup] is shed for you."[112] For if the cup was shed for us, that is, for our sins, it must needs be propitiatory, at least, by applying to us the fruits of the bloody sacrifice of the cross.

72. What other texts of the scripture do the fathers apply to the Sacrifice of the Mass?

First, the words of God in Malachias 1, where rejecting the Jewish sacrifice, he declares his acceptance of that sacrifice or pure offering which should be made to him in every place among the

---

[111] Lk 22:19
[112] Lk 22:19-20

gentiles.[113] Secondly, those words of the psalmist, "Thou art a priest for ever according to the order of Melchisedech":[114] why according to the order of Melchisedech, say the holy fathers, but by reason of the Sacrifice of the Eucharist, pre-figured by that bread and wine offered by Melchisedech.[115]

73. Why does the Church celebrate the Mass in the Latin, which the people for the most part do not understand?

First, because it is the ancient language of the Church used in the public liturgy in all ages in the western parts of the world. Secondly, for a greater uniformity in the public worship; that so a Christian, in whatsoever country he chances to be, may still find the liturgy performed in the same manner, and in the same language to which he is accustomed at home. Thirdly, to avoid the changes which all vulgar languages are daily exposed to. Fourthly, because the Mass being a sacrifice which the priest, as minister of Christ, is to offer, and the prayers of the Mass being mostly fitted for this end, it is enough that they be in a language which he understands. Nor is this in any way injurious to the people, who are instructed to accompany him in every part of this sacrifice by prayers accommodated to their devotion, which they have in their ordinary prayer books.

74. What is the best manner of hearing Mass?

The Mass being instituted for a standing memorial of Christ's death and passion, and being in substance the same sacrifice as that which Christ offered upon the cross, because both the priest and victim is the same Jesus Christ; there can be no better manner of hearing Mass than by meditating on the death and passion of Christ there represented; and putting one's self in the same dispositions of faith, love, repentance, etc., as we should

[113] Cf. Mal 1:10-11
[114] Ps 109:4
[115] Cf. Gn 14:18

have endeavored to excite in ourselves had we been present at his passion and death on Mount Calvary.

75. What are the ends for which this sacrifice is offered to God?
Principally these four, which both priest and people ought to have in view: First, for God's own honor and glory. Secondly, in thanksgiving for all his blessings conferred on us through Jesus Christ our Lord. Thirdly, in satisfaction for our sins through his blood. Fourthly, for obtaining grace and all necessary blessings from God.

Chapter 7

Of Purgatory

76. What is the doctrine of the Church as to this point?
We constantly hold that there is a purgatory; and that the souls therein detained are helped by the suffrages of the faithful: that is, by the prayers and alms offered for them, and principally by the Holy Sacrifice of the Mass.

77. What do you mean by purgatory?
A middle state of souls which depart this life in God's grace, yet not without some lesser stains or guilt of punishment, which retards them from entering heaven. But as to the particular place where these souls suffer, or the quality of the torments which they suffer, the Church has decided nothing.

78. What sort of Christians then go to purgatory?
First, such as die guilty of lesser sins, which we commonly call venial; as many Christians do, who, either by sudden death or

otherwise, are taken out of this life before they have repented for these ordinary failings. Secondly, such as having been formerly guilty of greater sins, have not made full satisfaction for them to the divine justice.

79. Why do you say that those who die guilty of lesser sins go to purgatory?

Because such as depart this life before they have repented of these venial frailties and imperfections, cannot be supposed to be condemned to the eternal torments of hell, since the sins of which they are guilty are but small, which even God's best servants are more or less liable to. Nor can they go straight to heaven in this state, because the scripture assures us, "There shall in no wise enter thither anything that defileth."[116] Now every sin, be it ever so small, certainly defileth the soul. Hence our Savior assures us, that we are to render an account "even for every idle word."[117]

80. Upon what then do you ground your belief of purgatory?

Upon scripture, tradition, and reason.

81. How upon scripture?

Because the scripture in many places assures us that God will render to everyone according to his works.[118] Now this would not be true, if there were no such thing as purgatory; for how would God render to everyone according to his works, if such as die in the guilt of any even the least sin, which they have not taken care to blot out by repentance, would nevertheless go straight to heaven?

---

[116] Apoc 21:27
[117] Mt 12:36
[118] Cf. Ps 61:13; Mt 16:27; Rom 2:6; Apoc 22:12

82. Have you any texts which the fathers and ecclesiastical writers interpret of purgatory?

Yes; "Every man's work shall be made manifest. For the day shall declare it, because it shall be revealed by fire. And the fire shall try every man's work of what sort it is. If any man's work abide which he hath built thereupon" (that is, upon the foundation, which is Jesus Christ[119]), "he shall receive a reward. If any man's works shall be burnt, he shall suffer loss: but he himself shall be saved, yet so as by fire."[120] From which text it appears, that such as both in their faith, and in the practice of their lives, have stuck to the foundation, which is Jesus Christ, so as not to forfeit his grace by mortal sin; though they have otherwise been guilty of great imperfections, by building wood, hay, and stubble upon this foundation;[121] it appears, I say, that such as these, according to the apostle, must pass through a fiery trial, at the time that "every man's work shall be made manifest": which is not till the next life; and that they shall be "saved" indeed, "yet so as by fire," that is, by passing first through purgatory.

Secondly, "Agree with thine adversary quickly, whilst thou art in the way with him: lest at any time the adversary deliver thee to the judge, and the judge deliver thee to the officer, and thou be cast into prison. Verily, I say unto thee, thou shalt by no means come out thence till thou hast paid the uttermost farthing."[122] Which text St. Cyprian, one of the most ancient fathers, understands of the prison of purgatory.[123]

Thirdly, "Whosoever speaketh against the Holy Ghost, it shall not be forgiven him, neither in this world, neither in the

[119] Cf. 1 Cor 3:11
[120] 1 Cor 3:13-15
[121] Cf. 1 Cor 3:12
[122] Mt 5:25-26
[123] Cf. Cyprian, Epistle 51, n. 20

world to come."[124] Which last words plainly imply that some sins, which are not forgiven in this world, may be forgiven in the world to come; otherwise, why should our Savior make any mention of forgiveness in the world to come? Now, if there may be forgiveness of sins in the world to come, there must be a purgatory; for in hell, there is no forgiveness, and in heaven, no sin.

Besides, a middle place is also implied, where Christ is said by his Spirit to have gone and "preached to the spirits in prison which some time were disobedient."[125] Which prison could be no other than purgatory; for as to the spirits that were in the prison of hell, Christ did certainly not go to preach to them.

83. How do you ground the belief of purgatory upon tradition?
Because both the Jewish church long before our Savior's coming, and the Christian Church from the very beginning in all ages and all nations, have offered prayers and sacrifice for the repose and relief of the faithful departed: as appears in regard to the Jews from 2 Machabees 12, where this practice is approved of;[126] which books of Machabees, the Church, says St. Augustine,[127] accounts canonical, though the Jews do not. And in regard to the Christian Church, the same is evident from all the fathers and the most ancient liturgies. Now such prayers as these evidently imply the belief of a purgatory; for souls in heaven stand in no need of our prayers, and those in hell cannot be bettered by them.

84. How do you ground the belief of purgatory upon reason?
Because reason clearly teaches these two things: First, that all and every sin, how small soever, deserves punishment.

---

[124] Mt 12:32
[125] 1 Pet 3:19-20
[126] Cf. 2 Mc 12:39-46
[127] Cf. Augustine, *City of God*, Bk. 18, Ch. 36

Secondly, that some sins are so small, either through the levity of the matter, or for want of full deliberation in the action, do not deserve eternal punishment. From whence it is plain, that besides the place of eternal punishment which we call hell, there must be also a place of temporal punishment for such as die in lesser sins, and this we call purgatory.

Chapter 8

Of the Veneration and Invocation of Saints

85. What is the Catholic doctrine touching the veneration and invocation of saints?

We are taught first, that there is an honor and veneration due to the angels and saints. Secondly, that they offer up prayers to God for us. Thirdly, that it is good and profitable to invoke them, that is, to have recourse to their intercession and prayers. Fourthly, that their relics are to be had in veneration.

Of the Veneration of the Angels and Saints

86. How do you prove that there is an honor and veneration due to the angels and saints?

Because they are God's angels and saints, that is to say, most faithful servants, courtiers, friends, and favorites of the King of Kings, who, having highly honored him, are now highly honored by him, as he has promised, "Them that honor me I will honor."[128]

---

[128] 1 Kgs 2:30

Secondly, because they have received from the Lord most eminent and supernatural gifts of grace and glory, which make them truly worthy of our honor and veneration, and therefore we give it to them as their due, according to that of the apostle, "Honor to whom honor is due."[129]

Thirdly, because the angels of God are our guardians, tutors, and governors: as appears from many texts of scripture. "He shall give his angels charge over thee to keep thee in all thy ways; they shall bear thee up in their hands, lest thou dash thy foot against a stone."[130] "Take heed that ye despise not one of these little ones; for I say unto you, that in heaven their angels do always behold the face of my Father that is in heaven."[131] "Are they not all ministering spirits, sent forth to minister for them who shall be heirs of salvation."[132] It is therefore evidently the will of God that we should have a religious veneration for these heavenly guardians. "Behold I send an angel before thee to keep thee in thy way, and to bring thee into the place which I have prepared; beware of him, and obey his voice, provoke him not, for my name is in him."[133]

Fourthly, because God has promised to his saints power over all nations, "He that overcometh, and keepeth my words unto the end, to him will I give power over the nations, and he shall rule them with a rod of iron . . . even as I received of my Father."[134] "Thou hast made us unto our God kings and priests, and we shall reign on the earth."[135] Therefore all nations ought to honor the saints, as having received from God this kingly power over them.

[129] Rom 13:7
[130] Ps 90:11-12
[131] Mt 18:10
[132] Heb 1:14
[133] Ex 23:20-21
[134] Apoc 2:26-28
[135] Apoc 5:10

Fifthly, because we have instances in scripture of honor and veneration paid to the angels by the servants of God.[136]

Sixthly, because the Church in all ages has paid this honor and veneration to the saints, by erecting churches and keeping holy days in their memory; a practice which the English protestants have also retained.

87. Do you then worship the angels and saints as gods, or give them the honor that belongs to God alone?

No, God forbid; for this would be a high treason against His Divine Majesty.

88. What is the difference between the honor which you give to God and that which you give to the saints?

There is no comparison between the one and the other. We honor God with a sovereign honor, as the supreme Lord and Creator of all things, as our first beginning and our last end. We believe in him alone, we hope in him alone, we love him above all things, to him alone we pay our homage of divine adoration, praise, and sacrifice. But as for the saints and angels, we only reverence them with an inferior honor, as belonging to him, for his sake, and upon account of the gifts which they have received from him.

89. Do you not give a particular honor to the Virgin Mary?

Yes, we do, by reason of her eminent dignity of Mother of God, for which "all generations shall call (her) blessed."[137] As also by reason of that fulness of grace which she enjoyed in this life, and the sublime degree of glory to which she is raised in heaven. But still, even this honor which we give to her is

---

[136] Cf. Jo 5:14-15
[137] Lk 1:48

infinitely inferior to that which we pay to God, to whom she is indebted for all her dignity, grace, and glory.

That the Saints and Angels Pray to God for Us

90. How do you prove this?

First, from Zacharias 1, where the prophet heard an angel praying for Jerusalem, and the cities of Judah: "The angel of the Lord answered and said: O Lord of Hosts, how long wilt thou not have mercy on Jerusalem, and on the cities of Judah, against which thou hast had indignation these threescore and ten years?"[138]

Secondly, from Apocalypse 5: "The four and twenty elders fell down before the Lamb, having every one of them harps and golden vials full of odor, which are the prayers of the saints."[139] And Apocalypse 8: "The smoke of the incense with the prayers of the saints ascended up before God out of the angel's hand."[140] From which text it is evident, that both the saints and angels offer up to God the prayers of the saints, that is, of the faithful upon earth.

Thirdly, because we profess in the Creed the communion of saints; and St. Paul, speaking of the children of the Church of Christ, tells them that they have a fellowship with the saints in heaven: "You are come unto mount Sion, and unto the city of the living God, the heavenly Jerusalem, and to an innumerable company of angels, to the general assembly and church of the first-born which are written in heaven, and to the spirits of just men made perfect, and to Jesus the mediator,"[141] etc. Therefore the children of the Church of Christ upon earth are

---

[138] Zac 1:12
[139] Apoc 5:8
[140] Apoc 8:4
[141] Heb 12:22-24

fellow-members with the saints in heaven, of the same body under the same head, which is Christ Jesus. Hence the same apostle calls the heavenly Jerusalem our mother;[142] and tells us that we are "fellow-citizens with the saints."[143] Therefore the saints in heaven have a care and solicitude for us as being members of the same body, it being the property of the members of the same body to be solicitous for one another.[144] Consequently, the saints in heaven pray for us.

Fourthly, because according to the doctrine of the apostle, it is the property of the virtue of charity not to be lost in heaven, as faith and hope are there lost: "Charity," saith St. Paul, "never faileth."[145] On the contrary, this heavenly virtue is perfected in heaven, where by seeing God face to face, the soul is inflamed with a most ardent love for God, and for his sake loves exceedingly his children, her brethren, here below; how then can the saints in heaven, having so perfect a charity for us, not pray for us, since the very first thing that charity prompts a person to do, is to seek to succor and assist those whom he loves?

Fifthly, because we find the rich glutton in hell petitioning in favor of his five brethren here upon earth;[146] how much more are we to believe, that the saints in heaven intercede for their brethren here?

Sixthly, because the souls of the martyrs pray for justice against their persecutors, who had put them to death;[147] how much more do they pray for mercy for the faithful children of the Church?

Seventhly, in fine, because our Lord tells us, "Make to yourselves friends of the mammon of unrighteousness; that when

[142] Cf. Gal 4:26
[143] Eph 2:19
[144] Cf. 1 Cor. 12:25-26
[145] 1 Cor 13:8
[146] Cf. Lk 16:27-28
[147] Cf. Apoc 6:10

ye fail, they may receive you into everlasting habitations."[148] Where he gives us to understand that the servants of God, whom we have helped by our alms, after themselves have got to heaven, help and assist us to enter into that everlasting kingdom.

Of the Invocation of Saints

91. What do you mean by the invocation of saints?

I mean such petitions or requests as are made to desire their prayers and intercession for us.

92. Do Catholics pray to saints?

If by praying to saints, you mean addressing ourselves to them as the authors or disposers of grace and glory, or in such manner as to suppose that they had any power to help us independently of God's good will and pleasure, we do not pray to them, but condemn all such addresses as superstitious and impious. But if, by praying to saints, you mean no more than desiring them to pray to God for us, in this sense we hold it both good and profitable to pray to the saints.

93. How do you prove that it is good and profitable to desire the saints and angels in heaven to pray to God for us?

Because it is good and profitable to desire the servants here upon earth to pray for us: "for the prayers of a righteous man availeth much."[149] Moses by his prayers obtained mercy for the children of Israel,[150] and Samuel by his prayers defeated the Philistines.[151] Hence St. Paul, in almost all his epistles, desires

[148] Lk 16:9
[149] Jas 5:16
[150] Cf. Ex 32:11-14
[151] Cf. 1 Kgs 7:8-10

the faithful to pray for him.[152] And God himself commanded Eliphaz and his friends to go to Job, that Job should pray for them, promising to accept his prayers.[153] Now, if it be acceptable to God, and good and profitable to ourselves, to seek the prayers and intercession of God's servants here on earth, must it not be much more so to seek the prayers and intercession of the saints in heaven; since both their charity for us, and their credit and interest with God, is much greater now, than when they were here upon earth?

94. But does it not argue a want of confidence in the infinite goodness of God and the super-abounding merits of Jesus Christ our Redeemer, to address ourselves to the saints for their prayers and intercession?

No more than to address ourselves to our brethren here below, as protestants do when they desire the prayers of the congregation; since we desire no more of the saints than what we desire of our brethren here below, viz. that they would pray for us, and with us, to the infinite goodness of God, who is both our Father and their Father, our Lord and their Lord, by the merits of his Son Jesus Christ, who is both our Mediator and their Mediator. For though the goodness of God and the merits of Christ be infinite, yet, as this is not to exempt us from frequent prayer for ourselves, so much recommended in scripture, so it is no reason for our being backward in seeking the prayers of others, whether in heaven or earth, that so God may have the honor, and we the benefit, of so many more prayers.

95. But is there no danger, by acting thus, of giving to the saints the honor which belongs to God alone?

No; it is evident, that to desire the prayers and intercessions of

---

[152] Cf. Rom 15:30; Eph 6:18-19; 1 Thes 5:25; Heb 13:18
[153] Cf. Jb 42:8

the saints is by no means giving them an honor which belongs to God alone; so far from it, that it would even be a blasphemy to beg of God to pray for us; because whosoever desires anyone to pray for him for the obtaining a grace or blessing, supposes the person to whom he thus addresses himself to be inferior and dependent of some other by whom this grace or blessing is to be bestowed.

96. Have you any reason to think that the saints and angels have any knowledge of your addresses or petitions made to them?

Yes, we have. First, because our Lord assures us that "there is joy in the presence of the angels of God, over one sinner that repenteth."[154] For if they rejoice at our repentance, consequently they have a knowledge of our repentance; and if they have a knowledge of our repentance, what reason can we have to doubt of their knowing our petitions also? And what is here said of the angels is also to be understood of the saints, of whom our Lord tells us, that "they are equal unto the angels."[155]

Secondly, because the angels of God, who, as we have already seen, are our guardians, are always amongst us, and therefore cannot be ignorant of our requests; especially since, as we have also seen from Apocalypse 5 and 8, both angels and saints offer up our prayers before the throne of God, and therefore must needs know them.[156]

Thirdly, because it appears from Apocalypse 11 and 19 that the inhabitants of heaven know what passeth upon earth.[157] Hence St. Paul, speaking of himself and his fellow-apostles, saith, "We are made a spectacle unto the world, and to angels, and to men."[158]

---

[154] Lk 15:10
[155] Lk 20:36
[156] Cf. Apoc 5:8, 8:4
[157] Cf. Apoc 11:15, 19:1-2
[158] 1 Cor 4:9

Fourthly, we cannot suppose that the saints and angels, who enjoy the light of glory, can be ignorant of such things, as the prophets and servants of God in this world have often known by the light of grace, and even the very devils by the light of nature alone: since the light of glory is so much more perfect than the light of grace or nature, according to the apostle, "For now we see through a glass darkly; but then face to face: now I know in part; but then shall I know even also as I am known";[159] that is, by a most perfect knowledge. Hence, it is written, "we shall be like him [God], for we shall see him as he is."[160] Now it is certain that the servants of God in this world, by a special light of grace, have often known things that passed at a great distance, as Elisha knew what passed between Naaman and his servant Gehazi,[161] and what was done by the king of Syria in his private chamber.[162] It is also certain that the devils, by the mere light of nature, know what passes amongst us, as appears by the correspondence they hold with magicians, and by their being our accusers.[163] Therefore we cannot reasonably question, but that the saints in heaven know the petitions which we address unto them.

Fifthly, in fine, because it is weak reasoning to argue from our corporal hearing (the object of which being sound, that is, a motion or undulation of the air that cannot reach beyond a certain distance) to the hearing of spirits, which is independent of sound, and consequently independent of distance; though the manner of it be hard enough to explicate to those who know no other hearing but that of the corporal one.

[159] 1 Cor 13:12
[160] 1 Jn 3:2
[161] Cf. 4 Kgs 5:20-27
[162] Cf. 4 Kgs 6:8-12
[163] Cf. Apoc 12:10

97. Have you any other warrant in scripture for the invocation of angels and saints?

Yes; we have the example of God's best servants. Thus Jacob begs the blessing of his angel guardian for his two grandsons, Ephraim and Manasseh. "God before whom my fathers Abraham and Isaac did walk, the God which fed me all my life long until this day, the angel which redeemed me from all evil, bless the lads."[164] The same Jacob "wept and made supplication to an angel."[165] And St. John, writing to the seven churches of Asia, petitions for the intercession of the seven chief angels in their favor: "Grace be unto you, and peace from him, which is, and which was, and which is to come, and from the seven spirits which are before his throne."[166]

Of Relics

98. What do you mean by relics?

The bodies or bones of saints, or anything else that has belonged to them.

99. What grounds have you for paying a veneration to the relics of the saints?

Besides the ancient tradition and practice of the first ages, attested by the best monuments of antiquity, we have been warranted to do so by many illustrious miracles done at the tombs and by the relics of the saints.[167] Which God, who is truth and sanctity itself, would never have effected, if this honor paid to the precious remnants of his servants were not agreeable to him.

---

[164] Gn 48:15-16
[165] Os 12:4
[166] Apoc 1:4
[167] Cf. Augustine, *City of God*, Bk. 22, Ch. 8

100. Have you any instances in scripture of miracles done by relics?
Yes; we read in 4 Kings 13 of a dead man raised to life by the bones of the prophet Elisha;[168] and Acts 19, "From the body of Paul were brought unto the sick, handkerchiefs or aprons, and the diseases departed from them, and the evil spirits went out of them."[169]

Chapter 9

Of Images

101. What is your doctrine as to images?
We hold that the images or pictures of Christ, of his Blessed Mother ever a Virgin, and of other saints, are to be had and retained; and that due honor and veneration is to be given them.

102. Do you not worship images?
No, by no means, if by worship you mean divine honor; for this we do not give to the highest angel or saint, nor even to the Virgin Mary, much less to images.

103. Do you not pray to images?
No, we do not; because, as both our catechism and common sense teach us, they can neither see, nor hear, nor help us.[170]

104. Why then do you pray before an image or crucifix?
Because the sight of a good picture or image, for example, of Christ upon the cross, helps to enkindle devotion in our hearts

[168] Cf. 4 Kgs 13:21
[169] Acts 19:12
[170] Cf. *Douay Catechism* (included in Volume II of this series)

towards him that has loved us to that excess as to lay down his life for the love of us.

105. Are you taught to put your trust and confidence in images as the heathens did in their idols; as if there were a certain virtue, power, or divinity residing in them?

No, we are expressly taught the contrary by the Council of Trent.[171]

106. How do you prove that it is lawful to make or keep the images of Christ and his saints?

Because God himself commanded Moses to make two cherubims of beaten gold, and place them at the two ends of the mercy-seat over the ark of the covenant in the very sanctuary.[172] "And there," says he, "will I meet thee, and I will commune with thee from above the mercy-seat from between the two cherubims which are upon the ark of the testimony, of all things which I will give thee in commandment unto the children of Israel."[173] God also commanded a serpent of brass to be made, for the healing of those who were bit by the fiery serpents; which serpent was an emblem of Christ.[174]

107. But is it not forbidden "to make the likeness of anything in heaven above, or in the earth beneath, or in the waters under the earth"?[175]

It is forbidden "to make to ourselves" any such image or likeness; that is to say, to make it our God, or to put our trust in it, and to give it the honor which belongs to God; which is explained by the following words, "Thou shalt not bow down

[171] Cf. Council of Trent, Session 25
[172] Cf. Ex 25:18-21
[173] Ex 25:22
[174] Cf. Nm 21:8-9; Jn 3:14-15
[175] Cf. Ex 20:4

thyself to them" (that is, "thou shalt not adore them," for so both the Septuagint and Vulgate translate it), "or serve them."[176] Otherwise, if all likenesses were forbid by this commandment, we should be obliged to fling down our sign-posts, and deface the king's coin.

108. **What kind of honor do Catholics give to the images of Christ and his saints?**
A relative honor.

109. **What do you mean by a relative honor?**
By a relative honor, I mean an honor which is given to anything, not for any intrinsic excellence or dignity in the thing itself, but barely for the relation it has to something else; as when the courtiers bow to the chair of state, or Christians to the name of Jesus, which is an image or remembrance of our Savior to the ear, as the crucifix is to the eye.

110. **Have you any instances of this relative honor allowed by protestants?**
Yes; in the honor they give to the name of Jesus, to their churches, to the altar, to the Bible, to the symbols of bread and wine in the sacrament. Such also was the honor which the Jews gave to the ark and cherubims, and which Moses and Joshua gave to the land on which they stood, as being "holy ground."[177]

111. **How do you prove that there is a relative honor due to the images or pictures of Christ and his saints?**
From the dictates of common sense and reason, as well as of piety and religion, which teach us to express our love and esteem

[176] Ex 20:5
[177] Cf. Ex 3:5; Jo 5:16

for the persons whom we honor by setting a value upon all things that belong to them, or have any relation to them; thus a loyal subject, a dutiful child, a loving friend, value the pictures of their king, father, or friend: and those who make no scruple of abusing the image of Christ, would severely punish the man that would abase the image of his king.

112. Does your Church allow of images of God the Father, or of the Blessed Trinity?

Our profession of faith makes no mention of such images as these: yet we do not think them unlawful, provided that they be not understood to bear any likeness or resemblance of the Divinity, which cannot be expressed in colors or represented by any human workmanship. For, as protestants make no difficulty of painting the Holy Ghost under the figure of a dove, because he appeared so when Christ was baptized,[178] so we make no difficulty of painting God the Father under the figure of a venerable old man, because he appeared in that manner to the prophet Daniel.[179]

Chapter 10

Of Indulgences

113. What do you mean by indulgences?

Not leave to commit sin, or pardon for sins to come: but only a releasing, by the power of the keys committed to the Church, the debt of temporal punishment which may remain due upon

[178] Cf. Mt 3:16
[179] Cf. Dn 7:9

account of our sins, after the sins themselves, as to the guilt and eternal punishment, have been already remitted by repentance and confession.

114. **Can you prove from scripture that there is a punishment often due upon account of our sins, after the sins themselves have been remitted?**

Yes; this evidently appears in the case of King David, where although the prophet Nathan, upon his repentance, tells him, "The Lord hath put away thy sin,"[180] yet he denounces unto him many terrible punishments which should be inflicted by reason of this sin; which accordingly afterwards ensued.[181]

115. **What is the faith of your Church touching indulgences?**

It is comprised in these words of our profession of faith: "I affirm that the power of indulgences was left by Christ in the Church and that the use of them is most wholesome to Christian people."

116. **Upon what scripture do you ground this faith?**

The power of granting indulgences was left by Christ to the Church: "I will give unto thee the keys of the kingdom of heaven: and whatsoever thou shalt bind on earth, shall be bound in heaven; and whatsoever thou shalt loose on earth, shall be loosed in heaven."[182] And we have an instance in scripture of St. Paul's granting an indulgence to the Corinthian whom he had put under penance for incest: "To whom ye forgive anything" (he speaks of the incestuous sinner whom he had desired them not to receive), "I forgive also; for if I forgave anything, to whom I forgave it, for your sakes forgave I it in

---

[180] 2 Kgs 12:13
[181] Cf. 2 Kgs 12:10ff
[182] Mt 16:19

the person of Christ";[183] that is, by the power and authority received from him.

Chapter 11

Of the Supremacy of St. Peter and His Successors

117. What is the Catholic doctrine as to the pope's supremacy?

It is comprised in these two articles: 1) That St. Peter by divine commission was head of the Church of Christ. 2) That the pope or bishop of Rome, as successor to St. Peter, is at present head of the Church, and Christ's vicar upon earth.

118. How do you prove St. Peter's supremacy?

First, from the very name of Peter or *Cephas*, which signifies a rock, which name our Lord, who does nothing without reason, gave to him who before was called Simon, to signify that he should be as the rock or foundation upon which he would build his Church. According to what he himself declared, when he told him, "Thou art Peter" (that is, a rock), "and upon this rock will I build my church, and the gates of hell shall not prevail against it."[184]

Secondly, from the following words, "I will give unto thee the keys of the kingdom of heaven, and whatsoever thou shalt bind on earth, shall be bound in heaven; and whatsoever thou shalt loose on earth, shall be loosed in heaven."[185] Where, under the figure of the keys of the kingdom of heaven, our Lord ensureth to Peter the chief authority in his Church; as when

[183] 2 Cor 2:10
[184] Mt 16:18
[185] Mt 16:19

a king gives to one of his officers the keys of a city, he thereby declares that he makes him governor of that city.

Thirdly, from Luke 22: "The Lord said Simon, Simon, behold Satan hath desired to have you, that he may sift you as wheat. But I have prayed for thee, that thy faith fail not, and when thou art converted strengthen thy brethren."[186] In which text our Lord not only declared his particular concern for Peter, in praying for him that his faith might not fail; but also committed to him the care of his brethren, the other apostles, in charging him to confirm or strengthen them.

Fourthly, from John 21:

> Jesus said to Simon Peter, Simon, son of Jonas, lovest thou me more than these? He saith unto him, Yea, Lord; thou knowest that I love thee. He saith to him, Feed my lambs. He saith to him again the second time, Simon, son of Jonas, lovest thou me? He saith unto him, Yea, Lord; thou knowest that I love thee. He saith unto him, Feed my sheep. He saith unto him the third time, Simon, son of Jonas, lovest thou me? Peter was grieved because he said unto him the third time, lovest thou me? And he said unto him, Lord, thou knowest all things; thou knowest that I love thee. Jesus saith unto him, Feed my sheep.[187]

In which texts our Lord, in a most solemn manner, thrice committed to Peter the care of his whole flock, of all his sheep without exception, that is, of his whole Church.

119. How do you prove that this commission given to Peter descends to the pope or bishop of Rome?

Because, by the unanimous consent of the fathers and the

[186] Lk 22:31-32
[187] Jn 21:15-17

traditions of the Church in all ages, the bishops of Rome are the successors of St. Peter, who translated his chair from Antioch to Rome, and died bishop of Rome. Hence the see of Rome in all ages is called the See of Peter, the Chair of Peter, and absolutely the See Apostolic: and in that quality has from the beginning exercised jurisdiction over all other churches, as appears from the best records of ancient history.

Besides, supposing the supremacy of St. Peter, which we have proved above from plain scripture, it must consequently be allowed that this supremacy which Christ established for the better government of his Church and maintaining of unity was not to die with Peter, no more than the Church, which he promised should stand forever. For how can any Christian imagine that Christ should appoint a head for the government of his Church and maintaining of unity during the apostles' time, and design another government for succeeding ages, when there was like to be so much more need of a head? Therefore we must grant that St. Peter's supremacy was by succession to descend to somebody. Now I would willingly know who has half so fair a title to this succession as the bishop of Rome?

120. Why do you call the Roman Church the mother and mistress of all churches?

Because, as we have already seen, her bishop is St. Peter's successor, and Christ's vicar upon earth; and consequently the father and pastor of all the faithful; and therefore the Church, as being St. Peter's see, is the mother of all churches.

Chapter 12

121. Have you anything more to add in confirmation of all these tenets contained in your profession of faith?

I shall add no more than this, that having already proved in the first chapter that the Church in communion with Rome is the true and only Church of Christ, and consequently her councils and pastors are the guides of divine appointment, which Christ has established to be our conductors in the way to a happy eternity, it follows that we should, without further hesitation, believe and profess what they believe and profess, and condemn and reject what they condemn and reject: assuring ourselves that by doing thus we shall be secure, since we shall follow those guides which Christ himself has appointed, whom he has commanded us to hear, and with whom he has promised to abide to the end of the world.

122. Why do you in your profession of faith make declaration of receiving in particular the doctrine of the Council of Trent?

Because this was the last general council called in opposition to the new doctrine of Luther and Calvin: and therefore we particularly declare our assent to the decrees of this council, as being leveled against those heresies which have been most prevalent in these two last ages.

May the God of unity, peace, and troth, by his infinite mercy conduct all Christians to unity, peace, and truth. Amen. Amen.

Appendix

I N which are briefly proposed the motives, or rational induce-
ments, to the Catholic faith, which, according to Dr. Jeremy Taylor, a learned protestant prelate, may "very easily persuade persons
of much reason, and more piety, to retain that which they know
to have been the religion of their forefathers, and which have had
actual possession and seizure of men's understandings, before the
opposite professions had a name."[188]

1. "I consider," says he, "that those doctrines that have had long
   continuance and possession in the church, cannot easily be supposed in the present professors to be a design, since they have
   received them from so many ages. . . . Long prescription is a
   prejudice oftentimes so insupportable that it cannot with many
   arguments be retrenched, as relying upon these grounds, that
   truth is more ancient than falsehood; that God would not for
   so many ages forsake his church, and leave her in an error; that
   whatsoever is new is not only suspicious but false: which are
   suppositions pious and plausible enough."[189] We have proved
   them not only to be pious and plausible suppositions, but the
   plain doctrine of the word of God.[190]

   He adds for other motives:

2. "The beauty and splendor of their church; their pompous services; the stateliness and solemnity of the hierarchy."[191]

---

[188] Jeremy Taylor, *A Discourse of the Liberty of Prophesying* (London: Royston, 1647),
251.

[189] Taylor, *Discourse*, 249.

[190] See above, Ch. 1, Sect. 1-3.

[191] Taylor, *Discourse*, 250.

3. "Their name of Catholic, which they suppose their own due."[192] They have certainly reason to suppose so, if the possession or prescription of seventeen ages can make it their due. I am sure it has fixed it so strongly upon them, that even their adversaries cannot help giving it them on many occasions.

4. "The antiquity of many of their doctrines."[193] He should have said *all*; but this could not be expected from a protestant.

5. "The continued succession of their bishops; their immediate derivation from the apostles."[194]

6. "Their title to succeed St. Peter; the supposal and pretense of his personal prerogatives";[195] grounded upon plain scripture, as we have seen,[196] and therefore no vain pretense.

7. "The multitude and variety of people which are of their persuasion."[197]

8. "Apparent consent with antiquity, in many ceremonials which other churches have rejected; and a pretended and sometimes an apparent consent with some elder ages in matters doctrinal."[198] Here he minces the matter for fear of allowing too much: yet cannot dissemble, that venerable antiquity is apparently on the Catholic side.

9. "The great consent of one part with another, in that part which most of them affirm to be *de fide* ("of faith"). The great differences commenced among their adversaries";[199] whose first fathers and teachers, from the very beginning of their pretended Reformation, went quite different ways, even to an utter breach of communion, which never since could be repaired.

10. "Their happiness of being instrumental in converting diverse

[192] Ibid.
[193] Ibid.
[194] Ibid.
[195] Ibid.
[196] See above, Ch. 11.
[197] Taylor, *Discourse*, 250.
[198] Ibid.
[199] Ibid.

nations";[200] whereas none of the reformed churches have ever yet converted one.

11. "The piety and austerity of their religious orders of men and women. The single life of their priests and bishops. . . . The severity of their fasts, and their exterior observances";[201] all of which the good-natured Reformation has laid aside.

12. "The great reputation of their first bishops for faith and sanctity. The known holiness of some of those persons, whose institutes the religious persons pretend to imitate."[202]

13. "Their miracles, true or false";[203] says the Doctor. *True*, say I, if any faith may be given to the most certain records of all nations.

14. "The casualties and accidents that have happened to their adversaries."[204] I suppose he means such as Luther's sudden death after a plentiful supper; Zwingli's falling in battle, defending his reformed gospel, sword in hand; Oecolampadius being found in his bed, oppressed, as Luther will have it, by the devil;[205] Calvin's dying of a strange complication of distempers, consumed alive by vermin, etc.

15. "The oblique arts and indirect proceedings of some who departed from them";[206] in manifestly corrupting the scripture, as the first protestants did in all their translations, to make it chime with their errors; in quoting falsely the fathers and ecclesiastical writers; in perpetually misrepresenting in their sermons and writings the Catholic Church and her doctrine; a fault from which the doctor himself is not exempt, etc.

I have passed over some other things of less weight, which he alleges in the same place; and shall only desire the reader to compare

[200] Ibid.
[201] Ibid.
[202] Ibid.
[203] Ibid.
[204] Ibid., 250-251.
[205] Cf. Luther, *De Missa Privata et Unctione Sacerdotum*, T. 7, Wit. fol. 230
[206] Taylor, *Discourse*, 251.

the motives by which the concessions of this prelate, so much esteemed by all protestants, may retain Catholics at present in the
religion of their forefathers, with these motives which St. Augustine
alleged 1,300 years ago against the heretics of his time, and by which
he declares himself to have been retained in the Catholic Church:

> Not to speak of that true wisdom which you do not believe to be
> in the Catholic Church; there are many other things which most
> justly hold me in her communion. 1) The agreement of people and
> nations. 2) The authority begun by miracles, nourished by hope,
> increased by charity, confirmed by antiquity. 3) A succession of
> prelates descending from Peter the apostle, to whom Christ after his
> resurrection committed his flock, to the present bishop. Lastly, the
> very name of Catholic, of which this Church alone has not without
> reason in such manner kept possession, that though all heretics
> desire to be called Catholics, yet if a stranger ask them where the
> Catholics go to church, none of them all has the face to point out
> his own church, or meeting-house.[207]

These were St. Augustine's motives for being a Catholic, and
these are ours.

Besides, we cannot dissemble that there are many shocking circumstances in the whole management of the pretended Reformation, which deter us from embracing it, whatever temporal incon-
veniences we are forced to sustain by this recusancy.

The first reformer, Martin Luther, had nothing of extraordinary
edification in his life and conversation. On the contrary, all his
work declares him to have been a man of an implacable nature,
rigidly self-willed, impatient of contradiction, and rough and violent
in his declamations against all those, of what quality soever, who
dissented in the least from him. But what was the most scandalous
in a pretended restorer of the purity of religion, was his marrying a

---

[207] Augustine, *Contra Epistulam Fundamenti Manichaeorum*, Ch. 4

nun, after the most solemn vows by which both he and she had consecrated themselves to God in the state of perpetual continence. In
which he was imitated by a great part of the first reformed ministers.

He and his first associates were certainly schismatics, because
they separated themselves from all churches, pure or impure, true
or false, that were then upon earth, and stood alone upon their
own bottom. Therefore, if there was any such thing then in the
world as the true Church of Christ (as there must always be, if the
scripture and Creed be true), Luther and his followers separating
from all churches, must have separated from the true Church, and
consequently must have been schismatics. "At first," says Luther, in
the preface to his works, "I was alone." Which is confirmed by Dr.
Tillotson,[208] and by Mr. Collier, in his *Historical Dictionary*, under
"Martin Luther," where he praises his magnanimity in having op-
posed himself alone to the whole earth.

It appears from his book that he learnt no small part of his Reformation from the father of lies, in a nocturnal conference, of which
he there gives his readers an account.[209]

Those that were the most busy in promoting the Reformation
here at home, were for the most part men of most wretched char-
acters, such as King Henry VIII and the leading men in the government during the minority of Edward VI, not to speak of the ministry of Queen Elizabeth, "the most wicked," says a late protestant
historian, "that ever was known in any reign."[210]

The foundations of the Reformation in England were laid in
manifold sacrileges, in pulling down monasteries and other houses
consecrated to God, rifling and pillaging churches, alienating church
lands, etc., as may be seen in the *History of the Reformation* by Dr.
Heylin.

The Reformation was everywhere introduced by lay authority,
and for the most part in direct opposition to and contempt of the

[208] Cf. Tillotson, *Sermon Concerning Resolution and Steadfastness in Religion*
[209] Cf. Luther, *De Missa Privata et Unctione Sacerdotum*, T. 7, Wit. fol. 228ff
[210] Cf. Bevil Higgons, *A Short View of the English History* (London: Edlin, 1723), 273.

bishops, the Church guides of divine appointment. A proceeding manifestly irregular and unjustifiable, that in Church matters the laity with a few of the inferior clergy, and those under the ecclesiastical censures, should take upon them to direct those whom Christ appointed to be their directors.

England herself, which glories most in the regularity of her Reformation, compared to the tumultuous proceedings of reformers abroad, owes her present establishment of the church to the lay authority of Queen Elizabeth and her Parliament, in opposition to all the bishops then sitting (who were all but one displaced for their nonconformity), to the whole convocation, and both the universities, that is, in a word, to the whole clergy of the kingdom; as appears from Fuller[211] and Dr. Heylin.[212]

Wheresoever the reformed gospel was preached, it brought forth seditions, tumults, rebellions, etc., as appears from all the histories of those times. Insomuch, that in France alone the reformed gospellers, besides innumerable other outrages, are said to have destroyed no less than twenty thousand churches.[213] How little does such a Reformation resemble the first establishment of the Church of Christ!

The fruits of the Reformation were such as could not spring from a good tree: 1) An innumerable spawn of heresies. 2) Endless dissensions. 3) A perpetual itch of changing, and inconstancy in their doctrine. 4) Atheism, deism, latitudinarianism, and bare-faced impiety: in fine, a visible change of manners for the worse, as many of their own writers freely acknowledge; and old Erasmus long ago objected to them, where he defies them to show him one who had been reclaimed from vice by going over to their religion, and declares he never yet met with one who did not seem changed for the worse.[214]

That religion is the best to live in, which is the safest to die in,

---

[211] L. 9

[212] Cf. Peter Heylin, *Ecclesia Restaurata* (London: Twyford, 1660), 120ff.

[213] Cf. Matthew Pattenson, *Jerusalem and Babel*, 2nd ed. (London: P.D.M., 1653), 158.

[214] Cf. Erasmus, *Epistola ad Vulturius Neocomus*

and that in the judgment of dying men, who are not like to be biased at that time by interest, humor, or passion. Now it is certain, that thousands who have lived protestants, have desired to die Catholics, and never yet one that had lived a Catholic, desired to die a protestant; therefore it must be safest for us to stay where we are.

That religion is preferable to all others, the doctrine and preaching of which is, and always has been, more forcible and efficacious in order to the taking off men's minds from the perishable goods of this world, and fixing them wholly on the great business of eternity; but such is the doctrine and preaching of the Catholic Church, as appears from those multitudes of holy solitaries in our Church, that have retired themselves from all the advantages to which their birth or fortune entitled them, and abandoned all earthly hopes for the love of heaven. Whereas the Reformation has never yet produced any such fruits.

There was a true saving faith in the days of our forefathers, before the pretended Reformation, by which great numbers are certainly arrived at the happy port of eternal felicity. Our histories are full of instances of the charity, piety, and devotion of kings, bishops, etc. of the old religion. Therefore, it is safer to follow their faith, than venture our souls in a new-raised communion.

All ancient pretenders to Reformation (i.e. all those that ever undertook to alter or amend the Church faith) were condemned by the ancient Church for heretics, and are acknowledged to have been such by protestants themselves. Therefore there is just reason to apprehend, lest protestants walking in the same path may be involved in the same misfortune.

In fine, protestants, to defend the Reformation, condemned in its first appearance by the Church guides of divine appointment, are forced to have recourse to a rule of faith, which if allowed of, would set all, both ancient and modern heretics, out of the reach of Church authority. They are forced to appeal to a tribunal at which it is not possible that any sectary should be condemned. Such a rule, such a tribunal is the scripture interpreted not by authority of

Church guides, but by everyone's private judgment; for this, in effect, is making everyone's private judgment the supreme judge both of the scripture and of all controversies in religion, and authorizing him to prefer his own whimsies before the judgment of the whole Church. Could it be consistent with the wisdom and providence of God, to leave his Church without some more certain means of deciding controversies, and maintaining unity? No, certainly.

ABOUT THIS SERIES

Tradivox was first conceived as an international research endeavor to recover lost and otherwise little-known Catholic catechetical texts. As the research progressed over several years, the vision began to grow, along with the number of project contributors and a general desire to share these works with a broader audience.

Legally incorporated in 2019, Tradivox has begun the work of carefully remastering and republishing dozens of these catechisms which were once in common and official use in the Church around the world. That effort is embodied in this *Tradivox Catholic Catechism Index*, a multi-volume series restoring artifacts of traditional faith and praxis for a contemporary readership. More about this series and the work of Tradivox can be learned at www.Tradivox.com.

SOPHIA INSTITUTE

Sophia Institute is a nonprofit institution that seeks to nurture the spiritual, moral, and cultural life of souls and to spread the Gospel of Christ in conformity with the authentic teachings of the Roman Catholic Church.

Sophia Institute Press fulfills this mission by offering translations, reprints, and new publications that afford readers a rich source of the enduring wisdom of mankind.

Sophia Institute also operates the popular online resource CatholicExchange.com. *Catholic Exchange* provides world news from a Catholic perspective as well as daily devotionals and articles that will help readers to grow in holiness and live a life consistent with the teachings of the Church.

In 2013, Sophia Institute launched Sophia Institute for Teachers to renew and rebuild Catholic culture through service to Catholic education. With the goal of nurturing the spiritual, moral, and cultural life of souls, and an abiding respect for the role and work of teachers, we strive to provide materials and programs that are at once enlightening to the mind and ennobling to the heart; faithful and complete, as well as useful and practical.

Sophia Institute gratefully recognizes the Solidarity Association for preserving and encouraging the growth of our apostolate over the course of many years. Without their generous and timely support, this book would not be in your hands.

www.SophiaInstitute.com
www.CatholicExchange.com
www.SophiaInstituteforTeachers.org

Sophia Institute Press® is a registered trademark of Sophia Institute. Sophia Institute is a tax-exempt institution as defined by the Internal Revenue Code, Section 501(c)(3). Tax ID 22-2548708.